20

Introduction to Marketing
Concepts

Introduction to Marketing Concepts

Graeme Drummond
John Ensor

ELSEVIER
BUTTERWORTH
HEINEMANN

AMSTERDAM • BOSTON • HEIDELBERG • LONDON • NEW YORK • OXFORD
PARIS • SAN DIEGO • SAN FRANCISCO • SINGAPORE • SYDNEY • TOKYO

Elsevier Butterworth-Heinemann
Linacre House, Jordan Hill, Oxford OX2 8DP
30 Corporate Drive, Burlington, MA 01803

First published 2005

British Library Cataloguing in Publication Data
A catalogue record for this book is available from the British Library

Library of Congress Control Number: 2005924636
A catalogue record for this book is available from the Library of Congress

ISBN 0 7506 5995 5

For information on all Elsevier Butterworth-Heinemann publications
visit our website at http://books.elsevier.com

Typeset by Newgen Imaging Systems (P) Ltd, Chennai, India
Printed and bound in Great Britain

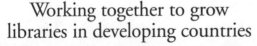

Contents

Preface

This text introduces the reader to basic marketing concepts and provides an attractive alternative to the traditional 'heavy-weight' marketing text. Equally applicable to students and industry practitioners, it focuses on the essential elements of marketing. The book cuts through much of the complexity and jargon surrounding the subject. The authors aim to provide a concise, but comprehensive text that is tightly written to accommodate the reading time pressures on students/practitioners. While 'reader-friendly' in nature, the book also aims to challenge the reader and stimulate debate by means of illustrative case examples and discussion questions.

Each chapter provides a structured approach to learning and features learning outlines. Additionally, numerous illustrative case examples are provided to highlight real-world examples of how marketing works in practice. The chapters build subject knowledge and provide a vital insight into the discipline of marketing.

The text is structured as follows:

Chapters 1–5 provide an overview of marketing and consider marketing in the context of the business environment. The primary emphasis relates to making the organization customer-focused. To this end, issues such as market research, segmentation and buyer behaviour are examined.

Chapters 6–9 consider the effective use of the marketing mix. Decisions relating to product, pricing, promotion and place (or distribution) are examined, and the overall aim of developing a winning marketing mix is central.

Chapters 10–12 consider marketing from a strategic perspective and examine how marketing activities generate competitive advantage. The importance of implementation and controlling strategic developments is highlighted.

Chapter 13 provides the control mechanisms aimed at translating strategic plans into specific actions. Behaviour, systems and operations that need to conform to corporate objectives are detailed.

Figures

1

Introduction to marketing

About this chapter

This chapter provides a basic introduction to marketing. It highlights key marketing concepts, which will be expanded upon in the rest of the text.

After reading this chapter, you will understand:

- The marketing concept.

- Marketing orientation as a business philosophy.

- Differences between marketing orientation and market orientation.

- The development and criticism of the marketing mix.

- Ethical issues relating to marketing.

- Benefits of e-marketing.

Marketing is essentially a simple process. Success stems from understanding customer needs. Given that this view makes intuitive sense, why complicate matters with the likes of segmentation, positioning, the 4Ps, the 7Ps and other associated jargon? The answer is that the concept is simple, but its implementation is highly complex and involves a range of interdependent variables. These variables must be given focus and direction in order to achieve the successful fulfilment of customer needs. Marketing is the means to provide such direction. Additionally, the provider must actually understand customers and their needs, as opposed to assuming they know what customers want. Marketing enables this understanding.

Therefore, marketing in its purist sense offers a mechanism that facilitates understanding, communication and the development of products as solutions to actual customer needs. Marketing is an interface between the provider and their customers.

1.1 What is marketing?

Numerous definitions of marketing exist:

Marketing is a social and managerial process by which individuals and groups obtain what they want and need through creating and exchanging products and value with others. (Kotler *et al.*, 1999)

Marketing is the management process responsible for identifying, anticipating and satisfying customers' requirements profitably. (Chartered Institute of Marketing – CIM)

Marketing is the process of planning and executing the conception, pricing, promotion and distribution of ideas, goods and services to create exchanges that satisfy individual and organizational objectives. (American Marketing Association)

The above definitions would appear to place marketing as a process, which looks to facilitate exchanges. To be sustainable, such exchanges must be mutually beneficial. Economic prosperity depends on the generation of such exchanges, assuming the CIM definition of '*profitability*' can be defined in a non-accounting sense (e.g. benefit or value). All the definitions emphasize the generation of value. Value is the benefit each partner in the exchange seeks (e.g. money, support, prestige). It drives the exchange process (see Figure 1.1).

Figure 1.1 also introduces the concept of time-scale into the equation. To be successful, exchange relationships must endure over the long term. Short-term, or one-off transactions are sales, whereas building a long-term on-going exchange relationship is marketing.

1.2 Marketing as a business philosophy

A number of generic business orientations exist. These orientations provide an underlying route to business success. They highlight the fundamentally

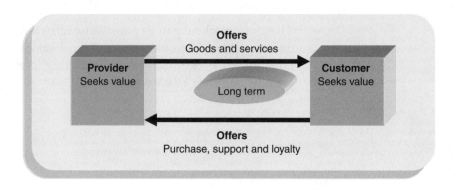

Figure 1.1
Long-term exchange
relationships

Illustrative example 1.1
Jazz^{fm}: exchange relationships

Radio station Jazz^{fm} provides a mix of music and intelligent presentation, including smooth jazz, blended with classic and contemporary soul. While having broad appeal during the day, the evening schedule offers many specialist shows covering numerous jazz styles. Jazz^{fm} has extended its activities into a Jazz^{fm} record label, events/concert booking and digital radio.

Media research shows a strong increase in audience figures, with over 1.4 million people tuning in each week. These listeners have, to use the marketing jargon, formed an exchange relationship with the company. Consider Figure 1.1. In order to form a viable exchange relationship, both provider and customers must offer something of value. So what is offered?

Jazz^{fm} provides more than just music. Head of marketing Nicola Thomson states: 'What unifies listeners – and attracts them to the station – is an attitude they identify with, which the brand and its presentation exemplifies; individual, intelligent, non-formulaic and unpredictable.' Strategically, Jazz^{fm} is a brand, based on a music format, that embodies an attitude and lifestyle. Listeners provide support, which drives audience figures – a key determinant for selling air-time to advertisers. Additionally, the audience provides a ready market for ancillary sales – music CDs, concert tickets etc.

most important element in business success. No one orientation is right or wrong. However, they may be inappropriate to a specific industry or business environment. Five basic orientations exist: production, product, financial, sales and marketing. Their key characteristics are summarized in Table 1.1.

Clearly all organizations will display elements of each. The question of orientation relates to which is the most significant for an organization. For example, no organization should neglect finance, but they may place greater (or lesser) strategic emphasis on marketing.

Adopting a marketing approach to business can generate many benefits, as products aim to provide solutions to specific customer needs. This approach:

• Generates products more likely to find a ready market.

• Encourages customer loyalty.

• Offers the opportunity to generate a price premium.

Table 1.1
Types of orientation

Orientation	Key success factor	Characteristic	Example
Production	Efficient production methods	Optimization of production and distribution methods/sytems in order to minimize unit cost and generate economies of scale and production volume	Commodity products where there is no differentiation, e.g. steel production
Product	Product quality and innovation of new ideas	The key focus is to generate innovative or superior quality products. Tends to be driven by technology as opposed to customer needs. The provider feels that good quality products 'sell themselves'	Leading edge technology-driven markets, e.g. biotechnology
Sales	Sales techniques and the ability to convince customers they have a need	Selling and promotional techniques are used to drive the business. Emphasis is on quick sales and sales volume. Often there is a need to convince customers that they need this product	Little/no differentation, e.g. life insurance
Financial	Return on investment and rigorous cost control	A balance sheet approach is taken, where the organization is simply judged by financial return	Organizations engaged in a diverse range of activity, e.g. conglomerate
Marketing	Understanding and meeting customer needs	Success stems from providing products that will meet specific customer needs. The customer is the focal point of product development activity	Branded products where consumers are likely to have a preference, e.g. designer label fashion brands

- Keeps organizations in-touch with ever changing customer needs.
- Promotes awareness of competitors' actions and product offerings.
- Provides potential to create differentiation where none previously existed.
- Gives marketing a greater impact on strategic planning.

It should be noted that a marketing orientation is not confined to the marketing department (if the organization has such a thing). It is a corporate-wide approach, with all employees having a role to play in generating customer value. For example, the office cleaner plays their part by creating a clean and efficient working environment, where customer contact staff can deliver high levels of customer care. As a simple exercise consider how the following employees could contribute in creating satisfied customers: receptionist, invoice clerk, canteen chief and managing director. Many organizations run customer care programmes for all members of staff, as opposed to just those with direct customer contact roles.

Given that marketing requires a corporate-wide adoption, a need exists to develop the marketing into a workable business strategy. Narver and Slater (1990) were influential in the concept of market orientation (as opposed to marketing orientation). Market orientation can be defined as:

> The organizational culture that most effectively and efficiently creates the necessary behaviours for the creation of superior value for buyers and, thus continuous superior performance for the business.

Narver and Slater proposed a model (see Figure 1.2) that identified the components of market orientation as:

- **Customer orientation** Understanding customers and creating valued solutions to actual customer needs.

- **Competitor orientation** Analysing the capabilities and ambitions of competitors.

- **Organizational culture** Developing employee behaviour and actions, which are customer focused.

- **Interfunctional coordination** Develop interaction between internal functional areas of the organization which best serve customer need and satisfaction.

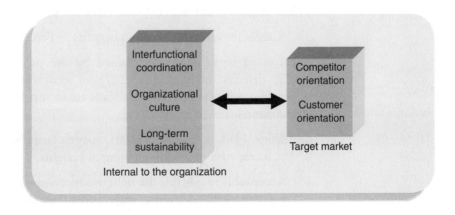

Figure 1.2
A model of market orientation

- **Long-term focus** Consideration of how the above can be sustained, and financially viable, over the long term.

Work by Kohli and Jaworiski (1990) supports the above view of translating marketing into a strategic orientation. Numerous studies (Jaworski and Kohli (1993) and Slater and Narver (1994)) have linked market orientation with enhanced organizational performance and associated internal benefits, such as increased staff morale.

Relationship marketing orientation

More modern approaches relating to marketing orientation, have suggested a relationship marketing approach. This recognized the importance of retaining existing customers and developing relationships with stakeholder groups (e.g. suppliers, distributors, etc.). The theory is based on the premise of building a relationship as opposed to simply generating transactions.

1.3 Creating customer value and satisfaction

Market-led organizations aim to generate customer value and satisfaction. Success is based on the ability to selectively (within target markets) deliver levels of customer satisfaction that exceed those provided by competitors. A precursor to this process is a detailed understanding of one simple question – What market are we in?

Organizations need to examine their product offering from the customer's viewpoint and understand, not the product offering from a technical perspective, but rather in terms of the benefits that are perceived by the potential customer. By thinking like customers, marketing becomes an interface between the provider and consumer. Ultimately, customers want benefits and these benefits determine the level of customer value derived from a product offering.

Jobber (2001) defines customer value as being dependent on perception:

Customer value = Perceived benefits − Perceived sacrifice

Perceived benefits are determined by the product, associated services (e.g. delivery, maintenance, etc.) and association/relationship with the provider, whereas perceived sacrifices are factors like cost, risk/uncertainty and time involved in purchase.

Adcock, Halborg and Ross (2001) suggest customers may use an intuitive 3As framework in assessing potential benefits. These are:

- **Acceptability** Is this the right product and will it provide a solution to my need while delivering some benefit? A need can be seen as simply

Illustrative example 1.2
Burberry: product association creates value

The Burberry brand has long been associated with exclusive, discriminating fashion design. Both Humphrey Bogart and Audrey Hepburn wore Burberry raincoats in their classic films *Casablanca* and *Breakfast at Tiffany's*. The brand's instantly recognizable 'signature' plaid fabric can rightly be considered a contemporary design icon, and has been extended from clothing to bags, shoes, swim wear and perfume. In the late 1990s, supermodel Kate Moss was featured in Burberry's promotional campaigns.

From a marketing standpoint, the above associations create customer value. The perceived benefits of style, classic design and association with cult figures, both past and present, greatly outweigh the perceived sacrifice – presumably high purchase cost. However, disturbingly, Burberry seems to have become favoured by the football hooligan fraternity, with images of Burberry-wearing soccer 'casuals' creating mayhem splashed across the media. Could such an undesired association damage the perceived value within the company's target market?

something that is missing, desirable or necessary. Many different product types can satisfy a need. For example: if the need is transport, potential products solutions could be private car, taxi, bus or train. These possible solutions are then considered in terms of the remaining As, as follows.

- **Affordability**   Is it available at the right price? Economic factors may override the most desirable option. For example, London has introduced congestion charging to access the road network in busy areas. This attempts to make the use of private cars less desirable. Additionally, affordability could be defined in psychological terms (e.g. stress, risk).

- **Availability**   Do I have access to this product/service at a convenient time/place? Again, availability may override the desired option. A potential passenger may resort back to using their car due to problems associated with the reliability of the rail network.

Benefits are what the customer actually receives from a product and the product's provider. (Note, the term product is taken to cover both goods and services.) Satisfaction is determined by how well the product performs relative to expectations. It is critical to consider expectations. Expectation derives from how well the customer expects the product to perform. This is often determined by past experience, the experience of, or association with, others or marketing communications (e.g. brand image,

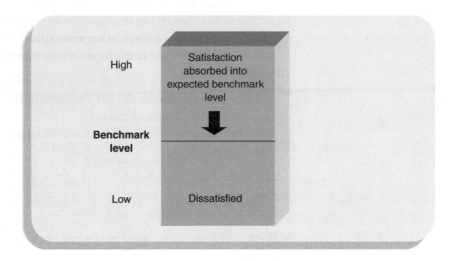

Figure 1.3
Customer satisfaction

advertising, sales promotion activity etc.). If expectation is higher than resulting benefits, the customer is likely to be dissatisfied. Conversely, satisfaction will exist when the benefits given by the product match or exceed the expected level. Hence it is important to manage expectation. A 'golden rule' of marketing is: never increase expectations above your ability to deliver. Additionally, marketing managers need to be aware that over time high levels of satisfaction become the norm. As opposed to adding value, satisfaction factors become an expected part of the basic product offering (see Figure 1.3). Customers will develop an expected 'benchmark' for acceptable levels of satisfaction.

1.4 An overview of the marketing mix

Given that the fulfilment of customer satisfaction is the key to business success, how do organizations achieve this? McCarthy (1960) suggested the concept of the marketing mix (the 4Ps) – product, price, place and promotion. These variables form the key elements within the marketing function, and can be adapted in order to generate, and sustain, customer satisfaction. Each 'P' contains various factors that can be emphasized to meet customer need. For example, price can be discounted depending on the target customer group. Remember, all elements of the mix are inter-related. A change in product formulation may need to be reflected in the promotional element of the mix. The 4Ps are the vital decision areas for marketing managers, as they offer controllable variables which can be innovatively applied to specific markets. Customers will view the marketing mix as an entirety, with all elements shaping perception. For example, a high-quality product will require a premium price to reinforce its desired market position.

In simple terms, marketing strategy involves splitting the market into like groups. This process is known as **segmentation**. Segmentation is the basis of much marketing – see later chapters. The target specific group is a specific marketing mix.

The following summarizes the key elements in the mix. Each will be discussed more fully in later chapters.

- **Product**   As previously stated, products are solutions to customers' needs. The provider needs to make various product decisions, including functionality, range offered, brand names, packaging, service and support. The product is normally the critical element in the mix, with all other decisions relating to this element.

- **Price**   This element determines what a provider is paid. Various price-setting models exist (see Chapter 7), with decisions relating to factors like market penetration, credit terms, discount policy and cost of provision. It should be noted that the price is not always paid directly by the consumer. For example, a charity may receive a government grant to provide services free of charge to worthy causes.

- **Place**   Place is perhaps more readily described as distribution. It is about making the product available. Some form of structured network is normally required – a distribution channel. However, true marketing power may lie with the control of this channel as opposed to control of the product. For example, large supermarket chains can largely determine which goods are made available to the consumer.

- **Promotion**   The promotional element of the mix provides communication with the desired customer group. A range of mechanisms can be deployed for this purpose: advertising, public relations, direct mail, Internet marketing, selling and sales promotion. The blend of methods is often referred to as the communications mix. Generally, promotion aims to make a target market aware of a product offering, develop a long-term relationship with the customer and create and stimulate demand. The effect of promotional techniques can be difficult to evaluate and organizations need clear aims and goals to obtain maximum benefit from a promotional budget.

Given that most developed economies are service-based as opposed to manufacturing-based, the mix can be adapted to consider elements particularly relevant to service-based products. Services display a number of characteristics, for example:

Intangibility   The service is not a physical object which can be examined, rather it must be experienced. Therefore, evaluating quality and suitability prior to purchase can be difficult. For example, the only real way to evaluate a hotel is to go and stay there.

Inseparability Unlike physical goods, services are often consumed as they are produced. They are inseparable from the provider. For example, getting a haircut.

Perishability Normally, services cannot be stored. This means that service supply needs to be carefully matched to demand. For example, if a hotel room is not booked its sale is lost for that time period. However, a fully booked hotel may need to turn away potential customers.

The above characteristics spurred the need to adapt the mix for service-based products. To this end, the mix can be expanded to the 7Ps by adding:

- **Physical evidence** Given the intangible nature of services, customers look for reassurance relating to required benefits and quality. They look for physical evidence (e.g. ambience, fixtures and fittings, appearance/attitude of staff, etc.) as an indicator of likely satisfaction.

- **Process** Process is the method by which the service is provided. It forms the facilitation element of the service offering, which deals with the customer at the point of contact. It covers request processes through to order fulfilment. In the Internet boom, during late 1990s, many 'dot.com' companies failed due to poor services processing and fulfilment.

- **People** Many services are people-based, therefore the quality of provision is totally dependent on the people providing the service. Their skills, attitude and motivation determine if the customer/staff interaction is positive or negative. Hence, people are an essential element of the marketing mix. Staff recruitment, training, development and empowerment to deal with problems become a critical element in ensuring a positive customer experience.

Table 1.2 summarizes key elements of the marketing mix.

1.5 Criticism of the marketing mix

While the mix provides a 'backbone' to marketing theory, which is both memorable and practical, it is not without its critics. Like any academic theory, the marketing mix does need to evolve in line with the business environment (e.g. the 7Ps for service marketing), and while criticism is both valid and healthy, it does not negate the importance of the concept. Common criticisms are:

- The 4Ps make no direct reference to forming, and sustaining, long-term relationships. If such relationships are critical to business success, why are they not directly addressed?

The 4Ps marketing mix	
Product	**Price**
Product range	Pricing model
Product performance	Discount policy
Branding	Credit terms
Packaging	Non-financial cost
Design	
Service support	
Place/distribution	**Promotional**
Channel selection	Advertising
Support supplied by	Sales force
channel members	Direct marketing/On-line
Market/customer coverage	public relations

The 7Ps extended marketing mix		
Physical evidence	**Process**	**People**
Market tangible assets	Fulfilment	Recruitment
Taken as quality	Administration	Training/skills
measure		Interaction with
		customers

Table 1.2
Key decisions relating
to the marketing mix

- The mix can promote a view of product, price, place and promotion as being separate entities, as opposed to the integrated product offering most customers evaluate.

- Internal resource constraints need to be considered, and without active acknowledgement of such factors, the inappropriate combinations of marketing mix variable may increase customer expectation beyond the organization's ability to deliver.

- Application of the 4Ps can promote standardization, or mass production, at a time when society increasingly values individuality.

- The mix can be viewed as manipulative. The right combination, and intensity, of factors could pressure the buyer into purchase.

1.6 Making the marketing mix effective

The above criticisms are more likely due to poor application of the concept, as opposed to any intrinsic flaw in the idea. Therefore, we need to

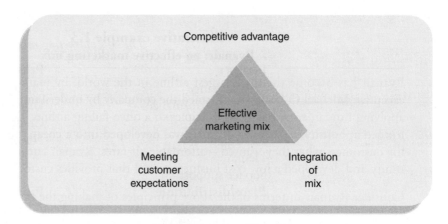

Figure 1.4
Making the mix
effective

ensure optimum use is made of the 4Ps, and its extended version. Figure 1.4 summarizes the factors that are normally deemed to create an effective marketing mix. Consider the following points, when reading the Ryanair illustrative example.

- **Competitive advantage** A competitive advantage is the generation of distinctive competencies relative to the competition. The key factor is to create an advantage, which creates customer value and is sustainable. Porter (1980) argues that there are two fundamental routes to competitive advantage: (1) cost leadership – pursuing the lowest possible operating cost within an industry; and (2) differentiation – creating a unique product offering which is seen by consumers as differentiated from the competitors. Commentators (e.g. Fuller and Goodwin, 1988) point out that these routes are not mutually exclusive and can be pursued in parallel. In developing a competitive advantage, it is important to consider internal resources. A company lacking in key skills, or financial resources, may be unable to sustain the desired competitiveness. A provider may be well advised to concentrate its resources in a limited range of markets, as opposed to spreading resources too thinly.

- **Meeting customer expectations** As stated above, expectations are vital to marketing success. Organizations need to segment and target specific customer groups, and then use the mix to create value. It is important to understand how customers evaluate rival product offerings. The aim is to score higher than competitors in the areas of greatest value to the consumer. For example, if customers place greatest value on economic criteria the organization would aim to be a price leader. However, if image, service and exclusivity were considered more important, a differentiation strategy would be followed, stressing branding image, service level and exclusivity (see the Ryanair example).

- **Integration of mix** The final component of effectiveness is to ensure the mix is well integrated. All the elements should support each other

Illustrative example 1.3
Ryanair: an effective marketing mix

Ryanair has become the third largest airline in the world, by market capitalization. Chief executive Michael O'Leary transformed the company by understanding customer need and applying fundamental business principles to a once-failing airline. Taking on board lessons learned at Southwest Airlines, Ryanair was developed into a cheap, no-frills operation, giving customers what they wanted – affordable air fares. Ryanair cut its costs at every opportunity and developed a low cost business model that provides customer value.

Consider Ryanair in terms of the above principles of making the marketing mix effective:

1 **Competitive advantage** The company has a clear low cost competitive advantage. Costs are minimized at all stages of the operation. While flying to popular destinations, Ryanair picks secondary airports. Such airports are far cheaper to operate from, and in some cases even pay Ryanair to fly there. Flying from Stansted as opposed to Heathrow saves an estimated £3 per passenger. Having aircraft on the ground is expensive, therefore Ryanair has perfected fast-turnarounds. Turnaround times are estimated to be half those of British Airways. Like most airlines, aircraft purchase represents a major cost outlay. O'Leary is credited with obtaining substantial discounts from Boeing. He states: 'I wouldn't even tell my priest what discount I got off Boeing!'.

2 **Meeting customer expectations** Ryanair is a 'no-frills' operation. As such, it provides a basic service at a highly competitive price. For example, unlike traditional airlines, passengers must pay for food and drink. The effect is to keep operating costs down, and turn a potential cost into a source of revenue. At check-in, Ryanair does not allocate seats. This speeds up boarding. Most customers feel the basic service is more than compensated for by the price paid.

3 **Integration of the mix** The company displays a well-integrated marketing mix, with low cost operations a key focal point. Consider promotional activity: Ryanair does not use an advertising agency. It does the work in-house, with simple newspaper and poster adverts emphasizing low fares. In terms of distribution, the company does not use travel agents. Tickets are booked directly, via the Internet. This saves Ryanair 15% of the ticket price. Additional revenue is generated by commission on car hire, hotel bookings, etc., made through the Ryanair website.

and have a common theme, which relates to the desired competitive advantage. The entire marketing mix provides a package of benefits to the consumer, and as such the benefits should be communicated by all mix elements. For example, a high price supports the assertion of a quality product.

1.7 Marketing and ethical issues

The 1990s saw the issue of ethics and corporate responsibility gaining prominence in the business world. Moral and ethical behaviour was no longer a peripheral issue. Rather, it became a 'cornerstone' of corporate policy. This was driven by numerous factors: increased consumerism (organized group pressure on behalf of consumers), legislative framework that enforced responsibility, increasing levels of management education and research linking ethical behaviour to positive business performance. Many situations required marketers to make moral judgement, while faced with conflicting commercial pressures and priorities. Ethics involves the application of moral principles as a guiding framework for business decision-making.

Lambin (2000) defines ethical marketing as the organization embracing an accountable marketing concept that

> defines clearly the rules of ethics it intends to follow in its relationships with the market.

This includes three main actions. First, replacing objectives relating to short-term satisfaction with objectives considering the well being of customers. Secondly, the organization needs to define, communicate and ensure implementation of internal rules of ethical conduct. Finally, the organization recognizes that being ethical may sometimes involve a trade-off with profit. Reidenbach and Robin (1991) identify several types of ethical behaviour within the organization. They term the final stage of this development as 'developed ethical' – the organization has a clearly articulated values statement, communicated, accepted and implemented by everyone in the organization.

The costs of non-ethical behaviour are summarized by Laczniack and Murphy (1993) as being:

- **Personal cost**   The individual can pay both a psychological (e.g. crisis of conscience) and financial cost (e.g. loss of employment) for unethical behaviour.

- **Organizational cost**   When ethical violations become public the price may be heavy – legal prosecution, loss of goodwill and consumer boycotts.

- **External cost**   Society in general can pay the price of non-ethical behaviour – pollution, waste and negative economic impact.

Societal marketing

No discussion of ethics is complete without the consideration of societal marketing. Here marketing approaches and techniques aim to enhance

> ### Illustrative example 1.4
> ### Greenpeace: consumerism protects the forests
>
> Environmental group Greenpeace has launched its 'Save or Delete' campaign, aiming to save some of the world's most ancient forests. The campaign highlights the threat to the world's rainforests and encourages consumers to buy wood and paper products bearing a Forest Stewardship Council logo. The logo denotes socially responsible environmentally based forest management. By providing such information and developing specific campaigns, organizations such as Greenpeace act as a vehicle for active consumerism.

the well being of society in general. Marketers can benefit society via the marketing of social ideas, concepts and values. Philip Kotler called for the marketing mix to include long-term consumer welfare.

1.8 e-Marketing perspective

Technology has had a fundamental impact on all aspects of business. Many of today's marketing activities are shaped by, and largely depend on, technology. e-Marketing encompasses all aspects of technology: Internet, database applications, text and mobile phone messaging.

e-Marketing is no different from any other form of marketing. It must be customer-orientated. However, the technology provides a massive leap both in capacity and capability. The benefits to the organization can be summarized as follows:

- **Lower costs** On-line transactions can mean substantially lower operating costs. For example, admin, people and promotional costs can all be reduced by Web-based sales processing.

- **Market access** It is possible to target/access new markets via new technology. For example, text messaging allows more direct communication with a desired target group, with the potential to customize promotional activity. The use of interactive technology can support marketing communication. For example, a retailer can place their catalogue on-line, allowing potential buyers to search for and combine items.

- **Market research/information** Information can be rapidly processed and drawn from a variety of sources to provide a comprehensive understanding

> **Illustrative example 1.5**
> *The Sunday Times*: **new media for new readers**
>
> *The Sunday Times* is reported to be developing plans to include a regular monthly CD-Rom in its traditional Sunday newspaper package. Known as 'The Month', the CD-based section will provide interactive entertainment (films, music, TV, etc.) coverage. From a marketing perspective, this format aims to reach a younger readership. Such readers have grown up in the digital/Internet age and regard traditional newspaper formats as outdated.

of customers. Data mining techniques allow the analysis of large-scale databases in order to determine potentially valuable links, associations and relationships. Statistical techniques can model and predict customer behaviour. Systems can be developed to aid customer relationship management (CRM). These relationship management systems provide an integration of all aspects of customer service and aim to build mutually beneficial relationships with customers. For example, Amazon, the Internet book retailer, uses CRM to suggest other titles buyers might be interested in.

Summary

Marketing is a process that satisfies customer needs via long-term exchange relationships. Marketing, and market orientation, promote the concept as a strategic business philosophy. Market orientation considers customers, competitors and interfunctional coordination over the long-term.

Customer value is based on perceived benefits. Such benefits are delivered via the marketing mix (the 4Ps), with the mix being extended for service based products (the 7Ps). Customers tend to make decisions based on acceptability, affordability and accessibility. The mix does have its critics. However, criticism is normally due to poor application of the concept, as opposed to any fundamental flaw. To be successful, the mix needs to (1) meet customer expectations, (2) deliver competitive advantage and (3) have a degree of integration.

Ethical issues have come to prominence in marketing. This is driven by consumerism, legal frameworks and good business practice. e-Marketing offers great potential to marketers. It can cut costs and open up new opportunities.

Discussion questions

1 Critically review the CIM definition of marketing.

2 Using Illustrative case 1.1: Jazz[fm], apply both a sales and marketing orientation. Which one fits best, and why?

3 Consider a recent purchase you have made and apply the marketing mix to this.

4 Porter cites two ways to gaining competitive advantage, cost leadership and differentiation. Select two organizations and discuss the appropriateness of the above strategies to each company.

5 Consider the criticisms of the marketing mix. How valid do you feel these are?

References

Adcock, D., Halborg, A. and Ross, C. (2001) *Marketing Principles and Practice*, 4th edn. Financial Times–Prentice Hall.

Fuller, W.E. and Goodwin, J. (1988) Differentiation: begin with the customer. *Business Horizons*, Vol. 31, No. 5, pp. 55–63.

Jaworski, B.J. and Kohli, A.K. (1993) Marketing orientation: antecedents and consequences. *Journal of Marketing*, Vol. 57, July, pp. 53–70.

Jobber, D. (2001) *Principles and Practice of Marketing*, 3rd edn. McGraw–Hill.

Kohli, A.K. and Jaworski, B.J. (1990) Marketing orientation: the construct, research propositions and managerial implications. *Journal of Marketing*, Vol. 54, April, pp. 1–18.

Kotler, P., Armstrong, G., Saunders, J. and Wong, V. (1999) *Principles of Marketing*, 2nd European edn. Prentice–Hall.

Laczniak, G.R. and Murphy, P.E. (1993) *Ethical Marketing Decisions*. Allyn and Bacon.

Lambin, J.J. (2000) *Market-Driven Management*. Macmillan.

McCarthy, E.J. (1960) *Basic Marketing: A Managerial Approach*. Irwin.

Narver, J.C. and Slater, S.F. (1990) The effects of marketing orientation on business profitability. *Journal of Marketing*, Vol. 54, October, pp. 20–35.

Porter, M.E. (1980) *Competitive Strategy*. The Free Press.

Reidenbach, R.E. and Robin, P. (1991) A conceptual model of corporate moral development. *Journal of Business Ethics*, Vol. 5, April, pp. 6–23.

Slater, S.F. and Narver, J.C. (1994) Does competitive environment moderate the market orientation-performance relationship? *Journal of Marketing*, Vol. 58, No. 1, pp. 46–55.

Strategic marketing: an overview

About this chapter

Strategic planning aims to integrate and coordinate activity and give focus to the organization. Recognizing that strategic decisions have behavioural, organizational and analytical elements enables many of the barriers to successful implementation to be overcome.

After reading this chapter, you will understand:

• The difference between corporate and marketing plans.

• Strategic and tactical approaches to marketing.

• The reason for, and barriers to, successful planning.

• Analytical, behavioural and organizational dimensions of planning.

• Structure of a typical strategic marketing plan.

2.1 Corporate and marketing plans

Marketing managers plan in order to complete tasks on time and without exceeding pre-set resource limits. It is likely that objectives, targets and budget will be set as part of the overall corporate planning and budgeting process. The task is to translate these factors into a workable marketing plan.

When developing a plan, the process involves choosing certain courses of action and ruling out other possible options. Planning should be systematic, structured and involves three key components: (1) objectives – what has to be achieved; (2) strategy (or actions) – defining how the objectives are to be achieved; and (3) resource implications – the resources required to implement the strategy.

Clearly, it is important to understand the interface between marketing and corporate strategy. This is best illustrated by considering the hierarchical structure of an organization. Senior management formulates objectives and strategy for the entire organization (or a strategic business unit – SBU). Managers in various functional areas, such as marketing, contribute to the process by developing specific functional strategies and ultimately tactics to achieve these corporate objectives. Effectively, the process involves a hierarchy of plans, with strategy at one level becoming the objective(s) at the next. Additionally, this process provides feedback on the success/failure of any strategy. Figure 2.1 illustrates the concept.

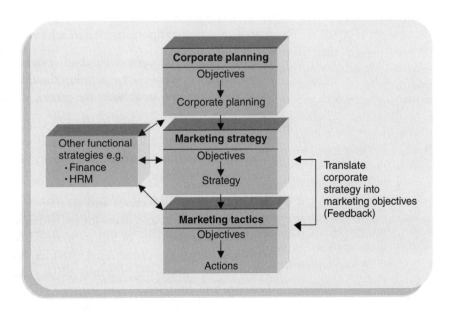

Figure 2.1
Corporate and marketing planning hierarchy

2.2   Corporate planning

The corporate plan will define objectives for the entire business and should coordinate the various functional strategies (e.g. Marketing, Operations, Human Resource Management, Finance, etc.) to deliver the overall corporate objectives. It is important that functional strategies are interrelated (see Figure 2.1). For example, if the marketing strategy focused on developing high levels of customer service in order to retain key customer groups, both the operations and human resource management functions would have a role to play in delivering this. Corporate strategy can be summarized as being:

- **Integrative**   The process **coordinates functional activity** towards a common goal and takes a 'whole organization' view of the corporation. By defining corporate targets, normally in financial terms, collective targets are set for the functional groups.

- **Provide focus**   Strategy defines the scope of the business – general nature of activities and markets served. This **strategic direction** allows functional areas to develop appropriate strategies and tactics.

- **Importance**   By its very nature, corporate strategy is the process of making major business decisions. It defines business direction over the **long term** and is critical in setting the overall resource profile available to the organization.

- **Matching**   There is a need to match the organization's activities and resource base to the current and future business environment.

A useful summation of corporate strategy management is provided in Figure 2.2. This model takes a top-down view of the overall strategy process. It identifies the five components vital in achieving corporate success:

1   **Vision**   Senior management and other stakeholders must establish an overall vision of what the corporation should be. This defines the basic need they fulfil and establishes the generic direction of the business.

2   **Corporate objectives and strategy**   Collective goals and strategy define the 'benchmarks' for success and ways of achieving success. This level coordinates corporate activity and initiates activities to achieve desired results.

3   **SBU/functional objectives and strategy**   Corporate strategy translates into objectives and plans for individual elements of the business. This may take the form of SBUs (Strategic Business Units – divisions within a company) or functional activities. For example, a hotel chain could divide its business into three SBUs – accommodation, food and beverage and conferences and leisure.

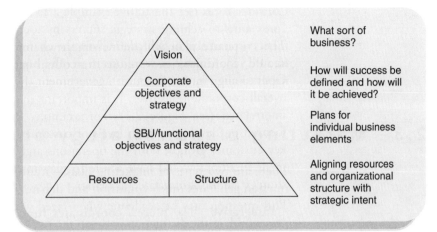

Figure 2.2
The strategic process

Illustrative example 2.1
Torex: marketing strategy and the 'drivers' of change

Rather than trying to cover all possible users, information technology company Torex has two distinct areas of operation – retailing and health care. Having adopted a clear segmentation and targeting strategy, Torex is able to establish a distinct competitive position, setting it apart from more general IT providers. A PEST analysis demonstrates how the organization can benefit from the 'drivers' of change. Consider the following statement in terms of **P**olitical, **E**conomic, **S**ocial and **T**echnological factors.

The UK government's commitment to modernize the health service (*political*) is excellent news for specialist information technology provider Torex. Growing demand for health care (*social*) will generate a need to modernize existing health service systems with specialized health service/care technology. As a provider of computer technology to the medical profession, Torex is well placed to benefit from increased government expenditure (*economic*). The company is also reported to be working on the 'Gpnet' project (*technological*) – an electronic information system which links doctors together.

---

4 **Resources**   For a given strategy, the need exists to match resources to strategic intent. This process normally involves annual budgeting.

5 **Structure**   Management must develop the appropriate organizational and staffing structures to facilitate success.

Successful businesses ensure these factors are aligned in order to turn strategic intent into business reality.

Consider Torex (see Illustrative example 2.1) in the context of Figure 2.2. Torex aims to achieve strategic success by focusing on two market segments – retail and health care. Given the changing business environment (see PEST), health care would seem to offer huge potential. The company needs to align its resources with government spending plans.

2.3   Marketing plans: strategy or tactics?

There are two types of marketing plan – strategic and tactical. This distinction generates much confusion and debate; is it a strategy or a tactic? This question may be academic when faced with the reality of the business world, as the distinction between the two will vary from organization to organization and manager to manager. However, much of the confusion can be removed if characteristics common to strategic plans and tactical plans can be identified.

- **Strategic marketing**   Takes a longer-term time frame and broadly defines the organization's marketing activities. The process seeks to develop effective responses to a changing business environment by analysing markets, segmentation and evaluating competitors' offerings. Strategy focuses on defining market segments and positioning products in order to establish a competitive stance. Marketing strategy tends to embrace all of the mix, or significant components of the mix (e.g. distribution strategy, communications strategy, etc.). Problems in this area tend to be unstructured and require external, often speculative, data.

- **Tactical marketing**   This takes a shorter-term time frame and concerns day-to-day marketing activities. It translates strategy into specific actions and represents the on-going operational dimension of marketing strategy. Tactical marketing tends to deal with individual components of the marketing mix elements (e.g. sales promotion, advertising, etc.). Problems are often repetitive and well structured, with data being internally generated.

Table 2.1 examines the differences between strategic and tactical marketing.

2.4   Why does planning matter?

The organization needs a strategic marketing plan in order to adapt to a changing business environment. Given the basic business premise of *success through effectively meeting customer needs*, it is clear organizations must continually adapt and develop to remain successful. Strategic marketing

	Strategic marketing	*Tactical marketing*
Time frame	Long-term	Short-term
Focus	Broad	Narrow
Key task(s)	Defining market and competitive position	Day-to-day marketing activity
Information and problem-solving	Unstructured, external, speculative	Structured, internal, repetitive
Example	New product development	Price discounting

Table 2.1
Strategic and tactical marketing

facilitates this process and provides robust solutions in an increasingly competitive world. Essentially, the plan should provide a systematic framework with which to analyse the market place and supply a well-defined way to pursue strategic goals.

However, the truly successful plan goes further than the simple process of planning. It is a vehicle to communicate, motivate and involve staff in fundamental business activities. Too often planning is viewed as a restrictive process based on programming events and generating paperwork. Remember, plans need employee commitment and 'ownership' to achieve results.

The key reasons for planning are summarized as follows:

- **Adapting to change**   Planning provides an opportunity to examine how changes in the business environment have/will effect the organization. It enables management to focus on strategic issues as opposed to day-to-day operational problems.

- **Resource allocation**   Planning allows us to deploy resources to effectively meet opportunities and threats. No plan can succeed without appropriate resources. When a strategic perspective is taken, organizations are better placed to marshal the resources required to meet strategic 'windows of opportunity'. Doyle (1994) defines strategic windows of opportunity as changes that have a major impact in the market place. Strategic windows include factors such as: (1) new technology, (2) new market segments, (3) new channels of distribution, (4) market redefinition – where the nature of demand changes, (5) legislative changes and (6) environmental shocks – sudden unexpected economic or political change. Essentially, the process involves aligning marketing activities with opportunities in order to generate competitive advantage.

- **Consistency** By providing a common base to work from (e.g. techniques and assumptions) the overall decision-making process can be enhanced. Additionally, common methods and formats should improve internal communication.

- **Integration** As a strategic process, planning should facilitate the integration and coordination of the marketing mix. By providing a strategic focus it should be possible to generate synergy from the individual elements of the marketing mix.

- **Communication and motivation** The plan should clearly communicate strategic intent to employees and other stakeholders. Clear objectives and an understanding of the individual, or group, contribution to the process serves to generate 'ownership' and motivation.

- **Control** All control activities are based on some predetermined plan. The planning process should set meaningful targets, thus defining the criteria by which success is measured.

To illustrate the above points, consider Illustrative example 2.2: Sainsbury. The company will need to adapt to change and have effective resource allocation if it is to reverse the downturn in its fortunes.

Illustrative example 2.2
Sainsbury: strategic return to core values

Major strategic decisions have to be made if Sainsbury is to regain its former glory. The UK's second biggest food retailer is looking to establish a more upmarket position, in order to reverse the recent downturn in fortunes. A new 'flagship' Sainsbury's store in London will feature new luxury product ranges. These include: a juice bar, upmarket bakery counter, a premium wine merchant – 'The Cromwell Cellar' – and a seasonal produce counter. The move sees the group attempting to return to its core competencies (see Figure 1.1) of being a top-quality food retailer. Sainsbury's traditional strength is not price, but rather quality, with the above developments aiming to position the company upmarket. Sainsbury struggled to compete in a price war with larger groups such as Asda and Tesco. Previous Sainsbury campaigns (e.g. 'Value to shout about' – featuring actor John Cleese) promoted price competitiveness, not something traditionally associated with the company. It is now committed to offering the highest quality food at the most competitive prices. This focus gives the group strategy a consistency of approach.

2.5   Barriers to successful planning

Few would argue with the concept of planning. In any activity, a plan provides a fundamental basis for success. Marketing plans should offer exactly what is required – optimizing the use of marketing techniques and resources in order to make the most of marketing opportunities. However, even the most charitable of marketing managers would view this statement as naive and unlikely to be fully achieved. If managers view planning as 'fine in theory' but failing, in practice, to deliver its full potential – where does it go wrong?

Clearly, barriers must exist to successful planning. Often, these barriers are more to do with the human aspects of the business management. They involve people, politics, skills and culture to a greater degree than formal systems, methodology and data.

Common barriers to successful planning are:

- **Culture**   The prevailing culture may not be amenable to marketing plans. If the fundamental principles of marketing are not accepted by the organization, any move towards being market-led and customer-orientated could be dismissed as 'not the way we do it'. Often we see considerable resistance to change and gradual regression back to old work practices.

- **Power and politics**   All organizations are subject to internal politics. The development of strategic planning becomes a battlefield where vested interests fight each other's proposals and squabble over status and resources. This process absorbs much management time and can result in ill-advised compromise and unnecessary delay.

- **Analysis not action**   Much time and energy can be wasted by the process of analysing data and developing rationales for action, as opposed to simply acting. While a rigorous process is commendable, it should not displace action. This 'paralysis-by-analysis' barrier tends to substitute information gathering and processing for decision-making. Perhaps surprisingly, many planning systems do not promote action and are more concerned with reviewing progress and controlling activity, rather than tackling strategic issues.

- **Resource issues**   In any planning situation, the potential exists to negotiate over resources. Indeed, a major aspect of the process is to match resources to strategic aims. Managers must take a realistic view of the resource position and endeavour to ensure resources are not over-committed or needlessly withheld.

- **Skills**   In some instances, managers do not have the skills (e.g. project management, forecasting, etc.) required to make the best use of the planning process. Here, planning takes on a ritual nature – a meaningless

25

but 'must-do' annual task. Often, planning is reduced to incremental increases/decreases in annual budget and fails to examine opportunities for business development.

Many of these barriers relate to the implementation of plans rather than the planning process itself. Chapter 12 deals with the issue of implementation in detail. However, the sound management practice would advocate the inclusion of implementation as part of the planning process. Indeed, Piercy (1997) suggests a multidimensional model of planning. This considers the analytical dimension, the behavioural dimension and the organizational dimension of any plan. Figure 2.3 summarizes the model.

- **Analytical dimension** Analytical tools, techniques and models are important, as they provide a framework to tackle issues and identify/solve problems. While formalized planning systems have the advantage of offering a common (corporate-wide) systematic approach, to be truly effective they must address behavioural and organizational issues.

- **Behavioural dimension** Here we focus on the people aspects of the planning process. Plans only become successful because of the support, participation, motivation and commitment of people. There is a need to understand and fully communicate the strategic assumptions underpinning the strategy. Plans must address behavioural factors in order to gain the support so vital to smooth implementation.

- **Organizational dimension** Strategic planning takes place within the context of a given organization. Therefore, it will be influenced by organizational factors, such as culture and style of management. Remember, organizational structures determine the flow of information, as well as defining responsibilities and reporting lines. Major strategic initiatives may require radical organizational changes.

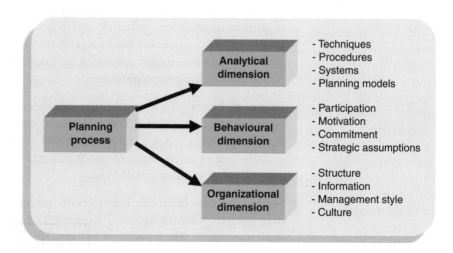

Figure 2.3
A multidimensional model of marketing planning (*Source:* Piercy, 1997)

By taking this 'multidimensional' approach to planning and actively considering behavioural and organizational issues within the planning process, it is possible to enhance the overall likelihood of success.

2.6 The structure of a strategic marketing plan

What does a strategic marketing plan look like? While the answer to this question will vary from organization to organization (in terms of structure and presentation), marketing plans perform a common function and have common components. Indeed, McDonald (1999) views marketing planning as a systematic way of identifying, selecting, scheduling and costing activities in order to achieve objectives. Such definitions focus on the purpose, as opposed to the structure, of planning.

Regardless of precedent and planning formats, strategic plans tend to have common elements. Marketing managers would expect a strategic plan to cover: (1) industry analysis, (2) internal analysis, (3) opportunity identification, (4) objective setting, (5) formulation of strategy, (6) proposed marketing programmes and actions and (7) implementation and control – including financial forecasts.

Figure 2.4 presents an annotated example of a strategic marketing plan. Note, Figure 2.4 does not attempt to portray the definitive marketing plan. It merely illustrates the component parts common to such plans.

Strategic marketing plans take on many different guises. The content, structure and complexity of a plan will vary. While planning formats and conventions are largely a matter of historic precedent within the organization, the key imperative is to generate action. Plans should address critical issues in a way that is relevant to the organization. For example, promoting decisive marketing initiatives within a limited time-scale.

2.7 Approaches to marketing planning

The development of a marketing plan is a significant and time-consuming activity. All planning is essentially objective-driven – objectives are translated into actions. A number of 'schools of thought' exist as to how the task is best approached. The standard approaches to planning are:

- **Top-down** Senior managers develop objectives and strategy. Managers at an operational level are then required to implement these strategies. This approach is said to encourage professionalism and promote a corporate strategic view of marketing activity.

Provides a link to overall strategy and illustrates marketing's contribution to achieving corporate goals

There is a need to define financial targets and translate these into specific measurable marketing objectives (e.g. market share, sales volume, customer retention)

Specific programmes are broken down into lists of activities. These are scheduled and given a time scale. Responsibility is assigned for each activity. A contingency (e.g. funds or time) may be set to cover any unforeseen problems

1 Executive summary
1.1 Current position
1.2 Key issues

Improves communication and staff involvement by summarizing key aspects of the plan

2 Corporate strategy
2.1 Corporate mission/objectives
2.2 Summary of overall position and corporate strategy

3 External and internal analysis
3.1 Overview of market
3.2 Competitor analysis
3.3 Future trends
3.4 SWOT

A picture of the competitive environment is developed. Internal factors (strengths and weaknesses) need to address external factors (opportunities and threats)

4 Marketing objectives
4.1 Financial objectives
4.2 Marketing objectives

5 Marketing strategy
5.1 Market segmentation
5.2 Competitive advantage
5.3 Marketing strategy
5.4 Specific marketing programmes
   - product
   - place
   - promotion
   - price

The overall strategic direction of marketing policy is defined. The strategy may vary according to market segment

Decisions are made relating to specific aspects of the mix. These may generate additional plans for each element of the mix

6 Implementation
6.1 Schedule of key tasks
6.2 Resource allocation
6.3 Budgets
6.4 Contingency

7 Control and forecasting
7.1 Assumptions made
7.2 Critical success factors
   - Benchmarks established
   - How measured
7.3 Financial forecasts
   - Costs
   - Revenue

A clear understanding of the assumptions underpinning the control process is required (e.g. projected market growth). The benchmarks measuring success must be assigned to critical activities. Profit and loss accounts may be forecast for the planning period

Figure 2.4
Illustrative example of a strategic marketing plan

• **Bottom-up** Here, authority and responsibility for formulation and implementation of strategy is devolved. Senior marketing managers approve, and then monitor, agreed objectives. It can be claimed that this approach encourages ownership and commitment.

Hybrid systems are also common, where objectives are 'top-down' and responsibility for the formulation/implementation of strategy is devolved.

2.8   e-Marketing perspective

e-Marketing is basically an interactive activity which is conducted via on-line systems. Virtually unheard of a decade ago, e-marketing has seen rapid growth and is quickly becoming central to much marketing planning. e-Marketing brings together a range of technologies: Internet, e-mail, electronic data/payment interchange and short message service (SMS) applications. The fusion, and wide adoption, of such technologies means marketers now have alternatives to traditional communications campaigns based on the mass media. It provides a mechanism to target and interact with key groups or individuals (see Illustrative example 2.3).

As a major driving force in future marketing activities, marketing planners need to consider the advantages and disadvantages of this new medium. Brennan, Baines and Garneau (2003) summarize these as follows:

Advantages:

- **Global reach**   Customers can now 'shop the world', with transactions being conducted across geographic boundaries. This provides much greater access to customers. Even small companies can now compete on a global basis. Additionally, e-marketing enables the targeting of groups who previously did not respond to traditional communications methods (e.g. teenagers).

- **Speed and flexibility**   The Internet is available '24/7' – all-day and everyday. Potential customers are not constrained by the availability of staff or shop opening hours. Buyers can conduct business when it is convenient to them.

Illustrative example 2.3
Heinz: using the Net as a strategic base

The recent creation of a consumer website for all its brands by Heinz is significant. This marks the increased importance attached to e-marketing by the company. HeinzOffers.co.uk will be promoted on packs and contain a series of promotional offers designed to be redeemed in-store. Consumers can register their details and receive a variety of customized promotions. The site aims to encourage brand loyalty and encourage users to try other Heinz products. This Web initiative should allow Heinz to communicate to a younger audience who are difficult to target via traditional mass media communication vehicles such as TV.

- **Low cost transactions** Individual transactions tend to have a much lower unit cost. For example, potential customers can access a brochure on-line, which is much cheaper than mailing out the equivalent paper-based product.

- **Interactivity** e-Marketing's greatest advantage is its ability to develop interactive engagement of customers. The technology allows a two-way dialogue to be established. For example, Amazon recommends an additional book of interest, based on the customer's previous buying habits.

Disadvantages:

- **Clutter and congestion** There is an argument that states people are simply overwhelmed by the sheer scale/volume of e-marketing – too many e-mails, a vast number of websites, etc. Marketing planners need to consider how to make their e-marketing standout in a congested cyber world.

- **Anonymity** By its very nature the Internet is anonymous. A Web presence may convey little about the actual provider. Traditional brand virtues – trust, loyalty and reputation – are far more difficult to convey in a virtual environment. Additionally, the question of security is ever-present. While websites are normally secure, they need to be perceived as secure.

- **Cost** While (as stated above) transaction costs are generally low, Internet set-up, maintenance and facilitation costs can be prohibitively high. For example, the organization needs a fulfilment system, which hands billing, stock control, logistics and distribution.

- **Sensory limitation** Sensory limitations do of course exist. A product can be viewed or described over the Internet, but cannot be touched, tasted or (generally) experienced. Moves towards broadband Internet connections will add improved sound, video capability etc.

Summary

Strategic planning offers a systematic and structured approach to choosing and implementing certain courses of action. Corporate plans define overall business objectives, while providing focus and coordinating functional activities. Such plans need to align the stakeholders' vision to the objectives, strategy, resources and structure of the strategic business units.

There is a need to differentiate between marketing strategy and marketing tactics. Essentially, strategic marketing focuses on defining segments, establishing competitive positions and coordinating all the elements of the mix. Tactics translate strategies into action and deal with day-to-day marketing transactions.

Planning allows organizations to adapt to a changing business environment and provides a framework for resource allocation. Additionally, sound planning promotes a consistency of approach and facilitates integration of activity, communication, motivation and control of activities. In order to achieve these benefits, we must overcome the numerous barriers to successful planning. These include: culture, internal politics or lacking the requisite skills to make planning a successful activity. Truly successful plans make use of analytical techniques but also address the behavioural and organizational dimensions of the process.

The structure and content of a strategic marketing plan will vary. However, plans tend to have common elements – industry analysis, internal analysis, opportunity identification, formulation of strategy, marketing programmes/actions and implementation/control.

Formulating marketing plans can take a top-down, bottom-up or hybrid approach.

e-Marketing is now a major driver of marketing strategy. As such, marketing planners need to be aware of both the limitations and advantages of this new medium.

References

Brennan, R., Baines, P. and Garneau, P. (2003) *Contemporary Strategic Marketing*. Palgrave.

Doyle, P. (1994) *Marketing Management and Strategy*, 2nd edn. Prentice Hall.

McDonald, M. (1999) *Marketing Plans*, 4th edn. Butterworth-Heinemann.

Piercy, N. (1997) *Market-Led Strategic Change*, 2nd edn. Butterworth-Heinemann.

3

Environmental factors

About this chapter

This chapter explores the environmental factors within which the marketing activities of an organization take place. The chapter also outlines the process of PEST analysis, industry analysis, competitor analysis and market analysis. The use of various approaches to facilitate an analysis of the environmental factors facing an organization, in particular the 'Five Forces' model and strategic groups, are covered.

3.1   Introduction

An analysis of the external environment is undertaken in order to discover the opportunities and threats that are evolving and that need to be addressed by the organization. A study by Diffenbach (1983) identified a number of positive consequences that stem from carrying out an organized environmental analysis (see Figure 3.1).

An analysis of the external environment can be broken down into three key steps, each becoming more specific to the organization. The first step is an analysis of the macro-environmental influences that the organization faces. This is followed by an examination of the competitive (micro) environment the organization operates within. Finally a specific competitive analysis is undertaken.

3.2   Macro-environmental analysis

The macro environment audit examines the broad range of environmental issues that may affect the organization. This will include the political/legal issues, economic factors, social/cultural issues and technological

Awareness of environmental changes by management:	Industry and market analysis:
• Enhanced ability to anticipate problems arising in the longer term • Senior management awareness of a range of possible futures and their effect on the organization • Greater inclination to act in advance of changes	• Quality of market and product forecasts improved • Identification of changes in buyer behaviour as a result of changes in social trends • Ability to identify future needs and anticipate new products
Strategic planning and decision-making:	Diversification and resource allocation:
• More flexibility and adaptability in plans as they reflect greater awareness of political events and economic cycles • Scope of perspectives broadened • Organization has greater ability to allocate resources to opportunities arising due to environmental change	• Ability to focus resources in business areas that have long-term attractiveness • Guides the acquisitions process • Move away from products exposed to greater social and political pressure (environmental issues etc.) towards other areas of the product portfolio
Relationship with government:	Overseas businesses:
• Improved understanding and relationship with government • Ability to be proactive on government legislation	• Improved ability to anticipate changes in overseas markets • Ability to anticipate changes in the way of undertaking business in overseas markets

Figure 3.1
A selection of benefits derived from organized environmental analysis (*Source:* adapted from Diffenbach, 1983)

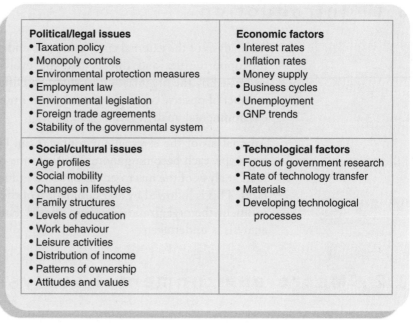

Political/legal issues	Economic factors
• Taxation policy	• Interest rates
• Monopoly controls	• Inflation rates
• Environmental protection measures	• Money supply
• Employment law	• Business cycles
• Environmental legislation	• Unemployment
• Foreign trade agreements	• GNP trends
• Stability of the governmental system	
• **Social/cultural issues**	• **Technological factors**
• Age profiles	• Focus of government research
• Social mobility	• Rate of technology transfer
• Changes in lifestyles	• Materials
• Family structures	• Developing technological
• Levels of education	processes
• Work behaviour	
• Leisure activities	
• Distribution of income	
• Patterns of ownership	
• Attitudes and values	

Figure 3.2
The PEST analysis of influences in the external environment

developments. This is normally referred to as a PEST (Political, Economic, Social and Technological) analysis, although some writers use the alternative acronym of STEP analysis (see Figure 3.2). The aim of this analysis is to identify the critical issues in the external environment that may affect the organization, before moving on to judge the impact they may have on the organization.

- **Political/legal issues**   There are a range of political organizations that have to be considered when looking at influences in this area of the audit. The structure of a political system defines the centres of political influence. A state with a federal political structure will differ from a unitary political system. In the UK there is a parliament for Scotland and an assembly for Wales. There are, however, a number of decision areas that are still the responsibility of the Westminster parliament. At the same time there is also an increasing range of decisions taking place both politically and legally within the framework of the European Union. Political pressure groups, such as Greenpeace, can also affect the political agenda. Therefore, when considering this area of the environment, a much wider view has to be taken than just the domestic national government or the legal process.

- **Economic factors**   Similarly, economic factors have to be viewed from a wider perspective than the organization's domestic economy. In the global economy, domestic economic conditions are heavily influenced by events in other areas of the world. Economics is concerned with the allocation of resources. Therefore, issues such as conservation of natural resources, costs

> ### Illustrative example 3.1
> ### Bluephone
>
> In May 2004, BT Retail, in response to new technological developments, announced that in partnership with Vodafone it was launching an innovative service called Bluephone. This service aims to offer a fully converged fixed and mobile phone service. The service consists of a mobile handset that contains the technology to switch calls automatically between BT's landline network and Vodafone's mobile platform. As a result customers can have access to the same services and information in any situation, be it at home, at work or when travelling. The customer would receive better reception, faster rates of data transfer, an overall lower level of charges and a single bill for the service. Many in the industry believe that there are still some question marks over whether the new technology can successfully deliver this type of service. BT, however, believes that within the next five years the Bluephone service will generate revenues of around £1bn.

of pollution, energy consumption and the whole area of the management of natural resources should be considered under this heading.

- **Social/cultural issues** Demographic changes are important and can be used as lead indicators in certain areas, such as health care and education. However, other critical areas such as social/cultural values and beliefs that are central to changes in consumer behaviour are harder to predict and can be subject to more dramatic shifts.

- **Technological developments** There is a great danger in using a particular technology to define an industry. In a situation where technological developments are fast-moving it is critical to understand the fundamental consumer needs which the organization's technology is currently serving. Identifying new technologies that can service that consumer's needs more completely or economically is the critical part of this area of the analysis.

The central role of this PEST analysis is to identify the key factors that are likely to drive change in the environment. Then the aim is to establish how these key factors will affect the industry in general and the organization in particular.

3.3   Industry analysis

An organization has to understand the nature of the relationship within its industry in order to allow the enterprise to develop strategies to gain advantage of the current relationships.

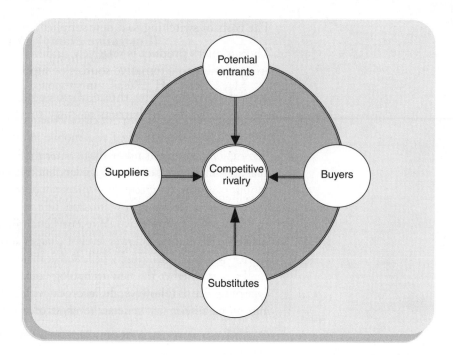

Figure 3.3
The Five Forces
model (*Source:*
adapted from Porter,
1980)

A useful framework that can be utilized when undertaking this analysis is Porter's 'Five Forces' model of establishing industry attractiveness for a business (see Figure 3.3). This analysis should be conducted at the level of the individual strategic business unit (SBU) rather than at the level of the organization as a whole, otherwise the range of relationships facing a company with several divisions causes the analysis to lose focus. Porter identified five factors that affect the level of competition and therefore profitability within an industry:

- **Suppliers**   The power of suppliers is liable to be strong where:
  - Control over supplies is concentrated into the hands of a few players.
  - Costs of switching to a new source of supply are high.
  - If the supplier has a strong brand.
  - The supplier is in an industry with a large number of smaller disparate customers.

- **Buyers**   The power of buyers is liable to be strong where:
  - A few buyers control a large percentage of a volume market. For example, grocery and electrical goods retailers in the UK dominate the market and are in a very strong position versus their suppliers as a result.
  - There are a large number of small suppliers. In the meat industry in the UK there are a large number of small farmers supplying a retail sector dominated by a small number of large supermarkets.

○ The costs of switching to a new supplier are low.

○ The supplier's product is relatively undifferentiated, effectively lowering barriers to alternative sources of supply.

• **Potential entrants**   The threat of potential entrants will be determined by a number of barriers to entry that may exist in any given industry:

○ The capital investment necessary to enter the industry can be very high in areas such as electrical power generation or chemical production.

○ A well-entrenched competitor who moved into the industry early may have established cost advantages irrespective of the size of their operation. They have had time to establish crucial aspects of their operation such as effective sources of supply, the best locations, and customer franchises.

○ Achieving economies of scale in production, distribution or marketing can be a necessity in certain industries.

○ Gaining access to appropriate distribution channels can be difficult. Peugeot/Citroen bought Chrysler's entire UK operations in order to gain an effective dealership network in Britain.

○ Government legislation and policies such as patent protection, trade relations with other states and state-owned monopolies can all act to restrict the entry of competitors.

○ The prospect of a well-established company's hostile reactions to a new competitor's entry to the market may be enough to act as a deterrent.

• **Substitutes**   Substitution can arise in a number of ways:

○ A new product or service may eradicate the need for a previous process. Insurance services delivered directly by producers over the phone or Internet are substitutes for the services of the independent insurance broker.

○ A new product replaces an existing product or service. Cassette tapes replaced vinyl records, only to be replaced by compact discs.

○ All products and services, to some extent, suffer from generic substitution. Consumers may choose to substitute buying a car in order to purchase an expensive holiday instead.

• **Competitive rivalry**   The intensity of competition in the industry will be determined by a range of factors:

○ The stage of the industry life cycle will have an effect. Natural growth reaches a plateau once an industry reaches maturity; the only way an organization can continue to grow in the industry is to take market share off its rivals.

○ The relative size of competitors is an important factor. In an industry where rivals are of similar size, competition is likely to be intense as they each strive for a dominant position. Industries that already have a clear dominant player tend to be less competitive.

○ In industries that suffer from high fixed costs, companies will try to gain as much volume throughput as possible, this may create competition based on price discounting.

○ There may be barriers that prevent companies withdrawing from an industry. This may be plant and machinery that is specialist in nature and therefore cannot be transferred to other uses. The workforce may have non-transferable specialist skills. If the industry is in maturity, moving towards decline, and rivals cannot easily leave the industry then competition inevitably will increase.

This model allows an organization to identify the major forces that are present in the industry sector. This can be related to the critical factors that were identified by the PEST analysis. Several issues then need to be considered:

• What is the likelihood that the nature of the relationships identified by the 'Five Forces' model will change given the trends in the external environment? Are there ways of benefiting from these potential changes?

• What actions can the organization undertake that will improve its position against the current forces in the industry? Can the company increase its power, relative to suppliers or buyers? Can actions be taken to reduce competitive rivalry, or are there ways of building barriers to dissuade companies from considering entering the industry? Are there ways of making substitute products less attractive?

• The organization will also need to consider its competitors. Given the forces in the industry, what is the relative position of the organization's rivals. Do conditions favour one particular operator? Could conditions change in favour of one particular competitor? Consideration of the relative competitive position of rivals is an important aspect of an audit and needs now to be considered in more detail.

3.4   Competitor analysis

The 'Five Forces' analysis has examined the overall industry and is a starting point in assessing a company's competitive position. This is likely to be a rather broad definition of an industry and contains a number of companies that would not be direct competitors. Toyota is likely to have a number of natural direct competitors, TVR is not likely to be one of them, although both companies are in the car industry. Toyota's scale is global and manufactures cars across the full range, TVR is a specialist, low volume prestige sports car manufacturer. Companies that are direct competitors in terms of products and customer profiles are seen as being in a strategic group. The car industry would be made up of a number of strategic groups.

Strategic groups

Strategic groups are made up of organizations within the same industry that are pursuing equivalent strategies targeting groups of customers that have similar profiles. TVR's strategic group is likely to contain Ferrari, Lotus, Lamborghini, Aston Martin etc. All these companies are following similar strategies and facing similar strategic questions. They are also aiming at very similar market segments. In the airline industry there are at least three strategic groups. One group consists of airlines with regional operations who offer scheduled flights and compete on cost. There is a group of major airlines who have global operations and offer scheduled flights with quality environments and service. The third group offer charter services to a range of holiday destinations (see Figure 3.4).

There are a range of attributes that can be used to identify strategic groups. Some examples are:

• Size of the company.

• Assets and skills.

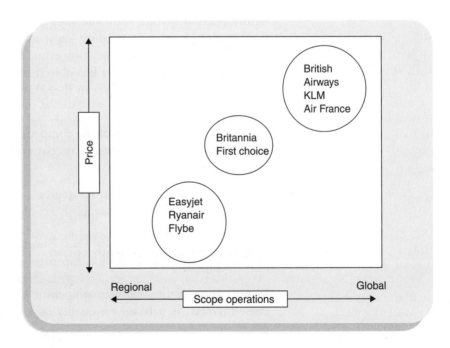

Figure 3.4
Strategic groups in the airline industry

- Scope of the operation.

- Breadth of the product range.

- Choice of distribution channel.

- Relative product quality.

- Brand image.

For many companies, analysing every competitor in its generic industry would be a difficult task in terms of management time and company resources. Defining an organization's strategic group allows a company to concentrate its analysis on its direct competitors and to examine them in more detail.

Tools that are used to analyse the internal environment, such as the Shell directional policy matrix (Shell, 1975), can of course be used to analyse competitors (see Chapter 6). For each competitor in their strategic group an organization needs, as far as possible, to establish the following:

- **Competitor's objectives**   Competitor's objectives can be identified by analysing three important factors:

  ○ Whether the competitor's current performance is likely to be fulfilling their objectives. If not, the competitor may initiate a change of strategy.

  ○ How likely the competitor is to commit further investment to the business. Financial objectives may indicate this. Investment is more likely from companies that have objectives which are long-term in nature, such as market share and sales growth, rather than organizations under pressure to produce short-term profitability. This also reveals potential trade-offs the competitor may be willing to take. If short-term profitability is the key objective then the rival is likely to be willing to lose market share in the short term in order to achieve its profitability targets.

  ○ The likely future direction of the competitor's strategy. The organization may have non-financial objectives, such as gaining technology leadership.

- **Competitor's current and past strategies**   There are three areas that should be explored in order to establish a competitor's current activities:

  ○ Identification of the current markets, or market segments, within which the competitor currently operates. This will indicate the scope of the business.

  ○ Identification of the way the competitor has chosen to compete in those markets. Is it based on quality of service, brand image or on price?

○ Comparison between the current strategy and past strategies can be instructive. First, it can illustrate the direction the competitor is moving, in terms of product and market development, over time. It can also highlight strategies that the organization has tried in the past and that have failed. The competitor is unlikely to attempt these approaches again without considerable reservations.

• **Competitor's capabilities** An analysis of a competitor's assets and competencies allows a judgement to be made about how well equipped they are to address the market, given the dynamics in the industry and the trends in the external environment. In order to evaluate a competitor's potential challenge to an organization a number of areas need to be examined (Lehman and Weiner, 1991):

○ *Management capabilities* The background and previous approaches of leading managers in a competitor company can give clues as to their likely future strategy. The level of centralization, or decentralization of management decisions will also affect decision-making. Recruitment and promotion policies, along with the remuneration and rewards scheme, all give an indication as to the culture and style of the management team.

○ *Marketing capabilities* An analysis of the competitor's actions, with the marketing mix, uncovers the areas where their marketing skills are high and also areas of vulnerability. There are a number of questions that can be asked: How good is the competitor's product line? Do they have a strong brand image? Is their advertising effective? How good are their distribution channels? How strong is their relationship with customers?

○ *Innovation capabilities* Evaluating a competitor's ability to innovate allows an organization to judge how likely the rival is to introduce new products and services or even new technology. Assessing the quality of a competitor's technical staff, its technical facilities and their level of investment in research and development, will all help indicate their likely potential in this area.

○ *Production capabilities* The configuration of a competitor's production infrastructure can highlight areas that may place them at an advantage or conversely point out areas that are problematic to a competitor. Such factors could be geographic spread of plant, level of vertical integration, or level of capacity utilization. Low capacity utilization can increase fixed costs per unit of manufacture. On the other hand, it offers a competitor production capacity for new products. The flexibility of production staff is also an important issue to identify. In the service sector, capacity and staff flexibility are just as important. Factors such as the ability to pull in additional staff on a temporary basis gives a service company an important capability.

○ *Financial capabilities*   The ability to finance developments is a critical area. Competitors that have strong cash flows, or are a division of a major group, may have the ability to finance investment not available to other competitors.

- **Competitor's future strategies and reactions**   One of the aims of the competitor analysis so far has been to gather information on rivals to establish their likely future strategy. Equally important is to evaluate a competitor's likely reactions to any strategic moves the organization might instigate. The reactions of organizations can be categorized into four types of response (Kotler *et al.*, 1996):

  ○ *Certain retaliation*   The competitor is guaranteed to react in an aggressive manner to any challenge. Market leaders, in particular, are likely to react in this manner against any threat to their dominant

---

Illustrative example 3.2
Wi-Fi

Between them the UK mobile phone operators paid £22.5bn to gain licences to run third generation, or 3G, telephone technology. There are now fears that, despite the fact that wireless fidelity (wi-fi) technology has been around for ten years, it may be able to offer the same services to users as 3G at a fraction of the cost. Wi-fi will let consumers access the Internet on a laptop at speeds 10 times faster than a standard dial-up service with the added advantage that there are no wires or cables involved. Currently consumers can access it through Local Area Networks (LANs) set up in areas such as airports, rail stations, cafes, pubs and hotels. These LANs are also sometimes referred to as wi-fi hotspots. Also consumers can set up wire-free IT equipment in their own homes. Experts believe wi-fi would be a third cheaper than 3G for Internet access and also offer the same level of savings for voice data. BT plans to have 4000 wi-fi hotspots installed by summer 2005. The Cloud, another wi-fi operator, plans to have 3000 hotspots in operation by the end of 2004. Each hotspot costs around £5000 to install and allows individuals access up to a range of 50–100 metres. In comparison, each 3G cell has a range of around 10–20 km. The scene seems to be set for a battle between these two technologies. It would be relatively cheap to distribute wi-fi technology across the UK. However, mobile telephone operators will not easily abandon the 3G technology upon which they have invested so heavily.

position. Companies that have an aggressive culture may also fall into this category.

○ *Failure to react*   Competitors can be lulled into a false sense of security in an industry that, over a long period of time, has seen very little change. In this situation companies can be extremely slow to react to a competitive move. The classic example is British motorcycle companies failing to react to the entry of Japanese manufacturers into the lower end of the market.

○ *Specific reactions*   Some competitors may react, but only to competitive moves in certain areas. For instance they may always react to any price reductions, or sales promotions, as they believe these will have an important impact on their business. But they may fail to respond to a competitor's increase in advertising expenditure. The more visible the competitor's move the more likely a competitor is to respond. Actions that are less visible, such as support material for the sales force or dealerships, are less likely to face a response.

○ *Inconsistent reactions*   These companies' reactions are simply not predictable. They react aggressively on occasion but at other times ignore similar competitive challenges.

3.5   Problems in identifying competitors

Analysing members of a strategic group provides crucial information on which to base strategic decisions. However, there are risks in the process of identifying an organization's competitors and a number of errors should be avoided:

• Overlooking smaller competitors by placing too much emphasis on large visible competitors.

• Focusing on established competitors and ignoring potential new entrants.

• Concentrating on current domestic competitors and disregarding international competitors who could possibly enter the market.

The competitive analysis has allowed the organization to establish its relative position versus its competitors on a range of important criteria. However, the organization has to judge itself and its competitors against the market it is operating within. At this stage in the external analysis it is useful to establish a range of information about the market. The customer and market segmentation would also be considered under a market analysis and this will be explored in detail in Chapter 5.

3.6 The market analysis

A market analysis will be made up of a range of factors relevant to the particular situation under review, but would normally include the following areas:

- **Actual and potential market size** Estimating the total sales in the market allows the organization to evaluate the realism of particular market share objectives. Identifying the key sub-markets of this market, and potential areas of growth, is crucial to developing a marketing strategy, as is establishing whether any areas are in decline.

- **Trends** Analysing general trends in the market identifies the changes that have actually taken place. This can help to uncover the reasons for these changes and expose the critical drivers underlying a market.

- **Customers** The analysis needs to identify who the customer is and what criteria they use to judge a product offering. Information on where, when and how customers purchase the product, or service, allows an organization to begin to understand the needs of the customer (Chapter 5 will look at consumer behaviour in more detail). Identifying changing trends in consumer behaviour may begin to signal potential market developments and opportunities.

- **Customer segments** Identifying current market segments and establishing the benefits each group requires allows an organization to detect whether it has the capability to serve particular consumers' needs.

- **Distribution channels** Identifying the changes of importance between channels of distribution, based on growth, cost or effectiveness, permits a company to evaluate its current arrangements. Establishing the key decision-makers in a channel of distribution also helps to inform strategic decisions.

Summary

The external auditing process creates the information and analysis necessary for an organization to begin to identify the key issues it will have to address in order to develop a successful strategy. The PEST analysis uncovers the critical areas in the external environment that the organization needs to consider. The industry analysis reveals the structure and strengths of players in the industry that any strategy will be required to address. The competitor analysis discloses the relative position of the direct competitors in the strategic group. Finally, the market analysis begins to explore current trends and areas of growth. More importantly it begins to build a picture of the consumer.

The external analysis is the initial step in the process of establishing the key issues facing an organization. The next stage is to examine the consumer, before establishing methods for segmenting markets.

Discussion questions

1   What are the benefits of undertaking an environmental analysis?

2   What does the acronym PEST stand for?

3   Identify an industry where the power of suppliers is very strong.

4   For an industry sector of your choice identify the key strategic groups.

5   Outline the content and structure of a competitor analysis.

References

Diffenbach, J. (1983) Corporate environmental analysis in large US corporations. *Long Range Planning*, Vol. 16, No. 3, pp. 107–116.

Kotler, P., Armstrong, G., Saunders, J. and Wong, V. (1996) *Principles of Marketing: The European Edition*. Prentice Hall.

Lehman, D.R. and Weiner, R.S. (1991) *Analysis for Marketing Planning*, 2nd edn. Irwin.

Porter, M.E. (1980) *Competitive Strategy*. The Free Press, p. 4.

Marketing research

About this chapter

Marketing research is undertaken by an organization in order to provide timely and relevant information that can be employed by managers to allow them to make fully informed decisions relating to marketing activities.

After reading this chapter, you will understand:

- The structure and role of a marketing information system.

- The internal sources of marketing data available to an organization.

- The difference between marketing intelligence and marketing research.

- The types of market research and market research methods that an organization can undertake.

- Approaches an organization can employ in carrying out marketing research activities.

- The stages in the marketing research process.

- The role e-marketing developments are having on marketing research activities.

4.1 Marketing information systems

Jobber and Rainbow (1977) describe a marketing information system (MkIS) as

> a system in which marketing information is formally gathered, stored, analysed and distributed to managers in accord with their informational needs on a regular planned basis.

All organizations require a marketing information system if they are to have the ability to make well-informed marketing decisions. Obviously the size and sophistication of the MkIS will depend on the size and scope of an organization's operations.

The aim of an MkIS is to seek out data from the external marketing environment and then sift and analyse this information to identify any salient issues of which the organization's managers need to be made aware. The MkIS will then distribute this relevant information to the company's marketing decision-makers. This, however, is not a one-way process. The organization's marketing decision-makers may also highlight areas where they require information in order to come to an informed judgement on an issue that requires action. This request will then initiate a specific investigation by the MkIS of various data sources in order to provide the manager with up-to-date and accurate information upon which to base a decision (for an overview of an MkIS system see Figure 4.1).

The type of information that feeds into a company's MkIS and assists management to make marketing decisions is derived from three key sources (Figure 4.1), as follows:

Internal sources of data

Companies produce internal information and reports on a regular basis. This information can originate from a number of areas within the organization, such as, finance, production, sales and marketing, or customer relations. Data from each of these areas will provide different perspectives on the day-to-day operation of the enterprise.

Much of this type of information is generated by organizations on a regular basis in the form of weekly or monthly reports. However, companies may also produce information on a 'one-off' basis if there is a reason for monitoring a specific aspect of the business. An organization may wish to monitor sales reactions to specific advertising campaigns or to a change in pricing policy.

Marketing intelligence

Marketing intelligence is developed by an organization through a continuous process of monitoring the external environment within which it operates.

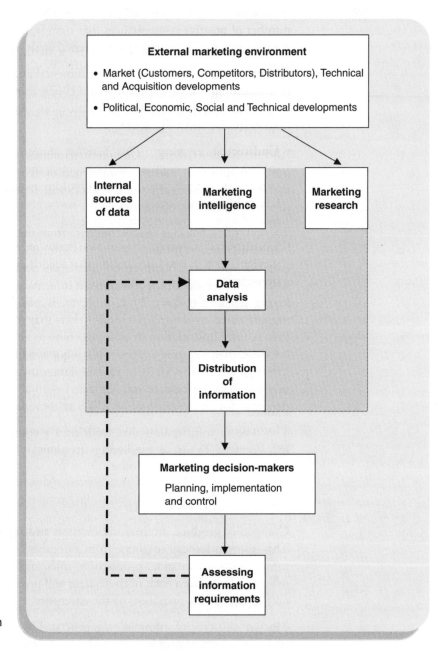

Figure 4.1
A marketing information
system

This is a process of environmental scanning and concentrates on the longer-term factors that will have an impact on the enterprise. It is critical that an organization forms this longer-term market intelligence by building on information from a wide range of sources. Much of this information will come from internal members of staff who are experts in their own area of activity but companies should also use external sources, such as research scientists, academics, sales people and distributors.

As discussed in Chapter 3, a study by Diffenbach (1983) identified a number of positive consequences that stem from carrying out this type of continuous and organized environmental analysis (see Figure 3.1).

The process of undertaking an environmental analysis is normally referred to as scanning. According to Aguilar (1967), there are four forms of environmental scanning that an organization can undertake in order to form market intelligence. These are:

- **Undirected viewing** This activity concerns the viewer exploring information in general without carrying a specific agenda. The viewer is exposed to a large amount of varied information but this is not an active search looking for particular issues, just a broad attempt to be aware of factors or areas that may have changed.

- **Conditional viewing** Again this is not an organized search but the viewer is sensitive to information that identifies changes in specific areas of activity.

- **Informal search** This is an organized but limited search for information to support a specific goal.

- **Formal search** This type of search is actively pursued and specifically designed to seek particular information.

There is, of course, an unlimited amount of information that can be scanned. Any organization can only scan a certain amount of this information. A balance has to be struck between the resources allocated to this activity and the potential benefits. More information also does not necessarily lead to better decision-making. Understanding the dynamics of the environment is the critical aspect to this activity, not the volume of information reviewed.

Managers search for data in five broad areas (Aguilar, 1967; see Figure 4.2):

- Market developments.

- Technical developments.

- Acquisition developments.

- Broad issues.

- Other developments.

(*Note:* Aguilar uses the word tidings rather than developments.)

The study showed that 58% of managers saw issues in the market development category as the most critical area for obtaining external information, three times more important than the next most significant area, technical developments, at 18%. The importance placed on market developments was true across all functional areas. The most significant

Area of external information	Category	General content
Market developments	• Market potential	→ Capacity, consumption, imports, exports
	• Structural change	→ Mergers, acquisitions, new entries
	• Competitors and industry	→ Competitor information, industry policy
	• Pricing	→ Effective and proposed prices
	• Sales negotiations	→ Information on specific current or potential sales
	• Customers	→ Current or potential customers, markets and problems
Technical developments	• New product, processes and technology	→ Technical information relatively new or unknown to enterprise
	• Product problems	→ Involving current products
	• Costs	→ For processing, operations, etc. for suppliers, customers and competitors
	• Licensing and patents	→ Products and processes
Acquisition developments	• Leads for mergers, joint ventures, or acquisitions	→ Information concerning possibilities for the organization
Broad issues	• General conditions	→ General info political, demographic etc.
	• Government actions and policies	→ Decisions affecting the industry
Other developments	• Suppliers and raw materials	→ Purchasing information
	• Resources available	→ Availability of people, land, other resources
	• Miscellaneous	→ Any other information

Figure 4.2
Critical areas of external information (*Source:* adapted from Aguilar, 1967)

categories of information within this area were market potential, accounting for 30% alone, and structural change, accounting for 10%. The only other category that reached double figures was for the category of new products, process and technology under technical developments.

One crucial aspect of this scanning activity is to detect weak signals. That is, identifying fragments of information that indicate significant changes, but whose potential impact has generally not been perceived. This is obviously difficult, especially as many organizations fail to recognize major signals in the environment.

Many of the factors that Aguilar states managers see as significant fall into the broad categories of political/legal issues, economic factors, social/cultural issues as well as the specific area of technological developments. As discussed in Chapter 3, these factors fall into what is normally referred to as a PEST (Political, Economic, Social and Technological) analysis, although some writers use the alternative acronym of STEP analysis (see Figure 3.2).

The central role of building marketing intelligence is to identify the key factors that are likely to drive change in the organization's area of activity. The aim is then to analyse how these key factors will affect the industry in general and the organization in particular.

Marketing research

Unlike marketing intelligence, which focuses on the long-term environmental factors affecting an organization, the focus of marketing research is on the immediate issues that an organization is facing in the short term.

4.2 Importance of marketing research

Burns and Bush (2000) define marketing research as:

> the process of designing, gathering, analysing and reporting of information that may be used to solve a specific marketing problem.

The aim of marketing research is to assist managers in their decision-making. David Ogilvy is quoted as saying 'an advertiser who ignores marketing research is as guilty as a general who ignores the decodes of enemy signals' (cited in Adcock *et al.*, 1998). Although Ogilvy is referring to advertisers, in fact this observation applies to any manager making any type of marketing decision. However, management decisions cannot be based purely on marketing research information. Even high quality data can be misinterpreted. Managers have to apply judgement, skill and initiative in interpreting marketing research data. Research data can play a significant role in reducing the level of risk associated with management decisions but it does not absolve managers from thoroughly testing this information before reaching any conclusions as to future action.

4.3 Types of marketing research

Marketing research falls into two major categories: continuous and ad hoc research.

- **Continuous research** involves collecting information from external sources on a continuous basis. Reports are produced on a regular basis, normally either monthly, quarterly or annually. This type of data allows an organization to consistently compare trends over time. The key types of continuous research that organizations employ are consumer panels, television viewership panels, marketing databases, retail audits, customer relationship management systems and website audits.

- **Ad hoc research** is employed when an organization wishes to gain information when making a non standard or one-off decision. This could occur during the development of a new product. The findings of this type of research are usually presented as a formal report. As a result many managers associate this type of research as the main activity of a market research department. Although specialist one-off research reports may look impressive it is important not to underestimate the usefulness of the data produced through continuous research.

4.4   Research methods

Secondary, often called desk research, and primary research are the two main categories of research data.

Secondary research

Secondary data is information that is already available as it has been collected, and in some cases analysed, by other parties for reasons other than for use in the research project that is currently being undertaken. This type of data may be external information or it may be internally available within the organization. Normally, the first stage of any research project would be to search for secondary data before undertaking any primary research. Before using secondary data the researcher has to evaluate its relevance and reliability to the research project being undertaken. Burns and Bush (2000) claim that a researcher should examine five factors when evaluating a piece of secondary data. These are:

1   The reason the study was undertaken. Sometimes a piece of research is not independent in nature but has been carried out to support a specific point of view. Obviously, an organization should try to avoid taking decisions based on information that has been produced as a result of a biased piece of research.

2   The credibility of the organization or individuals who undertook the research.

3   What specific information was collected and what method the researcher employed to measure or evaluate the data.

4   How the data was collected. There are many different methods for collecting data, which will be discussed later in this chapter. Each method may have an affect on the quality of the findings of a piece of research.

5   The consistency of the findings of a piece of research with other studies. If several studies report similar results, that may provide support for the reliability of any findings. If a report contradicts a number of other studies it may be an indication that the research is not reliable. However, in both cases the researcher has to evaluate a specific piece of research across all criteria and not merely agree with or discount a report's findings on the basis that it does not agree with the majority of the results from other secondary research sources.

Secondary data can be obtained from a number of sources (see Figure 4.3).

Primary research

Secondary research may have provided some useful data but it is likely that there will be gaps in this information which an organization will need to fill by undertaking some primary research. Primary research, sometimes referred to as field research, involves the organization in directly undertaking, or commissioning a research company to specifically undertake a piece of research. A range of approaches to carrying out primary research is available to an organization. These research methods fall into two key categories, qualitative and quantitative.

Qualitative research

Qualitative research at a basic level could be described as the collection, analysis and interpretation of data obtained by studying the behaviour and language displayed by individuals in a particular situation. The key aim of qualitative research is to provide a rich insight into the perceptions, attitudes and motivations of consumers. Chisnall (1991) states that this type of research is appropriate to answer the questions What? Why? and How? Unlike quantitative research, qualitative techniques do not provide large sets of numerated data that can be statistically tested for their reliability and validity. However, qualitative techniques do provide highly sophisticated and subtle insights into the phenomena being studied. A number of techniques are available to the researcher in undertaking a qualitative study. Each will now be discussed in detail.

• **Depth interviews**   This is a popular method of qualitative research and involves structured or semi-structured interviews that are normally around an hour long. The interviews are generally confidential in nature, undertaken face to face and respondents are encouraged to talk openly about the topic under discussion. The interview would normally be audio recorded so that a full transcript can be typed after the session has ended. The advantage of a depth interview is that the respondent is not influenced by other individuals, as can happen in focus groups. This type of interview also allows a deeper discussion to take place on a

Information domain	Information source	Type of information
External	Newspapers	Up-to-date articles in quality newspapers can often provide pointers to other useful sources of information. Newspaper articles are very much of the moment, reflecting issues that are currently in vogue
	Books	Can provide useful background information on a specific topic
	Academic journals	Published research findings that have been independently evaluated by other academics and therefore should demonstrate validity and reliability. Journal articles can tend to be dated rather than of the moment
	Conference proceedings	Conference papers are generally evaluated by other academics and therefore should demonstrate validity and reliability. Research findings are likely to be more recent than the data found in journal articles
	Directories and indexes	These sources provide information on organizations in specific industry sectors
	Government statistics and reports	Provide a number of statistics on economic and market performance as well as census information
	Company reports	Companies' annual shareholders reports can provide some useful information about the situation of an organization's competitors
	Trade association reports	Provide information on trends in the industry sector
	Commercial research agencies	Provide reports on business sectors and also market reports on specific countries; will tend to charge a commercial rate for allowing access to this information
Internal	Sales reports	Provide details of the trend of an organization's sales over time. Also the profile of sales made by specific categories of customers can be obtained
	Payment records	Provide details on customers' payment profiles. This allows an organization to identify credit profiles and good credit risks
	Stock records	Provide a profile of stock holding trends, changes in consumers' tastes in fashion, etc.
	Research reports	Valued information can be gleaned from previous research undertaken by the organization

Figure 4.3
Sources of secondary research data

particular topic. The key disadvantage is that normally a series of interviews with a range of individuals would need to be undertaken and that can be a costly process, both in terms of time and money. The choice of the individuals to interview will be based on their fit with the consumer profile for a particular product or service.

- **Focus group discussions**   Focus groups are made up of six to eight respondents who undertake an unstructured or semi-structured discussion facilitated by the researcher who acts as moderator. These discussions have traditionally taken place face to face although Internet discussions are becoming more common. Once again the discussion is audio recorded and sometimes videoed. The researcher normally has a list of issues, relating to the overall focus of the research, that they wish to have discussed by the group, but the aim is to give as much freedom to the group as possible in order that they can discuss the issues that they deem to be important. Analysis of these discussions should allow a researcher to identify the beliefs, attitudes, motivations, behaviours and preferences of the respondents and thereby gain a detailed understanding of the organization's consumers. Focus groups provide information that allows researchers to form questionnaire items that have been identified as important by focus group respondents rather than by the researcher. It also allows the researcher to construct any items on a questionnaire in the language used by the respondents themselves. As the focus group members are representative of the wider population in some way, this decreases the potential for misinterpretation of the question by respondents when filling in a questionnaire return.

- **Expert consultation**   Although much qualitative research is focused on the actual consumer, an alternative approach is to interview individuals with relevant expert knowledge. Various types of expert can be found in the academic community, financial services or the specialist press. Although they may not be a direct consumer of a particular product or service, they can be a rich source of specialist background knowledge. Experts may also be able to provide a valuable perspective on possible future developments in a product or service area.

- **Observation**   Observation is a qualitative technique that finds its roots in the social anthropological approach of studying a society over periods of months or years. Consumer researchers employ a similar approach in taking detailed observations of consumers; however, normally their observations are taken over relatively shorter periods of time. This technique can be employed to find out how consumers behave in a particular retail store, allowing the researcher to build up a picture of what factors may be affecting customers' purchase decisions. A number of observation methods can be employed including direct observation by the researcher, video recording and electronic monitoring of traffic in supermarket aisles.

Quantitative research

Quantitative research focuses on gathering data that is quantifiable and, some would argue, therefore unlike qualitative research in that it is less open to interpretation. Quantitative data includes information available through secondary sources, such as, market size, market share, sales figures (see Figure 4.3). However, not all information is available through these sources and in that case primary research has to be undertaken. In these circumstances the majority of organizations will collect quantitative data through questionnaire-based surveys.

These surveys are generally undertaken to establish information that is statistically tested to provide evidence that the findings are reliable and valid, as demonstrated by the rigour of the analysis undertaken. In many circumstances, in order to demonstrate that the findings are representative of a larger population, large-scale surveys have to be undertaken. Surveys themselves can be administered in a number of ways.

- **Survey methods**   There are a number of approaches available to a researcher in carrying out a survey. These are:

  - *Face to face interviews*   When administering a survey, a personal interview is very different from the depth interview employed in qualitative research. In the case of a survey, a structured interview is undertaken employing a standard questionnaire that is administered to every respondent in the same way. Therefore the wording, layout and order of the questions is rigorously adhered to by the interviewer. This approach means that a large number of respondents can be interviewed in a relatively short period of time. Once the data is collected there is no requirement for qualitative interpretation of the individual's responses. The questionnaire is designed in such a way that the respondent has to make a choice from a limited number of prescribed answers to any specific question. Once the survey is complete a statistical analysis of the respondent's replies is undertaken based on a numeric coding of each of the prescribed answers contained on the questionnaire. It is therefore critical that the questionnaire is designed and tested in such a way as to ensure that the respondents actually interpret the questions being asked in a manner consistent with the researchers' intentions and the respondents' answers are not overly constrained by the limited range of answers from which they are allowed to make a choice. A weakness of this approach can therefore be an inappropriately designed questionnaire.

  - *Telephone interviews*   Telephone interviews are less expensive than some other methods and provide a mechanism to collect information quickly. Participation is more likely if a limited amount of information is sought from the respondent. However, there are problems with this approach. Most respondents would be reluctant to supply personal details to an unknown researcher over the phone. The sample is likely to show some bias as only individuals listed in a telephone directory can be contacted. The sample may be further biased by only including those individuals who actually respond. In recent times this type of survey has been further compromised by consumers' negative reactions to the growth in unsolicited telesales. This has made them less likely to answer any questions posed by an individual in an impromptu telephone call.

○ *Postal surveys* Postal questionnaires offer the advantages of speed, extensive distribution and relative inexpense and can be used for any size of sample. Where respondents can be ensured of anonymity these methods can produce candid replies, eliminating the potential of bias associated with surveys undertaken using personal interviews. However, there are a number of problems linked with this method. Postal surveys often have quite high non-response rates, especially with longer questionnaires. Researchers using this method can face a problem in placing respondents into meaningful categories. There can also be a problem with ambiguity, unless very straightforward questions are asked, or questions are framed in such a way that they offer respondents the choice between highly polarized positions. Respondents may not be able to perceive the supposed subtlety of a question or indeed the researcher may not be able to interpret the respondents' subtle answers.

○ *Panel surveys* There are a number of consumer panels that are run continuously by commercial research agencies. Companies can pay to have questions about their products or services included in the regular survey. Several approaches are employed in carrying out these surveys, such as, questionnaires, consumer diaries or audits carried out in the consumer's home.

• **Questionnaire design** There are two key stages in the development of a questionnaire. These are:

○ *Planning stage* The aim of undertaking a questionnaire is to obtain relevant information to help an organization make appropriate marketing decisions. The first stage in constructing a questionnaire is therefore to establish the decisions that will need to be taken and the information that is required in order to make an informed choice. It is then necessary to construct a questionnaire that will reveal the necessary information.

○ *Design stage* There are several important factors that have to be considered when designing a questionnaire. Each of these is discussed below:

1 Sequencing of questions The order in which questions are posed on a questionnaire is critical. In order to allow the respondent to relax, simple questions that are general in nature are usually placed at the beginning of a questionnaire. The questions that follow should funnel down towards the detailed information that the

researcher wishes to identify. In order not to waste the respondent's time and also to avoid potentially alienating them, filter questions should be employed. These questions allow a respondent to avoid being asked individual questions or whole sections of the questionnaire that are not relevant to them.

2   Nature of the questions   There are three types of questions that can be employed on a questionnaire. These are:

(i) Open questions – which allow the respondent the freedom to provide an answer in his or her own way using their own words. The responses to this type of question are difficult to analyse statistically and most surveys that aim to use a quantitative analysis will concentrate on different versions of closed questions. However, open questions are often used in conjunction with closed questions and they can offer additional qualitative data for managers to study before making marketing decisions.

(ii) Closed questions – which offer the respondent a choice between pre-determined answers. This may be a simple choice between two opposing options or offer a range of choices through various multiple choice options. An alternative to simple multiple choice questions is the use of questions that employ scales in their responses. A number of scaling techniques are available to employ in a questionnaire, one of the most common being Likert scales. Using this technique a respondent may be asked a question such as, 'On a scale of one to five (where one equals strongly agree and five equals strongly disagree) how far would you agree with the statement that product X offers outstanding value?' These types of question can reveal quite subtle insights into consumers' attitudes and beliefs about marketing issues. Whatever closed question technique is employed the pre-determined options offered to the respondents can be numerically coded to facilitate a detailed statistical analysis of the total survey data.

(iii) Control questions – which are placed on a questionnaire to test whether the respondent's answers are consistent and this can be used as a way of confirming that a respondent's answers can be taken as genuine.

Whatever type of questions employed on a questionnaire it is crucial that they are tested to ensure that they are:

(i) Easy to understand, using straightforward day to day language.

(ii) Not leading the respondent into a particular response.

(iii) Not ambiguous or asking two questions at the same time.

(iv) Not based on assumptions about the likely views of respondents.

3 Layout A questionnaire needs to be structured in such a way that all the questions are well spaced out, ensuring that it is easy for respondents to read and navigate their way around.

- **Probability sampling** Generally, in quantitative research a probability sample is formed so that it can be thoroughly analysed using rigorous statistical tests. The aim is to create a sample that demonstrates no significant differences between itself and the target population. The target population is made up of everybody in the group the researcher wishes to focus upon. In market research many of these groups will be based on specific market segments as defined using criteria discussed in Chapter 5. The aim of forming a probability sample is in effect to attempt to construct a model representing the wider population. The data received from the respondents in the sample can then be statistically analysed and the findings can be considered as being representative of the wider population's opinions within specific degrees of confidence.

  - *Simple random sampling* Random sampling is a method of sampling that offers every member of a population identified as the focus of a research study an equal chance of being included in the survey. Simple random sampling involves assigning each individual in the sampling frame a number. The sample is then constructed by drawing numbers at random from the total numbers available.

  - *Stratified random sampling* In this method of sampling a similar approach to random sampling is employed. However, the identified population, which will be the focus of the research study, is divided into discrete homogeneous groups (strata) of individuals based on what are deemed by the researcher to be key criteria. These criteria could be factors such as age, income, gender, educational qualifications etc., or indeed combinations of these and other factors. Once the groups have been identified the sample is then constructed by drawing numbers at random from each of the groups. Each group therefore has representation in the sample. Normally within the overall sample the number of individuals drawn from each group will be in proportion to the group's size relative to the overall population.

  - *Cluster sampling* This method of sampling is employed where the researcher considers the target population to be made up of natural groupings, normally termed clusters. Thus an organization may be seen to be made up of a number of clusters in terms of its business units or administrative departments. In this situation a random sample of departments is taken and then a complete census of every member of each of those chosen departments is undertaken.

- **Non-probability sampling processes** Questionnaires can be administered using other sampling techniques rather than probability samples. However, these techniques do not allow the researcher to employ the same level of statistical rigour that probability samples allow. One of these alternative techniques is quota sampling.

  ○ *Quota sampling* Quota sampling is a common method employed in marketing research studies; however, as already stated, this is not a probability sampling technique and therefore statistically not as rigorous as the methods discussed earlier. Under quota sampling the approach is similar to stratified sampling in that the identified population being studied is divided into discrete homogeneous groups. Once again the criteria used to identify these groups are likely to be factors such as age, income, gender, educational qualifications etc., or indeed combinations of these and other factors. In quota sampling, however, the researcher decides that a specific percentage of the total sample will be made up of each of these groups. Therefore the researcher might decide that 20% of the sample should be women aged 18 to 24 who are in employment. While this approach may be easier to administer than random samples, and allows the researcher more flexibility, the results may not be representative of the wider population and lack the statistical rigour of a probability sample. However, quota samples are widely used and many researchers feel they can produce results that are a useful aid to decision-making.

  ○ *Sample size* If the intention is to undertake a rigorous statistical analysis of a survey's results then the size of the sample is critical. Calculations can be undertaken that determine the sampling error, that is the error that is caused by not interviewing everyone in the target population. The sampling error will depend on the size of the sample and of the target population. The researcher will need to undertake a cost–benefit analysis about the level of sampling error they are content to live with compared with the time and expense of undertaking a more extensive study. Generally, a sample of around a 1000 will provide reasonably statistically sound results for a target population of several millions. However, undertaking a random sample of 1000 is still an expensive and time-consuming exercise.

4.5 Approaches to marketing research

An organization has three options in choosing how to undertake a marketing research project. These are:

- **Undertake the work in-house** This is an option in the case of small scale research projects or where an organization is large enough and employs specialist marketing staff.

- **Employ a fieldwork agency**   Even for an organization with specialist market research staff that can design a questionnaire and coordinate a survey they may find that, for a large survey, they don't have the resources to actually carry out all the interviews. In this situation they can employ a specialist fieldwork agency who will undertake the interview then hand back the data for the organization to analyse. Many marketing research agencies will offer fieldwork administration as one of a range of services they offer clients.

- **Employ a marketing research agency**   Another option available to an organization is to contract out all aspects of the research project to an outside agency. The agency then would complete all the stages of the research project as laid out in section 4.6 of this chapter. In order for this approach to work successfully there has to be very clear communication between the client and the agency about the objectives of the research.

4.6   Stages in marketing research

In undertaking a marketing research project there are a number of distinct stages that should be followed, as outlined in Figure 4.4. Each of these stages will be discussed in turn:

- **Problem definition**   As has already been stated, the aim of undertaking marketing research is to obtain relevant information to help an organization make appropriate marketing decisions. The first stage in undertaking a marketing research project is therefore to establish the decisions that will need to be taken and the information that is required in order to make an informed choice. This should lead to the identification of a series of research objectives.

- **Develop research objectives**   Research objectives need to be established in order to provide a clear focus to the development of a research plan. The objectives should provide a clarity of vision for the individuals working on the project that allows them to develop an effective research brief.

- **Prepare a research brief**   A research brief is developed by the client in order to provide the researcher, whether they are in-house or an outside agency, with a clear definition of the organization's precise requirements. It is likely to contain the following elements:

  - Background information on the nature of the problem the organization wishes to address.

  - An account of the issue that is to be the focus of the research.

  - A statement of the specific research objectives the organization has developed.

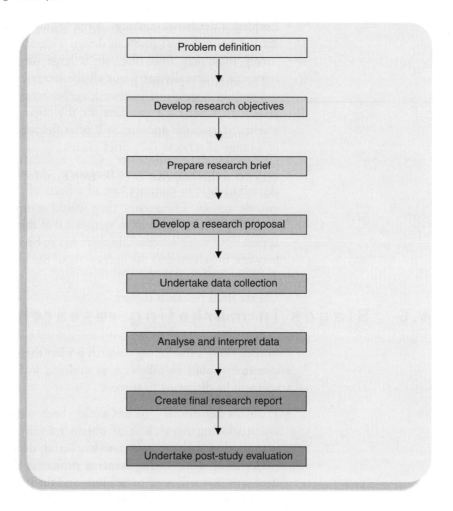

Figure 4.4
The market research
process

○ The time-scale that the research has to be completed within.

○ The arrangements the organization requires for reporting the project's outcomes.

• **Develop a research proposal** The research team undertaking the project will then need to develop a research proposal that is approved by the client before any work commences. This proposal may build on and refine aspects of the research brief. It is a statement of the project team's interpretation of the client's requirements as a result of a thorough examination of the research problem. The project team's proposal should contain:

○ Background information about the research.

○ The research objectives.

○ The research method, or methods, to be employed.

- The techniques to be employed in analysing any primary data.

- The role of the client in the research project.

- The interim reporting procedures.

- The format of the final research report.

- A timeframe for the project and a budget outline.

- **Undertake data collection** Once a research method is established and the technique that is to be employed for data collection is agreed, the fieldwork can be initiated.

- **Analyse and interpret data** When the primary data has been collected the research team will need to employ an appropriate research technique in undertaking an analysis and developing any reliable information to assist management in making marketing decisions.

- **Create final research report** In order to disseminate the results of the research the team should construct a final report that presents the findings within a clear and logical structure. The normal format for this report would contain the following elements:

- Title page.

- Table and contents.

Illustrative example 4.1
Norwich Union

In addition to its traditional customer satisfaction and product testing studies, Norwich Union has started using an online access panel. Access panels are a source of samples for questionnaire surveys. The online panel members are invited to take part in a specific survey by an e-mail which contains a link to a Web survey. The access panel has 500 members who are recruited and managed on behalf of Norwich Union by a specialist company called Lightspeed Online Research. The advantage of online research such as this is that carrying out a survey is cheaper than other alternative methods and results can be gathered in real-time. However, there are dangers in that poor recruitment and management of a panel can produce inadequate data. Online marketing research has been growing steadily over the past few years. In 2004, in Europe and the USA, online research is expected to grow by 18% over the 2003 figures and it is estimated global expenditure will reach £674m.

◦ Executive summary.

◦ Introduction.

◦ Description and justification of the research method employed.

◦ Analysis and findings.

◦ Limitations.

◦ Conclusions and recommendations.

◦ Appendices.

• **Undertake post-study evaluation**   Once a project is completed it is crucial that a review is undertaken into whether the research actually provided the client's management with the quality and quantity of information they actually required to make effective marketing decisions. It is only by undertaking a post-study evaluation that both the client and the project team can revise and enhance their future marketing research activities.

4.7   e-Marketing perspective

Websites can be useful sources of marketing information. Organizations can analyse how individuals navigate through their site. In doing so they can establish the type of information clients are seeking, the length of time they spend on sectors within the site and their actual purchases. The organization can build up a profile of customers with similar interests or purchasing habits. Through monitoring their website usage companies can also analyse the effectiveness of promotional campaigns such as discount vouchers.

The Internet also offers a new approach in carrying out a questionnaire survey. The questionnaire can be circulated by e-mail. This provides a very low cost method of disseminating a survey. This approach has the added advantage that it can be more interactive than a traditional mail survey. Prompts on the questionnaire can provide the respondents with detailed clarification on particular points. However, there are some disadvantages with Internet surveys. The results may be skewed by the fact that Internet users are generally found among more affluent consumers and in younger age groups. The fact that an individual's e-mail address is attached to any returned e-mail questionnaire destroys their anonymity and therefore creates reservations about the reliability of their responses on personal issues.

Summary

Marketing research activities are central to developing marketing policies and practice within a company. Marketing research systems produce a range of outputs that allow marketing managers to make well-informed decisions about marketing activities. Whatever the nature of a specific marketing research project it is crucial that it is actively managed by the commissioning organization, or department, so that timely, relevant and accurate information is produced.

Discussion questions

1 What is the difference between marketing intelligence and marketing research?

2 What are the disadvantages of a telephone survey?

3 Discuss the proposition that a qualitative research method will produce more insight into a consumer's motivation to purchase a particular product than a quantitative research approach.

4 What is the difference between a research brief and a research proposal?

References

Adcock, D., Bradfield, R., Halborg, A. and Ross, C. (1998) *Marketing: Principles and Practice*, 3rd edn. Pitman Publishing, p. 111.

Aguilar, F.J. (1967) *Scanning the Business Environment*. Macmillan.

Burns, A. and Bush, R. (2000) *Marketing Research*, 2nd edn. Prentice Hall.

Chisnall, P.M. (1991) *The Essence of Marketing Research*. Prentice Hall.

Diffenbach, J. (1983) Corporate environmental analysis in large US corporations. *Long Range Planning*, Vol. 16, No. 3, pp. 107–116.

Jobber, D. and Rainbow, C. (1977) A study of the development and implementation of marketing information systems in British Industry. *Journal of the Marketing Research Society*, Vol. 19, No. 3, pp. 104–11.

Segmentation

About this chapter

The segmentation process is a crucial aspect of strategic marketing. This chapter explores both consumer and organizational segmentation. Initially both consumer and organizational behaviour is summarized to illustrate the areas from which segmentation criteria have developed. A full analysis of segmentation is then undertaken to provide the foundation of the targeting and positioning activities that will be addressed in Chapter 11.

5.1   Introduction

At a fundamental level an organization's marketing objectives become a decision about which products or services they are going to deliver into which markets. It follows that decisions about the markets to be serviced are a critical step in strategy formulation. The segmentation process is therefore central to strategy and it can be broken into three distinct elements: segmentation, targeting and positioning. This chapter will examine the segmentation aspect of both consumer and organizational markets.

Successful segmentation relies on a clear understanding of the market. Knowledge of consumer behaviour is the crucial foundation on which that market understanding is built. The chapter will briefly summarize both consumer and organizational buyer behaviour as an introduction to market segmentation criteria.

5.2   Why segment?

There are a number of reasons why organizations undertake segmentation (Doyle, 1994):

- **Meet consumer needs more precisely**   In a generic market customer's demands will differ; by developing a distinct marketing mix for each consumer segment an organization can offer customers better solutions for their needs.

- **Increase profits**   Different consumer segments react in contrasting ways to prices; some are far less price-sensitive than others. Segmentation allows an organization to gain the best price it can in every segment, effectively raising the average price and increasing profitability.

- **Segment leadership**   In any particular market the brands that have dominant shares of the market will be highly profitable. Their market leadership gives them economies of scale in marketing and production and they will also have established access to distribution channels. Small companies or new entrants in a market are unlikely to be able to gain leadership; they can however take a dominant share of a particular market segment. This focus can allow them to develop a specialist marketing mix to satisfy the needs of the consumers in that group while at the same time building a competitive cost position relative to other companies in that segment.

- **Retain customers**   Providing products or services aimed at different consumer segments allows an organization to retain that customer's loyalty as their needs change. As an individual moves through life their needs in financial services will change. For example, young single individuals may need a minimum of credit and banking facilities and car insurance, while younger families will need in addition life insurance policies and mortgages and in middle age these needs will turn to pension provision. If an organization can provide all these services they may retain a customer who otherwise would transfer to another brand. An organization may also be able to use segmentation as a way of moving a customer over time from entry level products or services to products at the premium end of the market.

- **Focus marketing communications** Segmentation allows an organization to identify media channels that can specifically reach the target groups. For example, young women interested in fashion are likely to read certain fashion magazines. Rather than spending money on mass-market media that reach far wider than the target group, organizations can target their money and effort by using media focused directly on their potential consumer group.

5.3 The segmentation process

The segmentation process involves establishing criteria by which groups of consumers with similar needs can be identified. These criteria have to identify consumer groups that have the following characteristics:

- The consumers in the segment respond in the same way to a particular marketing mix.

- The consumers within the segment have to react in a clearly different way from other groups of consumers to the marketing mix on offer.

- The group has to be large enough to provide the return on investment necessary to the organization.

- The criteria used to identify the segment have to be operational. The following experience illustrates this point. A small company in the magazine market identified a group of customers that had clear needs: overseas nationals living in the UK who wished to buy magazines from their home country. The organization's proposed marketing offer was to import magazines from overseas and mail them out directly to the consumers' homes. This was a potential customer group that all responded in the same way to the proposed marketing mix. They clearly acted differently from other groups in the magazine market. This potential segment was large and potentially profitable but this was a difficult group to make operational. Overseas nationals cannot easily be identified as there is no official organization or overseas institute that will supply the names and addresses. The only way of pursuing this opportunity was to persuade overseas nationals to identify themselves. This could have been accomplished by attracting consumers to respond to a promotional campaign, allowing the organization to build a customer database. However, for a small organization this was likely to be a costly operation and the idea was dropped in favour of other options.

Given the fact that segments need to demonstrate these four characteristics, the next step is to examine the variables that can be used to usefully segment a market (see section 5.4). Comprehension of consumer buyer behaviour theory is central to the successful development and application of segmentation criteria.

5.4   Consumer behaviour

Consumer buyer behaviour relates to the end customer, the individuals who purchase products and services for personal consumption. This section will summarize the main sources of influence on consumer buyer behaviour (see Figure 5.1), in order to illustrate the influences that affect consumers' purchasing decisions. These influences can be broken down into four major categories: social, personal, psychological and situational.

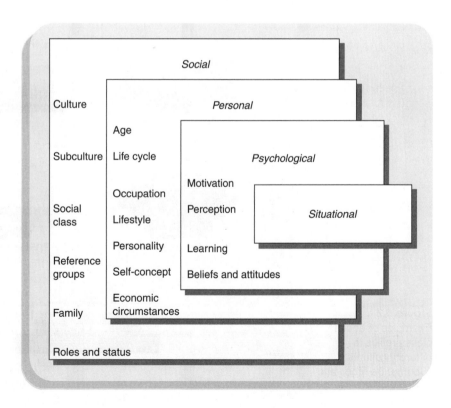

Figure 5.1
Influences on consumer behaviour

Social influences

There are a range of social influences on a consumer's purchasing behaviour:

- **Culture**   Behaviour is largely learned so the traditions, values and attitudes of the society an individual is brought up in will influence their behaviour. Cultural norms form the codes that direct behaviour. Therefore, in an informal culture, such as the USA or the UK, the use of first names in a formal business meeting may be acceptable. In other cultures, such as mainland China, more formal behaviour would be the norm. Within a larger culture there are obviously some subcultures; these may be based on religion, nationality, geographical areas or racial groups.

- **Social class**   An individual's social class has been seen as an important influence on consumer behaviour, with individuals in lower social groups generally being seen to be more culture-bound. Social class groupings are heavily dependent upon a society's cultural background. Some societies are more hierarchical than others; many have a few people in the top and bottom classes with the majority in the middle. However, some societies, such as Scandinavia and Japan, have much flatter structures (see Figure 5.2). Some societies are more open than others, that is individuals can move from one class to another, whereas in a closed society this is not possible.

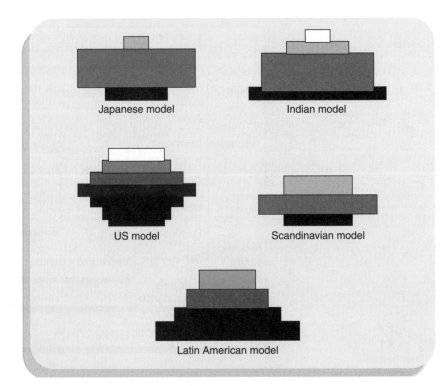

Figure 5.2
Examples of social class profiles in different cultures (*Source:* De Mooij and Keegan, 1991)

In Western societies social classification has been criticized as a predictor of purchasing behaviour. In the UK, a household in the higher AB category, after paying for a mortgage and private school tuition for their children, may have less disposable income than a lower category C2 or D household. There can also be wide discrepancies in purchasing patterns within social groups. Individuals are also influenced by smaller social groups, such as friends, co-workers and family. These can be categorized into reference groups and family:

- **Reference groups** Reference groups can be formal (be members of a professional association or society) or informal groupings (social friends etc.). These reference groups influence an individual's attitude or behaviour. Individuals will tend to exhibit purchasing behaviour that is deemed to be acceptable by their reference group. Group norms and the role an individual plays within a group exert considerable influence on their behaviour. Recent research into the behaviour of first-time mothers illustrated the power of reference groups in shaping their expectations of the quality of service they would experience during their stay in the maternity ward. For individuals from residential areas of lower economic status, doctors, midwives and information from antenatal classes were less influential than friends with young children – and more importantly, than the individual's sisters and mother. These reference groups influenced their subsequent behaviour in terms of length of stay and treatment (Tinson, 1998). This also underlines the power of one key reference group, the family.

- **Family** The family is a key group, not only because it is a primary reference group, but also because it is the group within which individual purchasing behaviour is socialized. Attitudes and beliefs in general and patterns of purchasing behaviour in particular are all learnt initially from the family into which an individual is born and raised (the family of orientation).

Once individuals start to have their own children they set up their own family unit (family of procreation). This developing family group also exerts an influence on the behaviour of individuals. There are, moreover, purchasing decisions that are taken by the household as a unit which reinforce the family as a key primary reference group.

Personal influences

An individual's personal attributes will have an influence on their purchasing behaviour. Factors such as the individual's age, occupation and financial situation, their personality, their family life cycle stage and their lifestyle in general will affect the pattern of their consumption decisions. These factors are commonly used as criteria to segment consumer markets and will be explored in greater detail in section 5.5.

Psychological influences

Four key psychological factors, those of motivation, perception, learning, beliefs and attitudes, are further influences on consumer behaviour.

- **Motivation** Individuals have a range of needs from basic biological needs, such as the need to satisfy hunger, thirst and physical distress, to psychological needs, like the need for social recognition, esteem or belonging. These needs may lie dormant at any particular time but, once aroused to a high enough level of intensity, they become a motivational force. A motive is a need that has reached a level that drives an individual to search for ways to alleviate its demands. There is a whole body of theory in this area that cannot be explored in this text, however, summarizing two of the most influential theories is worthwhile to illustrate their influence on marketing practice:

  - *Freud's theory of motivation* Freud proposed that individuals are motivated by unconscious psychological factors. Moreover, as an individual grows up they conform to social norms which requires them to repress a range of desires and passions (urges). This theory would suggest that an individual's consciously stated reason for buying a product may hide a more fundamental unconscious motive. An individual proposing to purchase an executive car may claim that this decision is based on the need for quality and reliability, whereas the unconscious desire may be for status.

  - *Maslow's theory of motivation* Maslow claimed that individuals have a hierarchy of needs. At the lowest level individuals are driven by basic physiological needs. When individuals are able to satisfy the needs at one level they will be motivated by the needs at the next level in the hierarchy (see Figure 5.3). The implication of the theory for marketers is that individuals will seek different products and services as they move up this hierarchy.

This theory is not universal and is biased towards Anglo-Saxon cultural values, in particular individualism and need for self-development. These needs would not have the same prominence in Japan or Germany, where the need for personal security and conformity take a higher priority.

Motivation theories relate to consumer needs and satisfying consumer's needs is a central tenant of marketing. These motivation theories therefore have influenced approaches to market segmentation. It should be noted that although Freud and Maslow's theories have been very influential in management and marketing theory and practice, they have been challenged on the grounds that the research evidence to support their utility as a psychological theory of motivation is weak (Steers *et al.*, 1996). However they are useful for

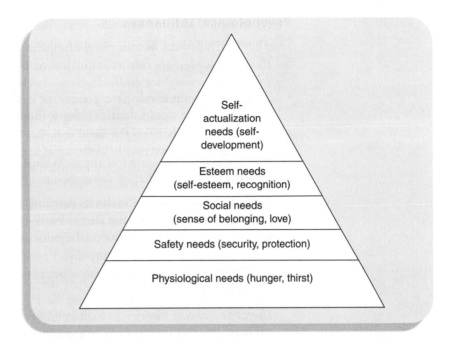

Figure 5.3
Maslow's hierarchy of needs (*Source:* adapted from Maslow, 1970)

marketers as they help to categorize consumers into groups based on needs.

- **Perception**   The way an individual perceives an external stimulus will influence their reaction. Individuals can have different perceptions of the same stimulus due to the process of selective attention, selective distortion and selective retention:

  ○ *Selective attention*   Individuals cannot observe all the potential stimuli in the external environment. Selective attention refers to the tendency of individuals to screen out the majority of stimulants to which they are exposed.

  ○ *Selective distortion*   Individuals process information within the confines of their current set of attitudes and beliefs. The tendency to adjust perceptions to conform to their current mindset is called selective distortion.

  ○ *Selective retention*   Individuals do not remember everything they perceive. Information that reinforces their attitudes and beliefs is more likely to be retained.

  Perceptual behaviour is relevant to the segmentation process because of its links with learning, attitudes and beliefs.

- **Learning, attitudes and beliefs**   Learning relates to any change in the content of an individual's long-term memory and is associated with how information is processed (covered under perception). There are various ways in which learning can take place, including conditioning, social learning theory and cognitive learning theory:

○ *Conditioning learning theories*   Such theories propose that reinforcement is necessary for individuals to develop attitudes and beliefs. Therefore, if an individual's experience of a particular product is positive this will reinforce their positive attitudes and beliefs about the brand. If the experience is negative, it is unlikely the consumer will buy the product again. The negative attitude that has been formed to the product could also affect the individual's attitude to other products and services offered by the company or linked to the brand.

○ *Social learning theories*   Such theories suggest that learning can take place without direct personal reinforcement. Individuals may remember the slogan associated with a brand name and form an attitude about its attributes without any direct reinforcement. An individual may learn from observing the behaviour of others and the recognition or rewards they receive.

○ *Cognitive learning theory*   In high involvement purchases an individual may use their own powers of cognitive reasoning to develop their attitudes and beliefs about a product.

Forming attitudes and beliefs about products effectively creates a position for the product or brand relative to other products and brands in the mind of the consumer. This lies at the heart of product positioning which is central to the successful implementation of segmentation strategy (see Chapter 11).

The buying situation

The buying process (see Figure 5.4) an individual goes through when making purchasing decisions is affected by the particular situational factors surrounding the activity.

High involvement purchases refer to situations where both the information search and the use of referent group consultation and post-purchase evaluation is extensive and occurs when the following factors are involved:

• **Self-image**   The purchase has a major effect on an individual's self-image, such as the purchase of a car.

• **Perceived risk**   The impact of a mistaken purchase would have a dramatic effect on the consumer. Expensive purchases would fall into this category, any mistake could have a major effect on an individual's financial position.

• **Social factors**   An individual's level of social acceptance may depend on the right purchasing decision.

• **Hedonic factors**   The purchase is concerned with products or services that are linked to providing personal pleasure.

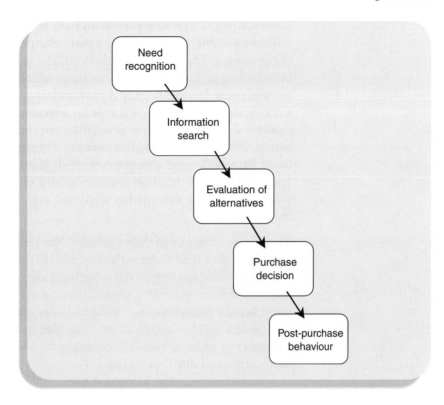

Figure 5.4
The buying process

Consumer behaviour theory is a complex area and only a brief overview has been provided here. Consumer behaviour is central to the segmentation, targeting and positioning process, in particular in establishing useful segmentation criteria.

5.5 Consumer segmentation criteria

Segmentation criteria can be divided into three main categories:

- **Profile variables**   Are used to characterize the consumer but in terms that are not expressly linked to, or predictive of, an individual's behaviour in the specific market.

- **Behavioural variables**   Relate to the behaviour of the consumer. Thus behavioural factors such as benefits sought, usage and the purchase occasion all come under this category.

- **Psychographic variables**   Identify individuals' attitudes, opinions and interests to build up a lifestyle profile that includes the consumer's consumption patterns. Thus these profiles are inextricably associated with specific purchasing behaviour.

Segmentation is a creative process and can be conducted using a range of different variables, each bringing a particular perspective to the dynamics of the market. The air travel market could be segmented according to the benefits sought (value or status), or usage occasion (business or holiday), or stage in the family life cycle (young and single or middle-aged, married with children). On occasion it may be relevant to use a single variable to segment a market, but more often than not they will be used in combination. For instance, a potential market segment in the air travel market could be middle-aged consumers with children who seek status benefits for business travel. Innovative combinations of variables from across the range can uncover new market segments, even in supposedly traditional markets.

There is no hierarchy to these variables. Marketers can use any variable as a starting point (first order variables), and then add further variables (second order variables) to give the grouping a clearer definition. Thus a segment of consumers seeking physical fitness may initially be determined using benefit segmentation. Profile variables may then be added such as age, gender, geodemographics etc., in order to more clearly identify the consumer in order to allow the company to develop specific media communication and distribution plans.

Profile variables

There are a range of demographic, socio-economic and geographic segmentation variables in this category.

Demographic segmentation

The key demographic variables consist of age, gender and the family life cycle.

Age Consumer's purchasing decisions will change with age. Older people are likely to be looking for different benefits from a holiday than younger people. However, age by itself may not be a sophisticated enough variable to help identify a consumer segment. Using the age range of 25–35-year-old individuals to identify a consumer group results in a rather unclear grouping. For instance, 25–35-year-old women will have different needs from 25–35-year-old men in certain markets. A 30-year-old woman who is single and has a professional job, is likely to have different needs to a 30-year-old woman who is married with three children and has chosen not to work outside the home. Both will have different needs to a 30-year-old unemployed woman who is single with a child.

There is also the issue of psychological age to be considered when using this variable. That is, consumers may perceive themselves to be in a different age group to their true chronological age. Therefore, a product or service aimed at 35-year-olds may attract older customers who still see themselves in this age range.

Age alone therefore has limitations as a method of breaking a market down into useful segments.

Gender   Sex, as a variable, has similar limitations to age. Clearly there are differences between consumer groups based on gender. However, this variable by itself only narrows the market down by 50%. There are still major differences within the gender category. Younger women may have different needs to older women. Cadbury, when designing a box of chocolates called Inspirations, which was aimed at the female market, found that older women did not like the contemporary design used on a prototype; however, younger women liked the modern packaging (Ensor and Laing, 1993).

Obviously age and gender variables can be used together to help define a segment. Therefore, we can define segments in terms of 25–35-year-old females, or 55–65-year-old males. However, this still gives us quite broad customer groupings that do not take into consideration wider factors that may affect consumers in these particular age and sex groupings. One way of attempting to overcome these deficiencies is to look at consumer life cycles.

Life cycle segmentation   The essence of the family life cycle is that consumers are likely to go through one of the alternative routes in the life cycle (see Figure 5.5). The classic route would be for a consumer to move from being young and single to young and married without children, to young married with children, to middle-aged married with children, to middle-aged married without dependant children, to older married, ending up finally as older unmarried.

At each stage a consumer's needs and disposable income will change. Someone who is young and single has very few commitments, so although their income in real terms may be low, they have high disposable income. Once an individual is married with children, commitments have increased. They are likely to have to move into the housing market, plus they are now buying products for young babies and children. The couple may well start to take out savings and insurance policies to protect their children's future. In middle age they will begin to be more interested in pension arrangements. Quite obviously, as an individual moves through these stages, their propensity to buy certain types of products will change. This approach is therefore useful in identifying these consumer groupings. In Western cultures there has been speculation that the family as a unit is of decreasing importance, however there is contradictory evidence on this issue. In 1985 a *Family Policy Studies Centre* report looking at the UK claimed that:

• Nine out of ten people will marry at some time in their lives.

• Nine out of ten married couples will have children.

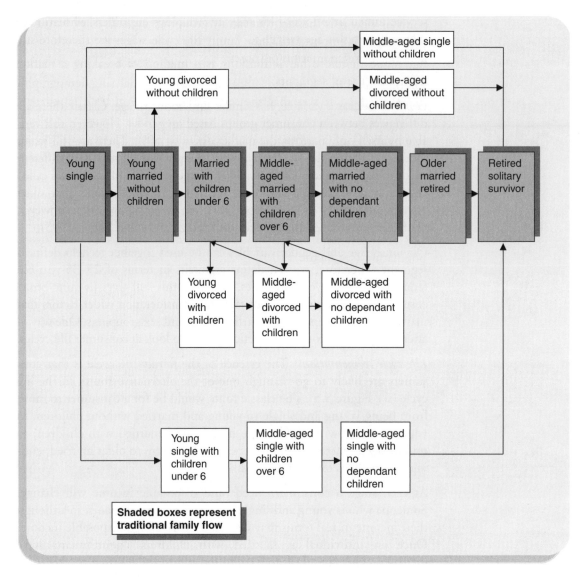

Figure 5.5
A contemporary family life cycle (*Source:* adapted from Murphy and Staples, 1979)

- Two in every three marriages are likely to be ended by death rather than divorce.

- Eight out of ten people live in households headed by a married couple.

There was one key change from earlier studies, however. This was a growing trend for individuals to go through the cycle belonging to more than one family group, that is, individuals were divorcing and remarrying. Therefore, both parental figures in a family grouping may not be blood relatives of the children. Also the siblings may not be blood relatives. From a marketer's point of view it is the fact that family groupings are still a key feature in society that is important. These family life cycle stages are therefore still relevant for segmentation purposes.

Another trend that Lawson (1988) identified after analysing demographic trends in the UK was that the stages have altered in both length and importance.

Full nest stages, when children live with their parents, are shorter due to the fact that couples are having fewer children and that these children are being born closer together. This means that individuals spend more time in the bachelor and empty nest stages and there are more people in these groups.

As a result of this study Lawson updated the family life cycle using the 1981 census, claiming this modernized version covers over 80% of the population (see Figure 5.6).

Stage	Percentage of Households
Bachelor	1.42
Newly married couples	3.11
Full nest 1 (with pre-school children)	11.91
Full nest 1 (lone parent)	1.26
Middle-aged no children	1.19
Full nest 2 (school age children)	16.97
Full nest 2 (lone parent)	1.92
Launching families (with non-dependant children)	6.3
Launching families (one parent)	1.45
Empty nest 1 (childless, aged 45–54)	9.45
Empty nest 2 (retired)	9.51
Solitary survivor under 65	2.66
Solitary survivor retired	14.17
Total	**81.32**

Figure 5.6
The modernized family life cycle (*Source:* Lawson, 1988)

> ## Illustrative example 5.1
> ## SKY TV
>
> In the UK 7.4 million households had a contract with SKY in 2004, that is 43% of the national market. By 2010 SKY aims to have increased that number to 10 million households. SKY's management believe that no household is beyond their reach. In order to achieve their aims SKY is embarking on a comprehensive market research exercise to ascertain consumer perceptions of their product offering in order to develop targeted marketing campaigns to overcome consumer's reluctance to subscribe to their channels. An interesting feature in the profile of SKY subscribers is the fact that only 21% of households that buy the *Independent* newspaper have a SKY contract. That is lower percentage than for any other group of national newspaper readers.

The 18.69% of households excluded from this table are made up of young people living in joint households, households with residents other than family and households with more than one family.

Indeed households can be a useful way of looking at social grouping. Individuals sharing a flat have to take part in group decision-making for products such as furniture, electrical appliances etc. Lawson claims, when discussing the 18.69% of the population that do not fit into the family life cycle, that households are likely to be a better unit with which to analyse consumer behaviour than the family.

Socio-economic segmentation

In socio-economic segmentation, factors such as occupation, educational background, place of residence and income are used to classify individuals into larger 'social class' groupings.

In the UK, JICNARS classification of social class has been a common tool to categorize an individual's social class (see Figure 5.7). JICNARS approach is heavily dependent upon income and occupation as the key factors used in determining its six major social groupings.

This is the traditional type of socio-economic classification system that was used in the UK for censuses since 1911. However, a new categorization system was used for the 2001 census (Rose and O'Reilly, 1999). This was as a result of major shifts in the make-up of the UK population. Currently 60% of the population are deemed to be middle class compared to 51% in 1984. The new categories also take account of the increased

Social grade	Social status	Occupations	Examples	Approximate % of households
A	Upper middle class	Higher managerial/ professional	Doctors, lawyers, professors, directors	3
B	Middle class	Intermediate managerial	Managers, teachers, computer programmers	10
C1	Lower middle	Junior managerial, supervisory, clerical administrative	Foreman, shop assistants, office workers	24
C2	Skilled working class	Skilled manual labour	Electricians, mechanics, plumbers and other crafts	30
D	Working class	Semi-skilled and unskilled manual labour	Machine operators, assembly workers	25
E	Subsistence	None	Pensioners, casual workers, unemployed, students	8

Figure 5.7
JICNARS social grade definitions (*Source:* JICNARS)

role in the workplace of women who now occupy 18% of all professional posts compared with 4% in 1984. Women, under the new system, will be categorized in their own right rather than according to their husband's occupation. The new classification was based on a survey of 65 000 people across 371 occupations (see Figure 5.8).

Despite this new classification there are still several problems with socio-economic approaches to segmentation for marketing managers:

• Social class is not an accurate gauge of disposable income. An electrician or a plumber who would be classified as social class C2 may well have a higher income than a junior manager who would be classified as social class C1.

• In Western societies there has been a major trend toward women working. Social classification has used the head of household's occupation to define social class; if both adults are working defining the head of

New social class	Occupations	Examples
1	Higher managerial and professional occupations	
1.1	Employers and managers in larger organizations	Bank managers, company directors, financial managers, senior local government officers
1.2	High professional	Doctors, lawyers, dentists, higher civil servants, academics, engineers, teachers, airline pilots, social workers, librarians, personnel officers, computer analysts
2	Lower managerial and professional occupations	Police officers, firefighters, prison officers, nurses, physiotherapists, journalists, actors and musicians
3	Intermediate occupations	Secretaries/PAs, airline flight attendants, driving instructors, computer operators, clerical workers, computer engineers, dental technicians, precision instrument makers
4	Small employers and own account workers	
5	Lower supervisory, craft and related occupations	Electricians, TV engineers, car mechanics, train drivers, printers
6	Semi-routine occupations	Drivers, hairdressers, bricklayers, plasterers, welders, cooks, shop assistants, garage forecourt attendants, supermarket check-out operators
7	Routine occupations	Car park attendants, cleaners, road workers, refuse collectors, labourers, road sweepers

Figure 5.8
New classes used in the 2001 UK census (*Source:* adapted from Rose and O'Reilly, 1999)

household becomes more difficult. Earlier in this chapter we have also seen that family structures themselves have become more complicated in the West. The new classification does attempt to address this issue but 'How does the new classification help to predict family purchasing behaviour?' Individuals from the same household may be in two completely different social classes.

- The variety and the changing nature of people's occupations make it increasingly difficult to apply social class categories consistently.

Most importantly in today's society social class is a less important predictor of behaviour than other methods of segmentation. For instance, an individual whatever their social class, who is interested in sport is more likely to buy products and services in the sporting area than an individual in the same social class who is not interested in sport. It may therefore be more important for marketers to identify individuals who share a common interest (i.e. sport) rather than identify social class groupings.

Geographic segmentation

Geographic   This variable was used more extensively in the past. There used to be clear consumer patterns in product areas such as food and alcohol across Europe, or even within a market such as the UK. Although some of these patterns still show through, mass communication and wider access to travel has tended to erode these regional differences. In the UK individuals are eating a much more cosmopolitan diet than 30 years ago. Pizzas and pasta dishes are common in many homes. Where geographic variables are used they tend to be used to reflect some wider cultural differences between markets. However, geographic variables can be useful if they are used in conjunction with other factors.

Illustrative example 5.2
Day Chocolate company

The market for fair trade chocolate and cocoa products has grown from sales of £1m in 1998 to £10.9m in 2003. It is a market segment that the Day Chocolate company dominates with its brands Divine and Dubble. Day Chocolate also supplies the Co-op with its own brand chocolate and much of the company's success is due to this relationship. In 2003 Co-op own-branded chocolate sales were up 26% on the previous year compared with 1% growth for the traditional branded products. In the first four months of 2004 own branded sales were up another 36% compared with a 15% decline for branded products. The overall chocolate market was worth £662m in 2003 so the ethical segment is a small percentage of the overall market. However, the Day Chocolate company, by focusing on this specialist market, is able to operate in a growth segment with limited direct competition. This is also against the background of an overall chocolate market that is maturing and showing signs of much lower levels of growth.

Geodemographics Geodemographic segmentation combines information on household location with certain demographic and socio-economic data. This approach relies on information that is gathered in census returns. In the UK, the census information on family size, household size, occupation and ethnic origin can be used to group residential housing into geographic areas that display similar profiles. There are several geodemographic forms of classification; one of the best known in the UK is ACORN (A Classification Of Residential Neighbourhoods). The ACORN classification identifies five major categories (one group is unclassified) that can be further subdivided into 17 groups (see Figure 5.9).

Categories	% pop.	Groups	% pop.
1 Wealthy achievers	25.6	A Wealthy executives	8.6
		B Affluent greys	7.7
		C Flourishing families	8.8
2 Urban prosperity	10.7	D Prosperous professionals	2.2
		E Educated urbanites	4.6
		F Aspiring singles	3.9
3 Comfortably off	23.6	G Starting out	2.5
		H Secure families	15.5
		I Settled suburbia	6.0
		J Prudent pensioners	2.6
4 Moderate means	14.5	K Asian communities	1.6
		L Post-industrial families	4.8
		M Blue-collar roots	8.0
5 Hard-pressed	22.4	N Struggling families	14.1
		O Burdened singles	4.5
		P High-rise hardship	1.6
		Q Inner city adversity	2.1
Unclassified	0.3	U Unclassified	0.5

Figure 5.9
The ACORN consumer targeting classification (*Source:* CACI Limited, © 2004; ACORN is a registered trademark of CACI Limited)

These 17 groups can be further subdivided into 56 neighbourhood types. For instance, ACORN category 2 (Urban prosperity), group D (Prosperous professionals) is made up of two neighbourhood types. One of these is neighbourhood type 13, which is categorized as 'Well-off professionals, larger houses and converted flats'. These types of neighbourhood areas are found in many urban centres in the UK but particularly in London, Edinburgh and university towns such as Oxford, Cambridge and Durham.

These neighbourhood areas allow specific patterns of consumption to be identified. For instance, ACORN type 2 'Wealthy working families with mortgages' is a sub-group of category 1, group A 'Wealthy achievers'. According to the ACORN profile this group is made up of families living in large detached houses, normally with more than four bedrooms. In many of these households both adults are working. These families are found all over the UK, including towns such as, Warrington, Milton Keynes and Northampton. These households have high levels of savings, good pension provision and are likely to have private health insurance. They are likely to lead an active lifestyle, going to the gym, walking and playing golf. The household also enjoys consuming wine, some of which they buy in cases by mail order. This type of detailed profile allows for highly sophisticated targeting.

This segmentation approach can be used to aid decision-making in a variety of areas:

• Identifying favourable retail locations for a specific retail format.

• The specific mix of products and services delivered in a particular retail location.

• Decisions on direct mail campaigns.

• The boundaries of specific sales territories.

• Location of poster sites.

• Selection of media.

There are criticisms of this approach. It is claimed that all these geo-demographic systems contain inaccuracies because of the difficulties in lining up the census enumeration districts with postal codes. There are also problems in reflecting the changes in housing that takes place between each census.

The geodemographic systems referred to so far are used at a relatively local level. There have been developments to try to use this approach at a much larger regional level. Geodemographic techniques have been used on a European scale to identify consumers who have common characteristics but may live in different countries. Using demographic (age),

Segment	Geographical boundaries	Description	pop. (m)
1	UK and Ireland	Average age and income profile; English as a common language	60.3
2	Central Germany, central and northern France, southern Belgium and Luxembourg	High proportion of older people and low proportion of middle-aged; average income; German and French languages	54.5
3	Portugal and Spain	Young population; below average income; Portuguese and Spanish languages	50.4
4	South-eastern France, southern Germany, northern Italy	High proportion of middle-aged people; above average income; French, German and Italian languages	71.5
5	Southern Italy and Greece	Young population; below average income; Italian and Greek languages	31.2
6	Northern Germany, the Netherlands, northern Belgium, Denmark, Sweden, Finland, Norway, Iceland and Switzerland	High proportion of middle-aged people; very high income; multilingual; German, French, Italian and Scandinavian languages	57.6

Figure 5.10
Euro-consumer segments using geodemographic segmentation (Note that Norway, Iceland and Switzerland are not currently members of the European Union) (*Source:* adapted from Vandermerwe and L'Huillier, 1989)

economic (income), cultural (language) and geographic (longitude and latitude) factors, six Euro-consumer segments can be identified (see Figure 5.10).

This approach illustrates the point that consumers in different countries can share similar characteristics. For instance, the consumers in segment 4 show more similarities to each other than to other consumers from their own country. This is the first step at European segmentation, it may well lead to the identification of sub-segments within these larger groups and to the ability for marketers to target relatively large geodemographic segments that transcend national boundaries.

Behavioural variables

The segmentation approaches that have been discussed so far are all using characteristics of the consumer as a way of identifying clear groupings. However, identifying consumer behaviour rather than their personal attributes can be a more effective way of identifying market segments.

The main behavioural variables in this category are benefits, usage and purchase occasion.

Benefit segmentation

Benefit segmentation uses the underlying reasons why an individual purchases a particular product or service, rather than trying to identify an individual's particular personal attributes.

Benefit segmentation is based on the concept that the key reason a consumer buys the product or service is for the benefit that product or service gives them. Identifying groups of consumers that are seeking a common benefit in a particular market allows a producer to develop specific products or service offerings. An example of benefit segmentation would be in the management education market. A survey in the USA found that there were several benefit segments in the market for MBA qualifications (see Figure 5.11).

Quality seekers wish to have the highest-quality education available. They believe a top-ranked education will benefit them during their entire business life, and will lead to job advancement or a career change

Speciality seekers wish to have a specialized education and to become experts in their areas of particular interest. Concentrated courses tend to fit their needs, and they will search for institutions that offer them

Career changers are seeking new jobs or employers and believe an MBA qualification will open up opportunities for career advancement and mobility. They have several years' work experience and feel that they are in a career cul-de-sac

Knowledge seekers wish to learn and feel increased knowledge will lead to power. They believe that an MBA will be an asset not only in their career but also in all aspects of their life

Status seekers feel an MBA will lead to increased income and prestige

Degree seekers believe that a first degree is no longer sufficient and that an MBA is needed in order to be competitive in the contemporary job market. These individuals tend to be active, self-oriented and independent

Professional advancers are striving to climb the corporate ladder. They are looking for professional advancement, higher salaries and job flexibility. They are upwardly mobile, serious, future orientated and wish to build a career within the current corporate structures

Avoiders look for MBA programmes that require the least effort to complete. They believe that all business schools will provide essentially the same education. Their motivation is 'other directed' and they will seek low-cost, 'lower-quality' programmes

Convenience seekers will join MBA programmes that are located near their homes or place of work and which have simple entry procedures. They are interested in any business school which provides these conveniences and is low-cost

Non-matriculators wish to undertake an MBA course without completing any formal application procedures. They are therefore attracted to a business school that allows them to begin an MBA programme without any formal application

Figure 5.11
MBA benefit segments (*Source:* based on Miaoulis and Kalfus, 1983)

The advantage of benefit segmentation is that it is a market-orientated approach which, by seeking to identify consumers' needs, allows organizations to set about satisfying them.

Usage segmentation

The characteristics and patterns of consumer usage is the essence of this segmentation approach. Consumers will generally fall into categories of heavy users, medium users, occasional users and non-users of a particular product or service. Identifying heavy users can be useful as they are likely to consume a larger percentage of an organization's sales than other groups, as the Pareto effect would suggest (see Figure 5.12). This can lead to the identification of new segmentation opportunities for an organization.

For example, mangers re-launched their cleaning product Sugar Soap, which was a universal non-silica-based household cleaner, by identifying that the heavy users of this product were professional household painters and decorators. In fact, the reason this group were heavy users of the product was because it could be used to clean surfaces that needed to be painted and, because it was a non-silica-based cleaner, they could paint straight onto the surface. Once managers had identified this group of heavy users they re-launched the product to the 'Do It Yourself' market for individuals wishing to decorate their own houses.

Airlines use frequent flyer programmes to retain the heavy users of their services. Many other companies in other sectors use incentives to retain this important customer grouping.

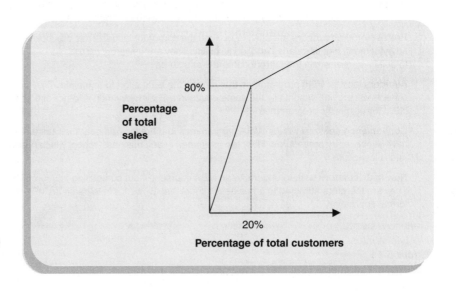

Figure 5.12
The Pareto effect, also known as the 80/20 rule

Banks and building societies may wish to have charging scales on their accounts that give incentives for heavy users while at the same time increasing relative charges for light users as they are relatively more expensive to manage.

Consumer groups can be further identified on the basis of **purchase occasion**, i.e. when they buy a particular product or service. Some products may be bought as individual gifts, or for a specific formal social occasion, such as a wedding. The convenience store concept is an example of occasion segmentation, where individuals can make purchases at a time and place that is agreeable to them.

Psychographic variables

The techniques that have been discussed so far have used either consumer characteristics or behavioural variables as the basis for identifying consumer groupings. Psychographics is a more recent approach that attempts to identify segments based on lifestyle characteristics, attitudes and personality. Rather than concentrating on single factors such as age, sex or marital status it attempts to build a broader picture of consumers' lifestyles. Asking a series of questions about consumers' activities, interests and opinions as well as questions about product and service usage identifies these lifestyles (see Figure 5.13).

Several models have been developed using this approach. These models do have broad similarities. There are a range of these models available, two will be discussed in more detail.

The VALs framework

The model was developed in the USA by asking 2713 individuals 800 questions. The VALs framework identified nine lifestyle groups in the American population. The model also identifies three developmental

Activities	Interests	Opinions	Demographics
Work	Family	Themselves	Age
Hobbies	Home	Social issues	Education
Social events	Job	Politics	Income
Vacation	Community	Business	Occupation
Entertainment	Recreation	Economics	Family size
Club membership	Fashion	Education	Dwelling
Community	Food	Products	Geography
Shopping	Media	Future	City size
Sports	Achievements	Culture	Stage in life cycle

Figure 5.13
Questions posed in lifestyle studies (*Source:* Plummer, 1974)

stages that individuals may pass through. Normally individuals would move from one of the need-driven stages to either an outer-directed or an inner-directed stage. This is a hierarchical model and relatively few would reach the integrated stage (see Figure 5.14).

The framework is divided into a series of segments:

- The needs-driven segment identified by this model have relatively little purchasing power and are therefore of marginal interest to profit making organizations. This is a declining group in Western societies.

- The outer-directed groups are more affluent and are interested in status products that other individuals will notice. They are therefore interested in brand names such as Rolex and Cartier.

- Inner-directed individuals in contrast are more concerned with their individual needs rather than external values. This is an important sector, as they tend to be trend-setters. This group is also the fastest growing group in Western societies.

- Very few individuals reach the integrated group.

Developmental stage	Grouping (% of US population)
Need-driven	**Survivors:** This is a disadvantaged group who are likely to be withdrawn, despairing and depressed (4%) **Sustainers** are another disadvantaged group, but they are working hard to escape poverty (7%)
Outer-directed	**Belongers** are characterized as being conventional, nostalgic, reluctant to try new ideas and generally conservative (33%) **Emulators** are upwardly mobile, ambitious and status-conscious (10%) **Achievers:** This group enjoys life and make things happen (23%)
Inner-directed	**'I-am-me'** tend to be young, self-engrossed and act on whims (5%) **Experientials** wish to enjoy as wide a range of life experiences as possible (7%) **Societally conscious** have a clear sense of social responsibility and wish to improve society (9%)
Nirvana	**Integrateds** are completely mature psychologically and combine the positive elements of outer- and inner-directedness (2%)

Figure 5.14
The VALs framework developed by Arnold Mitchell at the Stanford Research Institute

The Monitor framework

This framework was developed by the Taylor Nelson research agency. The model similarly divides consumers into three main groups, each with its own subgroups (see Figure 5.15).

The advantages of this lifestyle approach are:

• It takes into account factors other than status and class.

• Purchasing patterns are encompassed in the lifestyle profile.

• Well-defined communication channels may emerge as part of the lifestyle.

• Brand personalities can be built to appeal to specific lifestyles.

These models allow a more rounded view of consumer groups to emerge. Identifying the lifestyle of potential consumer segments allows the marketer to develop sophisticated marketing mixes that tie in with a particular lifestyle group. The lifestyle profile may highlight the type of

Groups	Subgroups (% of UK population)
Sustenance-driven are concerned about material security	**Aimless:** This group includes the young unemployed and elderly drifters (5%) **Survivors:** Working class people who retain traditional attitudes (16%) **Belongers:** This subgroup straddles the sustenance-driven and outer-directed groups. They are a conservative family-orientated group (The subgroup is 18% of the UK population in total: 9% in the sustenance-driven group)
Outer-directed	**Belongers** (9%)**:** This half of the subgroup are still conservative and family-orientated but are also status-driven **Conspicuous consumers:** are driven by a desire for status (19%)
Inner-directed	**Social resisters:** This group are caring and tend to hold doctrinaire attitudes (11%) **Experimentalists** are individualistic and are interested in the good life (14%) **Self-explorers** hold less doctrinaire attitudes than the social resistors and are less materialistic than the experimentalist subgroup (17%)

Figure 5.15
The Monitor framework developed by the Taylor Nelson research agency

Yuppies	Young upwardly mobile professionals
Dinks	Dual income no kids
Bumps	Borrowed-to-the-hilt, upwardly mobile professional show-offs
Silks	Single income lots of kids
Glams	Greying leisured affluent middle-aged
Jollies	Jet-setting oldies with lots of loot

Figure 5.16
Acronyms developed
from lifestyle groupings

retail outlets that the consumer group is attracted to, or the publications they are more likely to read, thus allowing managerial decisions to be made about the distribution and promotional aspects of the mix.

Weaknesses with psychographical models are that they currently tend to reflect a Western social hierarchy and culture. As a result these frameworks are not always easily transferred to different social settings. Cultural values may mean that aspirations are different than those represented by Western values of individualism, self-development and status. These models also do not easily represent the flatter social class structures that occur in certain cultures, such as Scandinavia.

Some critics of the approach would also argue that these broad lifestyle profiles are not accurate predictors of consumers' purchasing behaviour in any particular market sector. An outer-directed individual who may in general buy status products may not buy branded goods in a market area where there is very little risk of damage to their self-image. The soap powder they buy is unlikely to be of major significance to the way they feel about themselves or about the way other people see them. However, the car they drive, or the clothes they wear, is likely to be a much more significant indicator of their status to both themselves and others.

Lifestyle segmentation has led to the proliferation of acronyms to describe consumer groupings (see Figure 5.16).

5.6 Organizational/industrial segmentation techniques

So far this chapter has concentrated on segmentation of consumer markets. Obviously many companies' main markets lie in the organizational or industrial sphere. In these markets companies have to sell products and services directly to organizational purchasers. There are differences between the type of segmentation variables used in an organizational market and the ones that have so far been outlined for consumer markets.

The difference in approach lies in the nature of organizational buyer behaviour.

5.7   Organizational buyer behaviour

Organizations' purchase decisions are likely to be more complex because of the number of individuals and groups involved in the purchase decision and the possibility of the actual product/service being more expensive and sophisticated. All the individuals that participate in the decision-making process will have interdependent goals and share common risks, although they may face different systems of reward. What emerges is a decision-making unit (DMU) made up of all these individuals and groups. Individuals in the DMU will play one of six main roles:

- **Initiator**   Identifies a problem that can be overcome by the purchase of a product or service. An individual in a retail company may, for instance, identify a problem in the merchandising function of the company that could be resolved by a new piece of software. (The merchandise function develops the buying plan for a retail company, monitors sales and product margins amongst other things.)

- **User**   Will be the actual user of the product in the merchandising function of the company in this case. They may well be the initiators, although this role may be filled by someone outside the user group.

- **Buyer**   Actually undertakes the negotiation with potential suppliers. The brief for the technical requirements of the software needed, however, is likely to come from one of the other areas of the DMU.

- **Influencer**   Does not directly make the product or supplier choice but has a major impact on the decisions made. In this case an individual from the computer services unit in the organization will lay down the technical requirements of the software based on the need for it to integrate with the current hardware system.

- **Decider**   This is the individual who actually makes the decision to purchase. This individual may not have direct line management control of the merchandise or IT areas of the business but occupies this role because of the power and influence they have over the area being investigated. This is a crucial position in the DMU and yet it can be the most difficult to identify because several individuals may potentially play this role. In this case it may be the merchandise director, the finance director (many finance directors are responsible for the IT function) or the managing director.

- **Gatekeeper**   Determines the flow of information within the DMU without being directly involved in the buying decision. They control whether a potential supplier gains access to other individuals in the DMU. The flow of promotion material and information about suppliers is also under their guidance. Secretaries are very obvious gatekeepers but any individual in the DMU can potentially play this role. A technical person may favour one particular supplier and only passes their promotional material to other members of the DMU.

The size of the DMU will depend in part on the type of purchase decision being undertaken. Where a simple low-risk purchase is being made one or two individuals could undertake all the roles in the DMU. A high-risk expensive purchase may involve a large number of people from different functional areas in the company. Organizational purchases can be classified in terms of their level of risk as follows:

- **Routine order products**   These are used and ordered on a regular basis. The product or service is unlikely to pose any problems regarding its use or performance and is therefore low risk (e.g. office stationery).

- **Procedural problem products**   These products may involve some level of training in order for individuals to successfully adopt them. This will increase the risks associated with the successful introduction of the purchase to the company (e.g. personal computers or word processors).

- **Performance problem products**   The risks here lie with the question of whether the product can perform at the level required to meet the user's requirements. There may also be concerns about the product's ability to be compatible with the company's existing resources and current equipment (e.g. introducing new technology).

- **Political problem products**   Political problems could arise where a purchase takes away resources from another area within the organization. A high investment in a product for one area of the business may mean that another area has to forgo investment. Political problems can also take place where it is planned that the same product will be used by several different units, each having their own requirements (e.g. a new information system).

Political pressures also build up in the DMU because individuals look for different attributes from a particular product. This is partly based on the operational needs of their department. Individuals also pursue their own self-interest and are motivated by the formal rewards available to them. Individuals in different areas of the company may be given incentives in different ways. Buyers may be evaluated and/or given incentives to save the organization money. Production managers may be given quality and output targets. This can lead to strange effects. Bonoma (1982) talks of an organization that reduced its list price to well below that of its competitors, but gave only small discounts off this list price. All the competitors charged higher prices but gave larger discounts. Even though the company had lower prices organizations favoured the competitors. The main reason for this turned out to be that the buyers were evaluated and given incentives based on the price concessions they were able to obtain during negotiations rather than on the end price paid.

Figure 5.17 shows how each unit may have its own set of rewards. These disparate incentives can also lead to conflict within the DMU. Buyers may feel they cannot save money because the production engineers are setting technical specifications on a product that are too high. Alternatively production engineers may not be able to reach their output targets because the buyer has bought a cheaper product from a supplier who has less dependable delivery times.

This demonstrates that organizational buying decisions are more complex than general consumer buyer behaviour. Frameworks have been developed to give a more comprehensive view of the complex factors involved. These also act as a foundation for developing meaningful segmentation criteria in organizational markets. The Webster–Wind and the Sheth frameworks both try to develop logical models of this process.

Figure 5.17
Rewards/incentives as a source of conflict in organizational decision-making units (*Source:* adapted from Morris, 1988)

The Webster–Wind framework

This framework identifies four categories of variables that have an influence on organizational buying decisions (see Figure 5.18).

- **Environmental**   Any aspect of the external environment that may effect the organization buying behaviour is embraced under this heading.

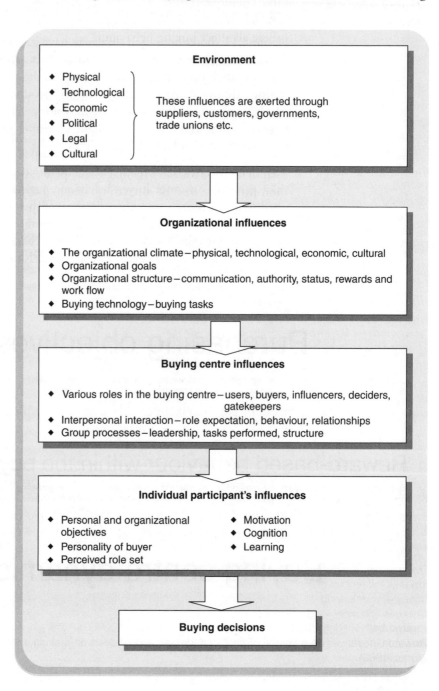

Figure 5.18
The Webster–Wind framework (*Source:* adapted from Webster and Wind, 1972. © American Marketing Association)

This includes political, economic, cultural, legal, technological and physical environments. Competitors' marketing actions are also deemed to be in the external environment.

- **Organizational**   There are several organizational factors that affect behaviour. The company's goals and objectives set parameters on activity. The organization's structure and resources act as constraints on its culture in terms of the type of policies and procedures that are followed; these all affect buying behaviour.

- **Interpersonal**   The relationship between the individuals in the buying centre are an important determinate of how decisions are reached. How coalitions are formed and where loyalties lie within an organization will be dependent on these relationships.

- **Individual**   Attitude to risk, creativity, competitiveness, style of problem-solving and locus of control will all be unique in each individual. The individual's personal goals, past experience and training will inform their way of operating. Each individual will influence the DMU's decisions to a greater or lesser extent.

Each of these categories has two subcategories of task and non-task-related variables. Task-related variables are directly related to the buying decision being undertaken; non-task variables are not directly concerned with the buying decision but nevertheless affect the decisions made (see Figure 5.19).

The Sheth framework

The Webster–Wind framework identifies and helps to assess key variables that influence organization's purchasing decisions, but it does not concentrate on the process to any great degree. Sheth (1973) developed a model that has some elements in common with the Webster–Wind framework but also has more of an emphasis on the psychology of the decision-making process.

Figure 5.19 Examples of task and non-task influences on organizational buying decisions (*Source:* adapted from Webster and Wind, 1972 © Copyright American Marketing Association)

	Task influences (Relate directly to the buying problem)	Non-task influences (Extend beyond the buying problem)
Individual influences	Goal of obtaining best price	Beliefs, values and needs of the individual
Interpersonal influences	Group dynamics during meetings to agree specifications	Informal off-the-job social interactions
Organizational influences	Company policies restricting supplier choice	Criteria used for personnel evaluation
Environmental influences	Potential changes in prices	Economic and political climate in an election year

He identified the importance of four main factors that influence organizational buyer behaviour:

- The expectations of the members of the DMU.

- The factors influencing the buying process.

- The character of the decision-making process.

- Situational factors.

The model is constructed so that the flow of the actual decision-making process can be illustrated (see Figure 5.20).

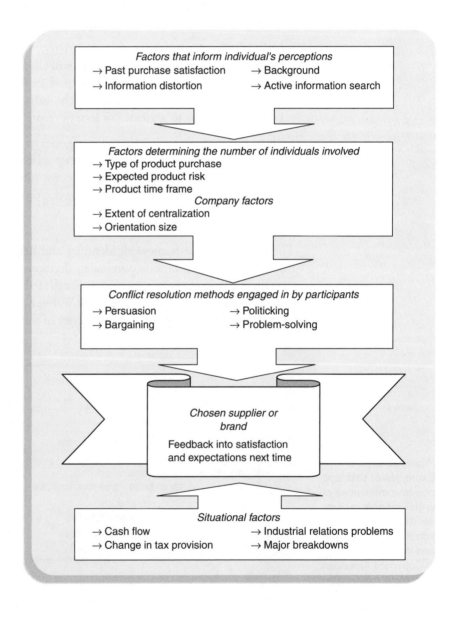

Figure 5.20
A model of organizational buyer behaviour (*Source:* adapted from Sheth, 1973)

Expectations of the members of the DMU

Every individual in the DMU will have their own attitudes and particular background that shapes the way in which they judge a supplier. An engineer will use different criteria to an accountant. Individuals' expectations will be determined by their educational background, their job or task orientation and their lifestyle in general.

Individuals will also be influenced by information from a range of sources. When the purchase being considered contains a high level of risk to the organization it is likely that a rigorous process will be undertaken to identify as many sources of information as possible. This information search is likely to be undertaken by the professional buyers and can lead them to play an important gatekeeping role by choosing what information is passed on to other members of the DMU.

The information provided, as with any communication, will be subject to perceptual distortion by the individuals in the DMU. Individuals' expectations will also be influenced by their previous experience of the product or service.

The factors influencing the buying process

The Sheth model outlines two sets of factors that will determine the particular buying process for a specific product or service. The first set of factors relate to the product itself:

- **Perceived risk**   If the purchase is high-risk then a detailed search for information will take place drawing more individuals into the DMU. This could occur if the purchase was a major capital expenditure.

- **Time pressure**   If a decision has to be made under time pressure a smaller number of individuals will be drawn into the DMU. The fewer people involved the quicker the decision.

- **Type of purchase**   A routine repurchase of a product is likely to be undertaken by an individual who has been delegated the responsibility.

The second set of factors that influence the buying process are related to the organization itself:

- **The organization's orientation**   An organization may be engineering-orientated or marketing-orientated. This orientation will, to an extent, reflect the balance of power within the DMU and have an important influence on its attitude to a purchase decision. An organization that has a dominant engineering orientation will perceive a purchase by using engineering values.

- **Size of the organization**   A small organization may have only one individual responsible for buying. This individual may undertake all the information searches themselves. Large organizations are likely to have more individuals involved in purchase decisions.

- **Degree of centralization/decentralization** A central buying department would be common in a strongly centralized organization. A much greater spread of individuals would be involved in a decentralized company.

Character of the decision-making process

Sheth's model identifies two types of decisions:

- Autonomous decisions are taken by an individual and are relatively straightforward.

- Joint decisions are undertaken by more than one individual. As the model has already indicated, each individual has a unique set of factors influencing them, so some level of conflict is likely.

The manner in which these conflicts are resolved affects the final decision. The model outlines four approaches to making decisions:

- **Problem-solving** This involves gathering information and using a systematic approach to weighing up the alternative options. A disadvantage of this approach is that it inevitably takes time.

- **Persuasion** Time is taken in order to get everybody to put the organizational needs and objectives above personal agendas. Again the disadvantage is this can slow down the decision process.

- **Bargaining** Is used in order to reach a compromise. Individuals in the buying centre trade concessions. This may result in a sub-optimal decision. Individuals may be satisfied but the decision may not be in the best interest of the organization as a whole.

- **Politicking** Power and influence are used to coerce individuals into supporting majority positions within the DMU.

The model would suggest problem-solving and persuasion are the most rational approaches to decision-making. Many practising managers will be well aware that the bargaining and politicking options are common practice in many organizations.

Situational factors

Finally the model highlights situational variables that are outside the control of the organization but influence the DMU. These variables would be such things as:

- A strike at a key supplier.

- A supplier is suddenly taken over by a competitor.

- Financial problems.

- Production breakdown.

- Changes in corporate taxation.

These two models illustrate the complexity of the buying process in organizations. They also give some insights into potential factors that can be used to identify organizational market segments.

5.8 Approaches to organizational market segmentation

Organizational markets can be segmented according to the characteristics of the organization; this is sometimes referred to as the macro level. Factors that would be analysed at this level would be:

- **Industry sector** Standard industry classification codes (SIC codes) will identify an organization's primary business activity. Different industry sectors may have unique needs from a product or service. In the computer hardware and software market the needs of retailers, financial services companies and local government will be different.

- **Size of the organization** This can be judged using several variables such as the number of employees, volume of shipments, market share. This method of segmentation has to be used with caution, just because an organization is large does not mean that it will be a large purchaser of your product. However, larger organizations will differ from smaller companies by having more formalized buying systems and increased specialization of functions.

- **Geographic location** Traditional industries can tend to cluster geographically, an example being the car industry in Detroit, USA. However, even emerging technologies show the tendency to locate in the same geographical area. The UK computer industry has clusters in central Scotland (Silicon Glen) and along the M4 motorway in southern England. Internationally there may well be different regional variations in purchasing behaviour, for example between Western and Eastern Europe.

- **End-use application** The way in which a product or service is used by a company has an important effect on the way the organization views its value. A truck that is used 12 hours a day by a quarrying company may represent great value. But for a construction company who only use the same piece of equipment two hours a day it may represent a much lower value for money purchase. Establishing end-use application can help establish the perception of value that will be used in particular segments.

Organizational markets can also be segmented according to the characteristics of the decision-making unit; this is sometimes called micro segmentation. The factors used include:

- **The structure of the decision-making unit** This is directly related to the models covered earlier in this chapter on organizational buyer behaviour. The type of individuals involved in the DMU of an organization will vary, as will its size and complexity.

- **The decision-making process** This can be short and straightforward or complex and time-consuming. This will largely be dependent on the size and complexity of the DMU.

- **Structure of the buying function** The buying function can be centralized or decentralized. Centralized buying allows an individual buyer to specialize in purchasing particular types of product categories. An individual is responsible for buying much larger volumes per purchase than under a decentralized structure. This allows them to negotiate larger discounts. In centralized structures the professional buyer has much greater influence within the DMU over technical advisers compared to buyers in decentralized systems.

- **Attitude towards innovation** There may be specific characteristics that mark out innovative companies. Identifying companies that exhibit this profile will allow a segment to be established at which new products can be initially targeted. There are organizations that are followers and only try a product once innovators have already adopted it. Identifying these companies can also be useful to a marketer.

- **Key criteria used in reaching a decision on a purchase** These can include product quality, price, technical support, supply continuity and reliability of prompt deliveries.

- **Personal characteristics of decision-makers** Factors such as age, educational background, attitude toward risk and style of decision-making can potentially be used to segment the market.

Figure 5.21 summarizes organizational macro and micro segmentation.

A more systematic method to organizational market segmentation has been developed, called the nested approach. This method moves through layers of segmentation variables starting with the demographics of the organization (the macro level) down through increasingly more sophisticated levels, reaching the complex areas of situational factors and personal characteristics. This approach effectively establishes a hierarchical structure in which to undertake the segmentation process (see Figure 5.22).

There is a balance to be struck with this approach between the macro level, which is generally inadequate when used in isolation, and the micro level, which may be too time-consuming and expensive to establish and operate in markets with limited potential.

Variables	Examples
Macro segmentation	
◆ Size of organization	Large, medium or small
◆ Geographic location	Local, national, European Union, worldwide
◆ Industrial sector	Retail, engineering, financial services
◆ End market served	Defined by product or service
Micro segmentation	
◆ Choice criteria	Quality, delivery, value in use, supplier reputation, price
◆ Structure of decision-making unit	Complexity, hierarchical, effectiveness
◆ Decision-making process	Long, short, low- or high-conflict
◆ Buy class	New task, straight or modified re-buy
◆ Importance of purchasing	High or low importance
◆ Type of purchasing organization	Matrix, centralized, decentralized
◆ Innovation level of organization	Innovative, follower, laggard
◆ Purchasing strategy	Optimizer, satisfier
◆ Personal attributes	Age, educational background, risk-taker/averse, confidence level

Figure 5.21
Organizational macro and micro segmentation

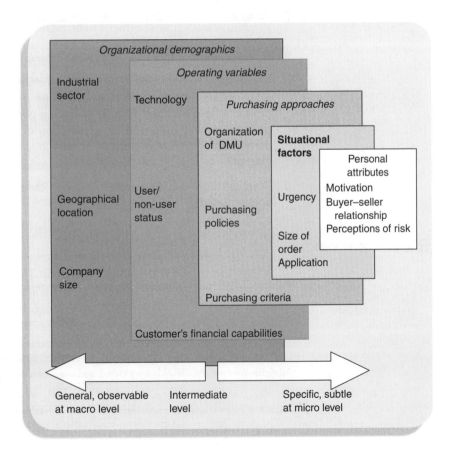

Figure 5.22
The major factors for segmenting organizational markets (a nested approach) (*Source:* adapted from Bonoma and Shapiro, 1983)

Summary

This chapter has illustrated how an in-depth knowledge of both consumer and organizational buyer behaviour is needed to successfully identify useful segmentation criteria. This led to an exploration of a wide range of criteria that can be used to segment both consumer and organizational markets. This is the first step in the critical strategic process of establishing market segments that are available for a company to serve. Companies have to evaluate the potential of these segments and to make choices about which groups to serve (targeting) and on what competitive basis (positioning). The next steps to successful segmentation will be explored in detail in Chapter 11 on targeting and positioning, and brand strategy.

Discussion questions

1 What are the potential problems associated with the socio-economic approaches to segmentation?

2 What are the main behavioural variables that can be used to segment consumer markets?

3 How is psychographic segmentation different from other methods?

4 A company is considering setting up a chain of 'coffee house style' retail outlets, which would offer chocolate drinks and other chocolate products, in a number of large shopping centres. What would be the potential advantages and disadvantages of employing either a geo-demographic or psychographic approach to segmentation in this new market?

5 What are the key differences between consumer and organizational segmentation?

References

Bonoma, T.V. (1982) Major sales: who really does the buying? *Harvard Business Review*, 60, May–June, pp. 111–19.

Bonoma, T.V. and Shapiro, B.P. (1983) *Segmenting the Industrial Market*. Lexington Books/D.C. Heath and Company.

CACI Limited (1993) (Data source BMRB and OPCS/GRO(s)). © Crown Copyright (1991) All rights reserved. ACORN is a registered trademark of CACI limited.

De Mooji, M.K. and Keegan, W. (1991) *Advertising Worldwide; Concepts, Theories and Practice of International, Multinational and Global Advertising*. Prentice Hall.

Doyle, P. (1994) *Marketing Management and Strategy*. Prentice Hall.

Ensor, J. and Laing, S. (1993) *Cadbury's Project Gift*. European case clearing house.

Family Policy Studies Centre Report, cited in Rice, C. (1993) *Consumer Behaviour*. Butterworth Heinemann.

Lawson, R.W. (1988) The family life cycle: a demographic analysis. *Journal of Marketing Management*, Vol. 4, No. 1, pp. 13–32.

Maslow, A.H. (1970) *Motivation and Personality*, 2nd edn. Harper & Row.

Miaoulis, G. and Kalfus, D. (1983) 10 MBA benefit segments. *Marketing News*, 5 August.

Morris, M.H. (1988) *Industrial and Organizational Marketing*. Merrill Publishing Company.

Murphy, P.E. and Staples, W. (1979) A modernised family life cycle. *Journal of Consumer Research*, Vol. 16 (June), pp. 12–22.

Plummer, J.T. (1974) The concept and application of life style segmentation. *Journal of Marketing*, Vol. 38 (January), pp. 33–7.

Rose, D. and O'Reilly, K. (eds) (1999) *Constructing Classes: Towards a New Social Classification for the UK*, ESRC/ONS.

Sheth, J.N. (1973) A model of industrial buyer behaviour. *Journal of Marketing*, Vol. 37, No. 4, pp. 50–6.

Steers, R.M., Porter, L.W. and Bigley, G.A. (1996) *Motivation and Leadership at Work*. McGraw-Hill.

Tinson, J. (1998) *Customer Service Interface: Implications for Maternity Service Provision*. Conference Paper, Academy of Marketing.

Vandermerwe, S. and L'Huillier, M. (1989) Euro-consumers in 1992. *Business Horizons*, Jan.–Feb., pp. 34–40.

Webster, F.E. and Wind, Y. (1972) A general model of organizational buying behaviour. *Journal of Marketing*, 36, April, pp. 12–17. © Copyright American Marketing Association.

Products, new product development and innovation

About this chapter

Decisions relating to the product offer that an organization chooses to present to the market are critical in determining the success of any enterprise. Organizations have to continually monitor the performance of their products in the market and react to changes in the external environment by developing and launching new competitive offerings to the consumer.

After reading this chapter, you will understand:

- The three levels of a product offering.

- The key attributes of a service product.

- The relevance of the product life cycle in product decision-making.

- The role of portfolio models in managing products.

- The main steps in the new product development process.

- The critical issues involved in managing the innovation process.

- The impact of e-commerce upon product management decisions.

6.1   What is a product?

The American Marketing Association defines a product as:

> Anything that can be offered to the market for attention, acquisition or consumption including physical objects, services, personalities, organizations and desires.

Jobber (2004) gives a more succinct definition by saying a product is anything that has the ability to satisfy a customer need.

6.2   Components of a product offering

Kotler *et al.* (1999) suggest that a product has three levels (see Figure 6.1). First, the core product addresses the fundamental need the consumer is trying to resolve. Fundamental needs are generic in nature and cover a wide spectrum of issues, such as, transport, data storage or self-esteem. Secondly, the actual product is the specific offering aimed at meeting a need. This includes attributes such as styling, branding, performance features and packaging. Finally there is the augmented product which enhances the actual product by offering additional services and benefits, making the product a more attractive proposition to the consumer. Examples of an augmentation include factors such as after-sales support, maintenance and affordable credit arrangements.

When developing products organizations have to consider each of the three levels described above. Companies must fully understand their core

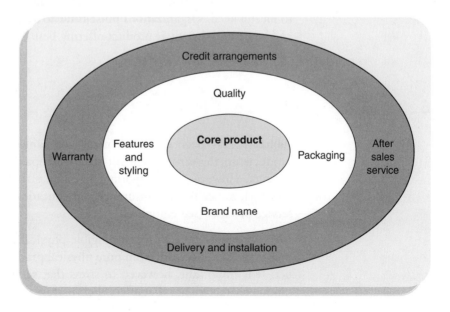

Figure 6.1
Three levels of a product

Table 6.1
Three levels of a product for Orange plc

Core	Actual	Augmented
Communications	Mobile phone network	Voice mail
	Handset	Insurance against loss
	Brand image	Monthly payment plans

product(s) and identify what need it is meeting. Organizations must then develop actual and augmented product offerings that are attractive to specific customer groups. Orange plc provides an illustration of this process, as shown in Table 6.1.

One school of thought has argued that in certain markets advances in quality management, manufacturing systems and information technology are leading to a tendency for organizations to develop competitive products that are indistinguishable from one another. Therefore, the only way for organizations to differentiate products is to concentrate on the augmented level by attempting to offer better service and support. Indeed, the augmented level may become such a vital part of the product offering that it is absorbed into the actual product. This has happened in the car industry where the warranty package on a new car is now seen as an integral part of the product offering.

Fundamentally, a product delivers a set of benefits to a customer in order to meet a need. Organizations must strive to understand this process fully and be certain that their product offering best matches not only need but customer expectation.

6.3 The service element

As has already been discussed, many companies now differentiate their products on the service element that accompanies the tangible physical product. However, it is important to emphasize that some market offerings such as health care, insurance and education, are made up of a pure service product (see Figure 6.2).

Many products are a mix of a tangible physical product and service elements across a spectrum from pure physical product to pure service product. It is important, however, to stress that service products hold some unique characteristics that affect their performance in the market.

Figure 6.2
Potential range of
product offerings

Intangibility

With a service product a consumer cannot be certain of what benefits they will accrue until after the purchase has taken place. This aspect of a service product applies equally to all services from items such as haircuts through to sophisticated financial products such as pension policies. In these circumstances consumers will attempt to reduce uncertainty in a number of ways. Consumers will seek out the recommendations of other individuals whose judgements they trust. Potential customers will also draw inferences about the service provided from such factors as the attitude of the staff providing the service or the ambience of the physical building within which the service is delivered. Lastly, consumers may make decisions based on the tangible elements a producer adds to the pure service product. These may include items such as warranty certificates, or glossy tickets and guidebooks provided when booking a holiday.

Lack of ownership

A pure service product cannot be owned as such, consumers can merely buy access to a particular service for a specific period of time. A consumer taking a flight on an airline experiences the service from the point of take off until landing at their chosen destination. The ticket is only a tangible physical symbol giving the consumer access to the airline's service. Once the ticket is exchanged with the airline in order to take a seat on the flight no tangible item remains. The service itself is intangible. An individual consulting an occupational psychologist will receive counselling about their chosen career path, but it is impossible for the consumer to touch or feel the advice given.

Theatre-goers can watch a play but they do not own the performance. Many institutions offering service products will try to augment their service with tangible attributes to reassure the consumer of the authenticity of their offering. Universities provide impressive physical environments, degree certificates and prestigious graduation ceremonies to augment the intangible service product they provide to their customers, which is knowledge. Banks operate out of large, imposing, physically robust premises to reassure consumers about their reliability and longevity as institutions.

Inseparability

The production of a service cannot be separated from its receipt by the consumer. The theatre performance is experienced by the audience as it is actually being produced by the actors. Thus the environment within which the product is being produced is critical in determining the consumers' reaction to the service offering. If the theatre is cold, dirty and damp the audience's reaction to the actors' performance may be adversely affected.

Perishability

Service products cannot be produced ahead of delivery and put into storage. This is not necessarily a problem if a service faces a constant level of demand but in markets with demand fluctuations this aspect of service products causes some problems. Many tourism visitor attractions have peak levels of demand during the summer but much lower levels of demand in the winter, yet they have an asset that has fixed capacity. With all service products if a customer cannot be found in a specific time period the product effectively perishes. Hotel rooms if not filled on a particular day cannot be stored and sold the following day. The service product that was available, that is of a room on that particular day, has perished and cannot be reclaimed by the producer.

Variability

There is one final aspect of services that marks them out as different from physical products and that is their variability. The play that is delivered by a group of actors is affected by their performance on any particular night. Every performance will be different to some degree. This aspect of service delivery is critical to the consumer's reaction to the product but it is actually very difficult for organizations to manage consistency of delivery. In fact, organizations that try too hard to control every facet of the behaviour of the individuals delivering their service can actually damage their products, as consumers can object to what they perceive as not being treated as a unique individual.

6.4 Uses and limitations of the product life cycle

Any company making decisions about products and markets will be influenced by the product life cycle (PLC). Organizations are advised to ensure that they fully understand the product life cycle for their products and industry segments. However, it should be noted that the product life cycle

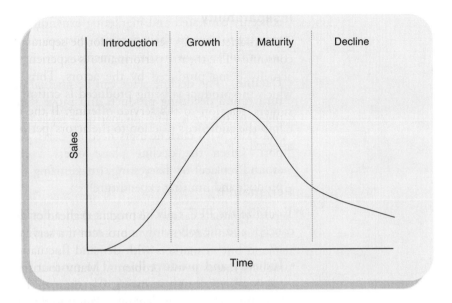

Figure 6.3
The product life cycle

(PLC) has been described as the most quoted but least understood concept in marketing.

In the PLC concept (Figure 6.3), products pass through four stages: introduction, growth, maturity and decline. Sales of the product vary with each of these phases of the life cycle.

- **Introduction** It takes time for sales to grow and the introductory phase sees awareness and distribution of the product increasing. Some organizations will specialize in innovation and aim to consistently introduce new products to the market place. Common strategies include:

  - *Skimming* Where a high price level is set initially in order to capitalize on the product's introduction and optimize financial benefit in the short term.

  - *Penetration* Pricing being used to encourage product usage and in order to build market share over time.

- **Growth** This phase sees a rapid increase in sales. Additionally, competition begins to increase and it is likely that prices will be static, or fall in real terms. The growth stage sees the product being offered to more market segments, increasing distribution and the development of product variations.

- **Maturity** Here product sales peak and settle at a stable level. This is normally the longest phase of the PLC, with organizations experiencing some reduction in profit level. This is due to the intense competition common in mature markets. As no natural growth exists, market share is keenly contested and marketing expenditure is increased. Marketers may try to expand their potential customer base by encouraging more use or finding new market segments.

- **Decline**   The decline stage can be gradual or rapid. It is possible to turn round declining products and move them back into the mature phase of the cycle. The alternative is replacement. A residual demand will exist, with current users needing parts, services and ongoing support. Often the decline phase offers a choice: reinvesting (turn around/replace) or 'harvesting' (maximizing financial returns from the product and limiting expenditure).

To utilize the PLC fully, managers need a detailed understanding of the concept and the following points merit consideration:

- **Industry and product line**   The product life cycle concept can also apply to overall industry sales. Clearly, the PLC for individual product lines needs to be considered in relation to this. For example, if an industry is entering the decline phase of its PLC, it may be unwise to launch new product lines. Currently, high technology industries, such as telecommunications, are in the growth phase. However, individual product lines have very short PLCs as they are rapidly replaced by more advanced technology. Make sure you understand where the industry is in terms of overall the PLC and how your portfolio of products fits into this overall pattern.

- **Shape of the PLC**   While the PLC normally conforms to the classic 'S-shaped' curve (see Figure 6.3), it is not always the case. Product life cycles can take different forms. They can display:

  ○ Cyclical and or seasonal trends.

  ○ Constant demand, where a steady level of sales is reached.

  ○ Rapid growth and fall, common to fashion or fad products (see Figure 6.4).

- **Volatility**   Any sales person will tell you that sales levels will fluctuate over time. The reality of the PLC is that sales will vary and the smooth graph shown in most textbooks will in fact display considerable volatility. This makes predicting your exact position in the life cycle difficult. Does a fall in sales mean we have reached the point of decline or is it a temporary blip? Only time will tell.

- **Duration of stages**   Some would argue that the length of each PLC phase is closely related to marketing decisions and not simply a natural cycle. Effective marketing should be able to extend and sustain the growth or maturity of a product offering. Equally, ineffective marketing would hasten its decline.

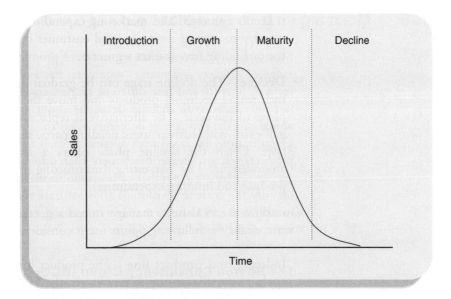

Figure 6.4
The product life cycle
for a fad product

Illustrative example 6.1
European low-cost airlines

In 1999 there were four low-cost airlines in Europe: Ryanair, easyJet, Virgin Express and Go. The huge growth of this market sector, plus the relatively low barriers to entry, has attracted a flood a new competitors. In 2004 there are more than 50 low-cost operators. The new competitors are generally 'me-too' operators offering nothing new in terms of their product or service apart from the destinations of their particular routes. Their brands tend to the lack the strength of the larger established low-cost operators, Ryanair and easyJet. At the same time their limited route networks offer limited economies of scale. This growth in undifferentiated competition has led to the airlines competing on price and the resulting price war has affected all the airlines' profitability. There have already been a number of casualties, with Duo, a Birmingham-based airline, ceasing to trade in May 2004 after only five months of operation. A number of smaller scheduled operators have also ceased trading elsewhere in Europe. The concept of the product life cycle would suggest as the low-cost airline market enters maturity there is likely to be a continued rationalization of airlines within this sector.

6.5   Managing product portfolios

Most organizations produce a number of products or services supplying a range of markets and market segments. Each of these products will perform differently and face different market conditions. Organizations are not only faced with making decisions about an individual product but also about the competing demands of all the products in their portfolio. Organizations are faced with dilemmas, such as the fact that maybe some products warrant greater investment than others because their potential is greater. There are a number of portfolio models that can be employed to identify the current position of an organization's product portfolio in the market and can assist a company in making decisions about the management of their products.

The Boston Consultancy Group (BCG) growth share matrix

This is one of the best-known portfolio models. The growth share matrix is concerned about the generation and use of cash within a business and can be used to analyse Strategic Business Units as well as products. The two axes on the model represent relative market share and market growth (see Figure 6.5). Relative market share is seen as a predictor of the product's capacity to generate cash, the proposition being, that products with a dominant position in the market will achieve high sales, but will need relatively less investment as they are already an established brand and should have lower costs through economies of scale advantages. Market

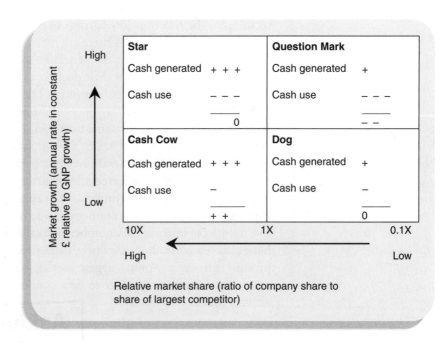

Figure 6.5
The Boston Consultancy Group's growth share matrix (BCG)

growth, on the other hand, is seen as a predictor of the product's need for cash. Products in high growth sectors require investment to keep up with the increased demand.

The model uses market share relative to competitors as an indication of the product's relative strength in the market. To do this the axis uses a log scale. At the mid-point of the axis, represented by 1.0 (or 1X) on the scale, the product's market share is equal to its largest competitor's market share. At the extreme left-hand side of the axis, represented by 10.0 (or 10X), a product has ten times the market share of the largest competitor. At the other extreme of the axis, represented by 0.1X, the product would only have a tenth or 10% of the largest competitor's market share.

Products are represented on the model by circles and fall into one of the four cells into which the matrix is divided. The area of the circle represents the product's sales relative to the sales of the organization's other products. The four cells in the matrix represent:

- **Cash Cows**   These products have high profitability and require low investment, due to market leadership in a low growth market. These products are generating a high level of cash. These products should be defended to maintain sales and market share. Surplus cash should be channelled into Stars and Question Marks in order to create the Cash Cows of the future. Current Cash Cows will inevitably over time lose their position as their market changes.

- **Stars**   Are market leaders and so are generating high levels of cash, but are in areas of rapid growth which require equally high levels of cash (investment) to keep up with the growth in sales. Cash generated by the Cash Cows should be channelled to support these products.

- **Question Marks**   These are also sometimes referred to as Problem Children or Wildcats. Question Marks are not market leaders and will have relatively high costs while at the same time these products require large amounts of cash as they are in high growth areas. An organization has to judge whether to use cash generated by the Cash Cow to try to develop this product into a Star by gaining market share in a high growth market or to invest in other areas of the business.

- **Dogs**   These are products with low levels of market share in low growth markets. Products that are in a secondary position to the market leader may still be able to produce cash (Cash Dogs). For others the organization's decision is likely to be a choice between moving the product into a defendable niche, harvesting it for cash in the short term, or divestment.

The overall aim of an organization should be to maintain a balanced product portfolio. This means investments should flow from Cash Cows into Stars and Question Marks in an effort to make products move round the matrix from Question Marks into Stars and from Stars into Cash Cows. This movement of cash and products round the matrix thus ensures the future cash flows of the business.

There have been a number of revisions and adaptations to this basic model in order to accommodate different factors. Figure 6.6 highlights the fact that products in the research and development stage also need investment, which cash generation provides – an issue the standard BCG overlooks. Figure 6.7 applies the basic portfolio analysis technique but in the context of the public sector. On one axis of this matrix is the organization's ability to effectively deliver a service within the constraints of current resources, on the other is the level of the political requirement to offer the service. This allows a key consideration of the public sector bodies, the need to provide services to satisfy political objectives, to be accommodated within a portfolio analysis approach.

The BCG is criticized for having a number of limitations, amongst them are:

- Market growth is seen as an inadequate measure of a market or of an industry's overall attractiveness. This measure doesn't consider such issues as barriers to entry, strength of buyers or suppliers or investment levels.

- Market share is an inadequate measure of a product's relative ability to generate cash. Other factors such as product positioning, brand image

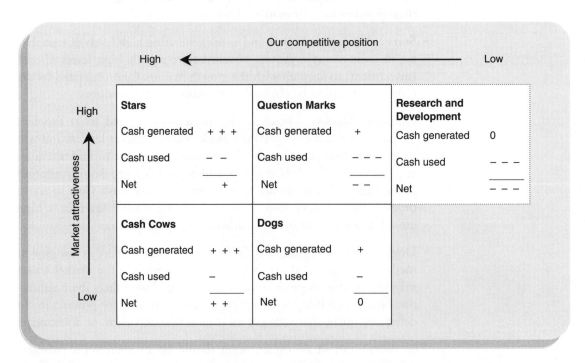

Figure 6.6
Matrix to accommodate research and development (*Source:* McDonald, 1985)

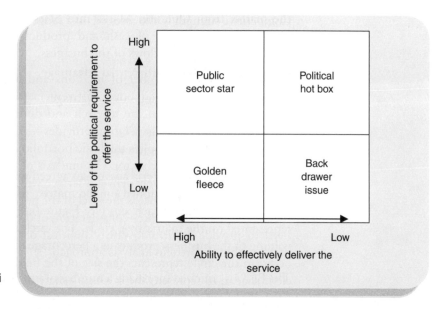

Figure 6.7
Public sector portfolio matrix (*Source:* adapted from Montanari and Bracker, 1986)

and access to distribution channels may allow an organization to gain higher margin and strong cash flows as a result.

- The focus on market share and growth ignores fundamental issues such as developing sustainable competitive advantage.

- Not all products face the same life cycle. Therefore for some stars facing a short life cycle it may be better for the organization to harvest them, rather than committing further investment.

- Cashflow is only one factor on which to base investment decisions. There are others to consider, such as return on investment, market size and competitors.

There are a number of models that use a range of weighted criteria in place of relative market share and growth in order to overcome some of the limitations of the growth share matrix.

The General Electric multifactor portfolio matrix

This model has two axes: market attractiveness on one axis and competitive strength on the other. Industry/market attractiveness is assessed on a range of weighted criteria including:

- Market size.

- Market growth rate.

- Strength of competition.

- Profit potential.

- Social, political and legal factors.

Competitive strength is also assessed on a range of weighted criteria such as:

- Market share.

- Potential to develop differential advantage.

- Opportunities to develop cost advantages.

- Channel relationships.

- Brand image and reputation.

On the basis of these criteria and on an agreed weighting scheme, an SBU or product is then positioned on the matrix, which is divided into nine separate cells, three on each axis (see Figure 6.8). The SBU or product is represented on the matrix by a circle. The circle's area represents the sales volume of the business/product as a percentage of the overall business. On occasion the circle represents the size of the market and a slice of the circle is shaded to represent the business's share of that market.

The Shell directional policy matrix

This takes a similar approach to the General Electric multifactor matrix (see Figure 6.9). In both models the cells contain policy recommendations for businesses/products that fall within their boundaries. For instance, for products that fall in the cell that represents high industry attractiveness and strong business strength, on the GE multifactor model, the policy recommendation is to invest for growth.

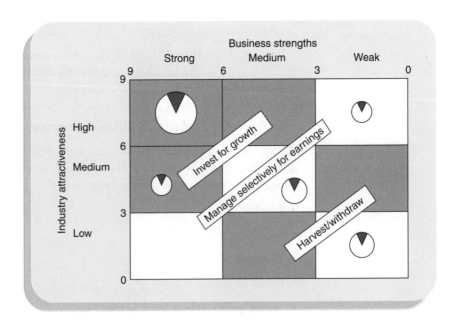

Figure 6.8
The General Electric
multifactor matrix

Figure 6.9
The Shell directional
policy matrix (DPM)
(*Source:* Shell
Chemical Co., 1975)

In both these models the number of factors considered as important on either axis, and their relative weighting, are based on managers' subjective judgements. This is a major criticism of these more sophisticated portfolio models. However, this ability to use judgement, based on their knowledge of their markets and industry, does allow managers to adapt the model to an organization's specific situation. The models are also criticized as being more difficult for managers to use and more time-consuming than the BCG matrix.

There are also wider criticisms of portfolio models in general, such as:

• They are based on an analysis of current areas of business and are therefore an inappropriate tool to employ in tackling the issue of new business development.

• They placed too much emphasis on growth, either through entering high growth markets, or through gaining high market share, whereas there are virtues to entering stable markets that have lower growth rates.

• These models can require information that can be difficult to obtain and are complex and time consuming to successfully execute.

In response to these criticisms, it should be pointed out that much of the information required for portfolio analysis should be collected by organizations anyway to support strategic decisions.

The reality is also that all models have weaknesses, their very role is to try to simplify relationships to foster understanding. Managers should be

---

Illustrative example 6.2
Häagen-Dazs

Throughout the 1980s and 1990s Häagen-Dazs was a hugely successful brand associated with the super-premium end of the ice cream market. The brand was associated with a number of innovations, including ice cream bars for adults, frozen yoghurt and sorbet offerings. However, in the year ending April 2004 Häagen-Dazs sales declined by 16.5%. Industry observers believe Häagen-Dazs has ceased to be the leader in the market in terms of innovation and has let rivals challenge its position. For instance, instead of Häagen-Dazs it was Richmond Food's Skinny Cow brand that opened up the low-fat segment for ice cream. Own label brands have also been gaining market share. Both Safeway, for its Best Simply Vanilla, and Waitrose, for its Belgian Chocolate line, have won praise for their new offerings. High-quality ingredients and packaging that in the past distinguished Häagen-Dazs from the rest of the market has now become the standard product offering. If Häagen-Dazs wishes to retain its premium positioning it will need to innovate in such a way as to mark itself out as still being a brand that is clearly differentiated from its rivals.

---

using a range of portfolio models along with other analytical tools in order to establish a rounded and comprehensive view of their organization's performance.

6.6 Managing new products

There is much debate relating to new product development (NPD) as to what is meant by the term 'new product'. The reality is that few products can be deemed to be truly 'new' in the sense of being innovative/unique or novel. Most 'new' products are updates and revamps of existing goods and services. Jain (1997) views new product strategy in terms of three categories:

- **Product improvement/modification** Unless products are to be replaced by completely new entities they must be upgraded and enhanced as a matter of necessity. The process can have two possible aims:

  ○ Maintaining the competitive position in an existing market, and/or

  ○ Adapting the product in order to appeal to other market segments. Major changes may result in the need to reposition a product offering within a given market. Conversely, organizations may only make minor changes aimed at ensuring the products remain up to date.

Illustrative example 6.3
NPD at Freeplay Energy

In the early 1980s Trevor Bayliss, the British inventor, developed the concept of a self-powered radio. Electricity for the radio would be provided by an integral wind-up generator. In the UK the Design Council awarded the wind-up radio 'Millennium Product' status. One national newspaper went as far as naming it as the most significant invention of a generation.

In 1994 the South African based BayGen Power company (later renamed Freeplay Energy) signed an exclusive agreement with Trevor Bayliss to develop and commercialize the product.

Freeplay Energy began to realize that volume sales could be developed by concentrating on the European and North American markets. Sales growth in these markets has allowed Freeplay to invest further in the technology, and as a result develop products that are smaller, lighter, more durable and less expensive. The FPR1 had to be wound for 20 seconds in order to produce 30 minutes of playing time. The FPR2, which Freeplay launched in 1997, weighs less, is more compact and supplies an hour of playing time after being wound for 20 seconds.

In 1999 the company added to the radio range with the launch of a new model, the Freeplay S360. The company also launched the 20/20 flashlight, which contains an integral energy storage unit to generate power for instantaneous or later use.

Freeplay Energy has a number of new product ideas under investigation. One initiative is the concept of a satellite telephone that can be charged up with energy provided by a 'self-powered' generator rather than costly disposable batteries. The company believes this product would overcome some of the problems faced by African economies. African states cannot afford to develop the landlines and other facilities needed for a modern telecommunications infrastructure. This approach would allow these states to make a technology leap and allow individuals access to the global communications network. Other product ideas include self-powered pull cord lights, water purification systems and even fetal heart beat monitors.

The company's philosophy is to attempt to create a range of products that will help improve communication across the developing world. This is reflected in its tagline, 'Powered by You'.

- **Product imitation** This strategy involves capitalizing on the initiatives of others and suits organizations that are risk-averse and/or have limited funds to invest. Clearly, there are potential ethical and legal problems with this option and organizations must define the line between imitation and copying. The strategy is most effective when the 'new' version of the product brings some additional dimension of added value.

Type of product development	Nature
New to world	Often scientific or technical developments, high risk, high return activities which can revolutionize or create markets.
New product lines or line additions	Such products can either be new to the provider, as opposed to the market place, or additions to the product ranges already on offer.
Product revision	These are replacements and upgrades of existing products. This category is likely to cover the largest single number of new product developments. Additionally, this may cover changes aimed at generating cost reductions – no perceived change in performance but more economic product/provision of the product.
Reposition	Aiming to diversify away from existing markets by uncovering new applications, uses or market segments for current products.

Figure 6.10
Types of 'new' product developments
(*Source:* adapted from Booz *et al.*, 1982)

- **Product innovation** This involves bringing new and novel ideas to the market place. Product innovation may be aimed at:

  ○ Replacing existing products with new approaches and items that enhance customer satisfaction.

  ○ Providing diversification in order to target opportunities in new markets. Clearly, organizations should expect a correlation between risk and diversification.

Booz *et al.* (1982) classified 'new' products using the categories shown in Figure 6.10. Again this demonstrates that truly original, innovative products represent only a small proportion of total development.

6.7   Why do products fail?

Most new products fail to provide a satisfactory return on investment for their organization. According to Doyle (1994) failure rates run at a level of about 80 per cent for consumer products, 30 per cent for industrial products and around 20 per cent for service-based products.

There are a number of common reasons why new products fail. They can be summarized as follows:

- **Under-investment**   Projects can be short of funds and therefore lack the investment required to establish and sustain a new product in the market place.

- **The product fails to deliver any customer benefit**   This tends to happen with products that contain some technical or scientific advance. While the technology may be innovative, it may not be seen as innovative by consumers or it may not be delivering benefits deemed worthwhile by the market place, therefore it fails to be adopted. Additionally, even though the product is using new technology it still has to perform to the required performance parameters. Remember, quality is defined as 'fit for purpose'. There needs to be a clear definition of the market segment and how the product offering is positioned.

- **Forecasting error is a common source of failure**   As the saying has it, 'Forecasting is difficult, especially if you're forecasting the future.' Amusing, but certainly true! Often, forecasting errors relate to over-optimistic forecasts of demand and/or underestimates of costs. Managers need to examine the assumptions supporting forecasts as well as the forecasting techniques employed. Also, timescales for planned developments have to be realistic.

- **Internal politics, trade-offs and compromise can result in problems**   A project may lack the support and commitment of staff and vested interests may conspire against its success. Equally, trade-offs, and other such factors, may result in the project drifting from its original target, as internal conflict distracts management from its original course of action. Internal conflict, in particular, has been the graveyard of many good product ideas.

- **Industry response is vital**   For example, success may be completely dependent on retailers stocking products or on the response of competitors – what happens if they drastically cut the price of their competing products? Such factors are not in the control of the organization; however, good quality market research and competitor intelligence can lessen the negative impact of any potential reaction from external parties.

An understanding of the pitfalls of new product development obviously helps organizations avoid them and increases their chance of success. When addressing this issue, organizations should consider the nature and background of their project, as some types of development activity are inherently more risky than others. Additionally, the organization's attitude to risk and investment has a bearing on the situation. While some factors are unpredictable, and projects can be a 'hostage to fortune', most issues are simply a matter of good management and sensible marketing. Applying

> ### Illustrative example 6.4
> ### The *Independent* compact edition
>
> In September 2003 the *Independent* newspaper's circulation figure was 218,000 copies. In October 2003 the newspaper launch a totally new concept to the UK market – the quality tabloid, or compact edition as they referred to it. Initially the compact was published along-side a broadsheet edition. By May 2004, however, the *Independent* ceased to publish the broadsheet format. *The Times* newspaper followed the *Independent*'s move, making two-thirds of its daily copies in a compact format. By September 2004, year-on-year sales of the *Independent* were up 21% to 264,000 copies, while sales of *The Times* were 4.5% higher. The only other daily national newspaper with increased sales was *The Financial Times*, with a 0.89% increase. Since the launch of the compact edition the *Independent* has consistently out-performed others in the quality newspaper market.
>
> Not only were the *Independent*'s overall sales figures higher, they gained share of significant segments of the market. Sales increased to women readers, ABC1s and to younger readers, all key segments for organizations making decisions about where to place advertising. In another key area for potential advertisers, readership has also increased. In the six months to June 2004, total Monday to Friday readership rose 24.3% to a total of 722,000. All other quality titles in that period showed a decrease.
>
> There were some problems associated with the move to a compact format, a key issue being that advertisers refused to pay broadsheet rates for smaller compact adverts. This resulted in some dif-ficult negotiations. The *Independent* was prepared for this situation as it had studied the experi-ences of the Swiss newspaper *Le Matin*. *Le Matin* had changed format some three years previously, and took a year to persuade its advertisers of the value of a compact format. Having been prepared for this eventuality, the Independent had persuaded most advertising agencies to agree to a new pricing structure by July 2004.
>
> The success of the *Independent* compact format in such a competitive market as the UK did not go unnoticed in other markets. In July 2004 the World Association of Newspapers was recorded as stating that at least 20 large newspapers across the globe were making plans to convert from a broadsheet to compact format.

a sound, structured approach to NPD and employing effective project management skills should move the odds in the organization's favour.

6.8   The new product development process

No matter what type of new product is under development – a 'new to world' product, a new product line or a development simply aiming to reduce cost – an organization requires some mechanism, or process, by which to evaluate ideas and, when appropriate, translate them into com-mercial products. Such a process provides a vital ingredient in the fight for

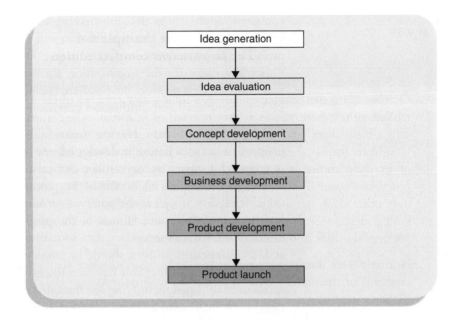

Figure 6.11
Stages in the NPD process

commercial success. Indeed, Davidson (1997) cites lack of rigorous process as a factor commonly contributing to the failure of new products.

NPD processes take many shapes and forms but it is vital that any process is driven by an overall NPD strategy. If this is not the case, development activities will lack coordination and focus. The majority of NPD processes employed by organizations will contain many of the stages shown in Figure 6.11 and discussed below.

- **Idea generation**   The critical first stage in the NPD process is the development of a new product idea. There are numerous approaches organizations employ in order to generate the initial new product idea. They may be generated via a formalized technical research and development process or from systems that scan the business environment, enabling the organization to identify trends, customer requests and competitors' intentions. Market research certainly has a role to play in this process. Equally, management should ensure that an environment is in place that encourages staff to suggest product development ideas and that systems are employed that reward such activity. Many companies use specific techniques such as brainstorming in order to generate ideas for new products.

- **Idea evaluation**   Once new product ideas have been developed they have to be screened in order to establish their feasibility. Ideally, ideas should be screened against the organization's strategic objectives by establishing whether they can demonstrate that they are likely to contribute to the achievement of these outcomes. It is important to establish criteria against which all ideas are evaluated. This provides a consistent approach to decision-making and the safeguards associated with rigorous testing. The organization will need to develop criteria to measure the attractiveness of the market for the new product idea. Other key measures the organization should employ to evaluate the potential of a new product proposal are likely to include financial, marketing, operational and production criteria.

- **Concept development**   Having successfully passed through a screening process, an idea has to be developed into a fully fleshed out product concept. This stage involves initial technical and marketing evaluations. The organization has to establish the product's technical and operational feasibility as well as the potential resource requirements necessary for the manufacture and launch of the proposed product. Marketing information, such as secondary data sources on general industry trends and key competitor profiles, should be employed to establish the potential of the product. Once this has been undertaken a marketing strategy needs to be outlined identifying the intended product positioning in the target segment(s), and a range of marketing goals, such as market share.

- **Business evaluation**   Business evaluation is undertaken with the aim of evaluating the commercial potential and investment requirements of the new product. Sales volume, revenue and cost projections will establish the viability of the project. Often organizations have predetermined returns on investment which projects must demonstrate they will meet. Clearly, this exercise is more difficult when an organization is dealing with a highly innovative product or situation that requires the diversification of their portfolio.

- **Product development**   This stage turns the concept into an actual product. The product development stage tends to be dominated by technical and operational issues. There is a need to examine both the development of the product (styling, features, performance/branding/etc.) and the means of its production and delivery (manufacturing, administration, after-sales support, etc.). This stage may see the building of a prototype and the use of market research to establish the final product offering. To gauge market-place reaction, products may be test marketed with groups of actual consumers.

- **Product launch**   Using the knowledge and targets generated in the previous stages of the NPD process, a final marketing plan is developed. This includes all the remaining elements of the marketing mix. Thus a final price is set, a promotion campaign is designed and the build-up of stock begins within the distribution channels. It is vital that the product has the correct marketing, operational and logistical support to make it a success. Competitor and customer reaction should be monitored and the product offering 'fine-tuned' if required. Where resources are limited, or where high degrees of uncertainty exist, the product may be introduced using a 'roll-out' strategy. This entails a phased launch, gradually building market coverage.

Given the importance of new product development, managers must endeavour to make the process as rigorous and objective as possible. Only in this way can organizations maximize the likelihood of success and minimize the chances of progressing with poor ideas. However, there is a dilemma: while robust development processes have their advantages, there is increasing commercial pressure to act quickly. This may result in corners being cut and ultimately mistakes being made in the new product development process. So, the reality of business life requires management to develop the right products in an increasingly shorter time frame. How can this be facilitated? Adhering to the following principles should help to optimize the NPD process:

- **Multi-functional teams** A range of studies suggest that projects go more smoothly when multi-functional teams are employed. Project teams made up of individuals from different functional backgrounds (e.g. production, marketing, design and finance) allow a more balanced evaluation of a new product idea to emerge. For example, problems relating to the manufacture of a product can be discussed at a very early stage of a project. Additionally, the multi-functional approach promotes 'ownership' of the project across the organization and as a result staff are more committed and motivated.

- **Completeness and evaluation** NPD can be viewed as a six-stage process, as outlined in the section above. The simple act of completing all these steps of the process can increase the likelihood of product success. Undertaking each stage in a systematic manner and building an ongoing evaluation into the process may not guarantee success, but it will reduce the chances of failure. So-called 'evaluation gates' at the end of each stage can review the potential product and whether the NPD process has been properly conducted.

- **Customer involvement** Although market research is used to evaluate possible ideas and to review products after launch, it may also be advisable to integrate the 'voice of the customer' into the entire project in a more sustainable manner. This is possible by having an ongoing process of market research that takes place during each development stage or even by having customer representation on the multi-functional team.

- **Parallel processing** Traditionally, NPD has been viewed as a sequential process with activities following each other in sequence. However, it may be possible to conduct some activities concurrently, in other words, undertaking a process of parallel development. Encouraging functional areas, departments and individuals to work more closely has a number

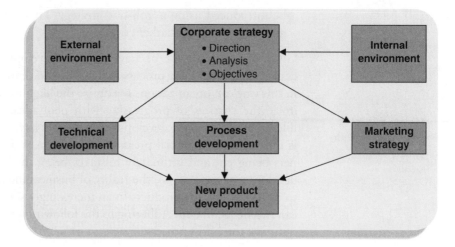

Figure 6.12
Strategic direction of
NPD

of advantages. First, this overlapping, parallel approach reduces overall development time. Secondly, as activities are being undertaken at the same time, they can share information and a more interactive approach can be developed. This can improve the overall quality of the process. An illustration of this approach would be where both a technical and marketing feasibility assessment are conducted as one process, thereby generating a more vigorous product and market specification.

• **Strategic direction**   NPD requires a strategic focus and clear links must be established between the organization's overall corporate strategy and the NPD process. As previously stated, the organization's strategic objectives should be used as a template against which new product ideas are evaluated. Additionally, the process of strategic analysis and audit should provide valuable information, both internal and external, relating to the development of product offerings. The aim should be to integrate three stages into one coherent framework (see Figure 6.12). These are:

  ○ Technical development – improving the technical capability of the product.

  ○ Process development – improving the provision/production of products and services.

  ○ Marketing strategy.

6.9   Managing innovation

The term 'innovation' covers a broad range of activity concerned with changing established products, processes and practices. Successful innovation blends creative thinking with the organizational ability to implement

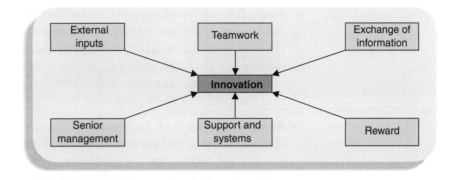

Figure 6.13
Factors that facilitate
organizational
innovation

the new idea. In order to be successfully implemented organizations have
to give new ideas support, commitment and resources.

Organizations cannot remain focused on the past. The static organization
that believes 'the old ways are the best' will, in the end, flounder. Senior
management has a key role in addressing the issue of innovation and creating an organizational culture and infrastructure to support the process.
Organizations that continue to learn and effectively translate this learning
into product offerings are the ones that will prosper.

There are a number of factors that can facilitate the innovation process, as
summarized in Figure 6.13.

- **Teamwork** Teamwork is vital, as successful innovation requires a
  combination of skills based across functional areas of activity, such as
  marketing, research and design. Innovation tends to flourish where frequent contact and good working relationships exist among groups.

- **Exchange of information** The exchange of information and ideas
  should be encouraged, as this not only facilitates innovation but also
  enhances teamwork. Information flow and effective communication
  contribute greatly to creativity. However, it is important to recognize
  that more information is not necessarily better. Information overload
  brings it own problems and should be avoided.

- **External inputs** Organizations should also focus on the external environment. External inputs relating to market trends, customer perceptions, technological developments and competitor activities are vital
  inputs into the overall innovation process. The organization must be
  receptive to new ideas and have the capacity to evaluate such concepts.

- **Senior management** Senior management has a critical role to play in
  the process of organizational innovation. They need to develop appropriate strategies and act as facilitators to the process. This normally
  involves taking calculated risks and allocating the required resources to
  any project (see the following section). Consequently, senior managers
  should be committed to long-term growth as opposed to short-term

profit. If it is to work properly, innovation requires the correct systems and support. Frequently, this relates to organizational culture. Creating the right organizational climate is important, as the wish is to challenge existing practices and generate creativity. Systems, such as communications networks, computer-aided design and project management structures, need to be in place.

- **Reward** Group and individual motivation are important factors affecting the ability of any organization to foster and exploit innovation. Reward and recognition for innovation help generate ideas and foster a collaborative atmosphere. Additionally, the role of the individual must not be neglected in the discussion of innovation. While the organization can facilitate and foster innovation, individuals have to take ownership. People need to have the courage, skill and motivation to make things better. Only this type of commitment will see the process to completion.

6.10 e-Marketing perspective

Increasingly, organizations are developing knowledge management strategies through the use of information technology. Mobilizing and managing the

---

Illustrative example 6.5
The Sony Librie

e-Books are already available for download onto standard laptops, desktop computers and hand-held personal digital assistants (PDAs). Sales have been growing as more mainstream titles, such as Dan Brown's *The Da Vinci Code*, become available. In May 2004 worldwide sales of 389,882 were up 5% on the same quarter the year before, while revenues were up 23% to £1.7 m. These sales are tiny compared with the sales of printed texts. Many observers believe that most readers would prefer the look and feel of the traditional paperback book than reading a text on a computer screen.

However, in early 2004 Sony, in conjunction with Philips and E-ink, launched Librie, a new type of electronic book reader. The product costs around £200 and contains a screen that provides an ink-on-paper look on a hand-held device that has the weight of a thick paperback book. The Librie is powered by four AA batteries and has 10 Mb of memory. The batteries will allow around 10 000 page turns. Currently, however, there are a limited number of titles available. The advantages of this type of product are that titles can be bought at any time of day or night. Newspapers can also be delivered in such a format.

Many publishers are sceptical about the potential threat of the e-book, however, time will tell if their judgement is accurate.

---

knowledge base of an organization is rapidly becoming a management priority. The collective experience and accumulated learning within an organization can be vital to successful NPD. The organization needs to facilitate the development of, and access to, information. Enabling technologies and techniques include computer networks, 'group-ware' software products that enable work and knowledge to be shared (e.g. Lotus Notes) and data warehousing. O'Connor and Galvin (1997) define data warehousing as constructing a high-level database available to support decision-making.

Products themselves are also affected by developments in information technology. The traditional book is now facing competition from the e-book concept. Compact discs are being replaced by music downloads over the Internet. Although in both cases the core product remains the same, new technology is changing the tangible elements of the product.

Summary

Decisions about the product offering an organization chooses to present to the market are critical to an enterprise's ability to meet its objectives. Organizations have to consider the whole offering not just the core product. Companies also have to review their product portfolio on a regular basis and consider the future prospects of individual products within their total range. The external environment is always changing and organizations have to adapt their products in line with these developments. In making decisions about the product area of the marketing mix, organizations have to be committed to continual innovation. In order for this to be successful, it is essential that structured NPD processes are created within an overall environment that encourages creativity.

Discussion questions

1   Why should marketing managers be cautious in using the concept of PLC as a basis for making decisions about a particular product in their portfolio?

2   Discuss whether the BCG model plays a useful role in management decision-making.

3   What are the strengths of the Shell directional policy matrix in analysing an organization's product portfolio? Are there issues with this model that would cause you concern as a marketing manager?

4   In what way can an Internet bank provide customers with tangible elements to any of their product offerings?

References

Booz, Allen & Hamilton (1982) *New Product Management for the 1980s*. Booz, Allen & Hamilton Inc.

Davidson, H. (1997) *Even More Offensive Marketing*. Penguin.

Doyle, P. (1994) *Marketing Management and Strategy*. Prentice Hall.

Kotler, P., Armstrong, G., Saunders, J. and Wong, V. (1999) *Principles of Marketing*, 2nd European edn. Prentice Hall.

Jain, S. (1997) *Marketing Planning and Strategy*, 5th edn. South-Western.

Jobber, D. (2004) *Principles and Practice of Marketing*, 4th edn. McGraw-Hill.

McDonald, M. (1985) Seminar Notes, Cranfield MBA Programme.

Montanari, J.R. and Bracker, J.S. (1986) The strategic management process at the public planning unit level. *Strategic Management Journal*, Vol. 7, No. 3, pp. 251–65.

O'Connor, J. and Galvin, E. (1997) *Marketing and Information Technology*. Pitman.

Shell Chemical Company (1975) *The Directional Policy Matrix: A New Aid to Corporate Planning*. Shell.

Price and pricing strategy

About this chapter

This chapter provides an overview of pricing as an element of the marketing mix.

After reading the chapter, you will understand:

- Pricing from an economic, accounting and marketing perspective.

- Pricing models/objectives and strategies.

- The 'non-price' dimension of price.

- Revenue management.

- Ethical decisions relating to pricing issues.

- e-Marketing perspective relating to pricing.

7.1   Introduction

Traditionally, pricing has been the poor relation of the marketing mix, with product, place and promotion seen as the main focus of marketing management. This is surprising, while the other 3Ps represent pure cost, price represents the generation of revenue. As Kotler (1999) states: 'Price differs from the other three marketing mix elements in that it produces revenue; the other elements create costs'.

Effective pricing strategy requires input from across the organization. Sales, finance, operation and marketing all have a role to play in the process. While price-related decisions are often multi-functional, it is important to remember they are an integral part of the mix and, as such, cannot be set without reference to the entire mix. Understand how pricing effects positioning strategy is central to many marketing decisions. It should also be noted that price is the most (in theory) flexible mix element. A price can be changed instantly! However, the consequences of a price change can be wide-reaching, affecting both the organization and its competitors.

Remember, pricing involves much more than a simple financial transaction in return for a product. It greatly influences buyer behaviour. For example, consumers often use price as a direct indicator of quality. Potential buyers are likely to balance affordability – able to pay – with acceptability – providing an acceptable solution to needs. Marketing planners need to understand the complex dynamics associated with such decisions.

The most commonly cited criticism of pricing is that it is too often cost-based. As such, it often fails to reflect market conditions, customer behaviour and organizational goals. Therefore, increasing importance is being attached to more dynamic pricing models which, while based on cost, are responsive to current circumstances and strategic objectives.

7.2   Pricing from an economic/accounting viewpoint

Much traditional economic theory derives from the relationship between price and demand. An economist would view demand as either: (1) 'elastic' – demand changes significantly with price or (2) 'inelastic' – little change in demand with significant price change. Price elasticity is often illustrated in terms of a demand curve – see Figure 7.1. Consider how the slope of the line (in Figure 7.1) would differ if illustrating inelastic demand.

In reality, few products have unlimited price elasticity. At some point a market will become saturated, with price cuts failing to attract additional buyers. In the case of inelastic demand, eventually price increases would

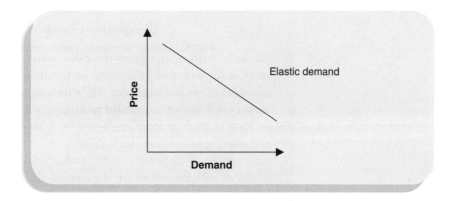

Figure 7.1
Example of demand
curve (elastic)

force buyers to seek substitutes. While the demand curve provides a useful conceptual model, it is not without its weaknesses. On the plus side, a basic understanding of market elasticity allows marketing managers to consider the likely effect of price cuts/increases. For example, in inelastic markets price cuts will have negligible effect on demand. However, on the negative side: (1) Demand curves are difficult, if not impossible, to plot accurately. (2) They do not consider actual buyer behaviour: for example, brand loyalty. (3) Demand curves fail to look at price as an integrated element of the marketing mix. (4) Price may not be completely under the organization's control: for example, suppliers may try to enforce a recommended price regardless of price/demand dynamics.

Consider the above point in relation to the 'easyCinema' case below.

Demand curves are often cited as 'explainers' of market behaviour as opposed to reliable marketing management techniques which support decision-making. Subsequently, organizations have tended to develop other pricing methods, models and strategies.

Accounting-based approaches to price tend to emphasize two key elements of managerial control. First, cost is perceived as the basis of price setting, with cost-based formulas being used to derive and allocate product cost to organizational activity. Once costs are calculated a margin can then be added to generate a level of profit. Often the biggest challenge, and area of most contention, is the allocation of overhead costs. These can be difficult to link to individual product lines. Secondly, return on investment is considered. When costs have been determined and demand forecast, pricing is set to achieve a required return on investment. Hence pricing needs to recoup investment and generate sufficient surplus revenues to make the investment attractive.

No one would argue that sound financial management does not matter. However, a solely accounting approach neglects the importance of the customer and their perception of value. Remember, customer value is the

> ### Illustrative example 7.1
> ### easyCinema: dynamic price model struggles
>
> easyCinema, owned by airline entrepreneur Stelios Haji-Ioannou, offers a 'no-frills' multiplex 10 screen cinema format with customers able to buy tickets for as little as 20p. There are no adverts, or trailers, and no food/confectionery concessions. In fact, there is not even a box office, with customers booking via the Internet. Like easyJet, a 'dynamic' pricing policy means bookings have to be made in advance to secure the best deals. It plans prices ranging from 20p to £5, with an average price of around £1.50, with pricing dependent on time, day of the week and film booked.
>
> However, the venture has hit a major problem – film distributors are opposed to easyCinema's aggressive pricing policy, fearing it would undermine other outlets and future film production. Consequently, the big Hollywood studios have refused to supply the latest release 'blockbuster' films to easyCinema, leaving the company to screen minor films and previously released, or so-called second run, films. The relationship with powerful Hollywood players has made the easyCinema business model – the cheaper the product, the more people will buy – difficult to operate successfully. Ultimately, customers may opt for latest releases as opposed to ultra-low admission prices.

difference between perceived benefits minus perceived sacrifice. As such it includes factors that can't be readily quantified in financial terms – e.g. risk, convenience, loyalty and image. As Adcock, Halborg and Ross (2001) state, costs are about production, whereas price is about value. Therefore, effective pricing strategies would seem to require a multi-functional approach that emphasizes strong financial management and customer value. Marketers need to have as strong an understanding of customer-driven value as accountants have of cost.

7.3   Pricing objectives

When considering how a price should be set, there is one fundamental question to address: What is the organization trying to achieve? In other words, what is the objective of setting a price? The obvious answer – to make a profit – is overly simplistic. Pricing can look to deliver a range of objectives. Shapiro and Jackson (1978) highlight three areas relating to pricing objectives. First, cost, where the focus is on internal/product related factors. Secondly, a competition focus that concerns industry

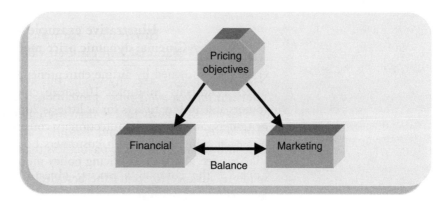

Figure 7.2
Pricing objectives

benchmarks and rivalries. Finally, a marketing approach that emphasizes marketing strategy and the customer's perceived value. However, careful consideration of pricing sees price fall into two main areas: financial and marketing. This redefines Shapiro and Jackson's view of marketing, by taking the term to mean both a customer and competitor viewpoint, and financial to embrace both cost- and revenue-generating elements (see Figure 7.2). It should be noted that financial and marketing objectives are not mutually exclusive. They need to be balanced.

Financial objectives

These can be summarized as follows:

- **Return on investment** As stated above, there is a basic need to cover cost and generate some additional revenue. This additional revenue is the organization's return on investment. Basically, the return has to be high enough to justify the risk. Therefore, the more risky a venture the higher potential returns need to be.

- **Profit optimization** Here we look to generate the optimum level of profit. Optimization is often different from maximization. Maximization being the absolute maximum price achievable in the short term, while optimization takes a longer-term view. As such, it aims to retain customers.

- **Generating cash flow** Cash is the 'life blood' of any business. As such, it may be a pricing objective simply to generate sufficient cash.

Marketing objectives

These relate to customers and competitors. Additionally, they should conform to legal frameworks and ethical policies operating within a given market place.

- **Gaining market share** Often organizations wish to increase, or at least maintain, their market share. As market share is a key indicator of

> ### Illustrative example 7.2
> ### National Express: best value fares
>
> National Express – the city-to-city bus company – launched an '... *easily the best value going*' promotion. This announced a series of £1 (yes £1!) fares to London from destinations like Leeds, Manchester, Birmingham and Cardiff. The fares were only available on-line, with passenger paying less than a penny per mile!
>
> Consider the company's pricing objectives in relation to this campaign.

business success, companies may accept lower financial returns in order to develop their position within a market place. Profit impact of market share (PIMS) analysis has been influential in such objectives. This suggests that acquiring market share leads to profitability. However, blindly gaining market share at any cost is highly questionable, and may damage the long-term viability of the organization. While other mix factors can influence market share, pricing is often seen as the major weapon in the battle.

- **Market stability**   A pricing objective could be to maintain the 'status quo' within an industry. Accepting a 'going-rate' and not acting in an aggressive fashion has one key advantage – stability. By avoiding direct price challenges to competitors, the industry is unlikely to find itself in a price war, which damages everyone. Within stable markets it is possible to plan for the future.

Legal/ethical factors

Organizations need to act both ethically and legally. Hence objectives need to reflect the legal, cultural and moral frameworks applying to their area of operation. Given that competition is the major driver of lower prices, it would be (in theory) beneficial for suppliers to collude and agree to keep prices artificially high. To protect consumers from such actions, most developed economies have laws to prevent such price fixing. Ethical pricing issues are discussed more fully later in the chapter.

7.4   Pricing strategies

A basic business maxim is that strategy should follow objectives. Put another way, objectives define *what* we want to achieve, while strategy defines *how* we are going to achieve it. Pricing follows this pattern. Section 7.3 outlined basic pricing objectives. We now examine pricing strategies. There are two important factors to consider when developing a pricing strategy. First,

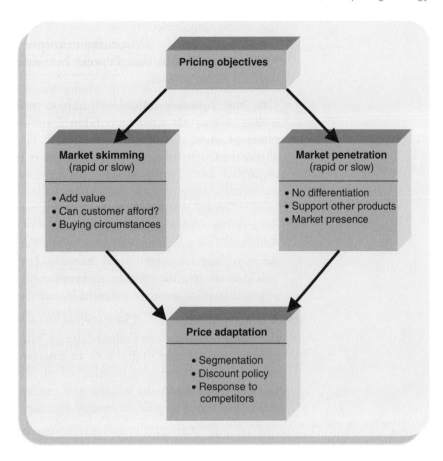

Figure 7.3
Elements of pricing strategy

any pricing strategy must be compatible with strategies associated with other elements of the mix. Secondly, there must be a willingness to adapt pricing according to the prevailing market conditions and potentially different customer segments. Key pricing strategies are: (1) market skimming, (2) market penetration and (3) price adaptation (Figure 7.3).

Market skimming

Marketing skimming tends to involve charging the highest possible price for a given product. Basically, the provider is making a judgement as to how much customer value is associated with the product. While charging a price premium, it is important that the price is perceived as fair as opposed to exploitative. It is likely that the product will be aimed only at a small section of the available market and will be perceived as 'exclusive' in nature.

When is a skimming strategy appropriate? To answer this question, marketing managers need to look for the following criteria:

• **Does the product generate added value?** The added value may be functional (e.g. more reliable, faster, ease of use, safer) or perceived (e.g. brand name, celebrity endorsement). For successful price skimming the offering must be sufficiently distinctive from its competitors, or have no meaningful competition. For example, an anti-ulcer drug which a patent protects.

- **Can the customer afford it?** There must be sufficient buyers willing/able to pay a price premium. Extreme price skimming simply prices products out of the market, with buyers seeking lower-priced alternatives or simply declining to purchase. It should be noted that an organization can opt to gradually make products affordable by progressively reducing price over time, thus widening affordability. Initially, 'early adopters' would be charged a price premium, with prices being reduced as competition builds up, to generate market share. Additionally, we need to consider who the buyer actually is. Remember, the buyer and user may not be the same. For example, travelling business class on an airline will be more expensive because corporations, as opposed to price-sensitive individuals, pay the bill!

- **Buying circumstances** The situation the buyers find themselves in at the time of purchase can radically change price sensitivity. For example, calling out a plumber to deal with an emergency is likely to prove more expensive than getting a number of plumbers to quote for a job! Equally, a bottle of wine bought in a restaurant normally costs much more than the same product bought in a supermarket.

If one or more of the above criteria apply, skimming is feasible. Managers need to consider whether a rapid or slow skim is appropriate. A **rapid skimming** pricing strategy involves setting a high price combined with high levels of promotional activity/spend. The aim is to capitalize on the buyers' willingness/ability to pay, with heavy levels of promotion creating awareness, understanding and preference. Alternatively, a **slow skimming** price strategy, using high price and relatively low levels of promotion, can be deployed. This may be applicable when the product/provider is already well established, or when intensive promotion could damage the product position (e.g. exclusive goods). Additionally, the strategy can be used when resources are too limited to commit to expensive promotional campaigns.

Market penetration

A market penetration strategy means keeping prices relatively low in order to gain market share. As above, this can be combined with promotional elements of the mix to give a rapid or slow penetration strategy. A penetration strategy is likely when one, or more, of the following apply:

- **No product differentiation possible** Where there is little to differentiate the product from its competitors, buyers see no added value. This means organizations have little option but to compete on price. Additionally, the strategy would be applicable when price-sensitive buyers are targeted. A 'no-frills' cost-effective product could widen a product's potential customer base.

- **Support other products/services**   Prices can be set low (even below cost) in order to support the sale of other products. A classic example is supermarket 'loss leaders', where the supermarket sells a few selective lines at cost to attract customers. Additionally, an organization could discount product prices in order to make money from providing maintenance, after-sales servicing and parts.

- **Market presence**   Highly competitive prices tend to gain market share. Therefore, organizations aiming to establish a presence in a market, or indeed establish a dominant position within a market (e.g. market leader), may opt for a price penetration strategy. Once a targeted market share has been gained, prices may be systematically increased to reflect awareness, customer loyalty and market position. Also, a defensive view can be taken, with low prices acting as a barrier to others who would otherwise challenge for market share.

Price adaptation

The organization needs to recognize price adaptation is a complex issue. Whilst it is a powerful marketing tool, it can be controversial in nature. As such, careful consideration is needed to develop effective adaptation strategies. Given that segmentation is the basis of much marketing strategy, it is reasonable to expect segmentation to strongly influence pricing. Prices may be adapted to meet the needs of various customer groups (e.g. student discounts, off-peak travellers, those buying in bulk). However, care must be taken, as those paying full price may perceive adaptive pricing negatively. They could perceive themselves as subsidising other segments. For example, some banks have been criticized for providing mortgage discounts only to new customers.

Price adaptation often extends into discount policy. The creative use of discount can be a major marketing tool. Discounts can stimulate demand and can be applied both directly (e.g. a price reduction) and indirectly (e.g. interest free credit, extended payment terms, optional extras provided at no additional charge).

The final area of price adaptation is in response to competitors' actions. It is more likely that organizations will follow competitors' price cuts when there is excess supply within a market, or when customer loyalty is deemed to be weak. Price increases are likely to be matched when there is excess demand, or industry costs are rising. Table 7.1 summarizes typical responses to competitor price increases/decreases, for given industry conditions.

Table 7.1
Response to competitors' price changes

Organizational response	Competitor cuts price	Competitor increases price
Match price change	Excess supply	Rising industry costs
	Price-sensitive buyers	Excess demand
	Falling industry costs	Non-price-sensitive buyers
Ignore price change	Strong buyer loyalty	Excess supply
	Excess demand	Price-sensitive buyers
	Rising industry costs	Falling industry costs

7.5   Revenue management

More recent thinking relating to pricing has adopted a revenue management approach. This approach attempts to identify which segments generate the most revenues for the business as a whole (Burgess and Bryant, 2001). The approach is well established in service sectors such as the hotel and hospitality industry, where differential pricing is used to optimize overall revenue. For example, hotel room prices would increase during the week when the market is mainly business travellers (not price-sensitive), and decrease at the weekend to attract the short break holiday market (price-sensitive). The process also focuses on using accounting/cost-related information to support marketing decisions.

7.6   The 'non-price' price

A commonly asked question is: What about circumstances where no price is charged (e.g. charities providing services)? The answer is quite simple: there is always a price to pay. However, those benefiting from the service may not be the ones who pay. In the case of the charity, services are provided free to worth while groups, but are paid for via donations and grants. Most not-for-profit organizations serve multiple groups. In general terms these groups fall into two categories; supporters who provide funds and clients who receive benefits. It is likely the term price will be replaced by terms such as fee, donation, taxation, grant, subsidy, etc.

The not-for-profit sector is unlikely to follow traditional pricing models. For example, the National Health Service (UK) is free to all at the point of delivery, but paid for via taxation. A voluntary group may provide child care services at the lowest possible price, thus giving low-income single parents access to nursery provision. While such organizations are not aiming to generate a profit, they are judged and scrutinized by the public. Public funded bodies need to provide evidence of cost management and financial prudence in order to show the money raised has been spent wisely.

Price can also be viewed from an individual point of view. By defining price in terms of psychological factors, as opposed to money, marketers may gain a deeper insight into 'customer' behaviour. Consider the process of internal marketing. Here, a marketing mix approach is taken within the organization to facilitate change. The 'product' could be a new customer service policy the company wishes to implement. The promotional campaign would involve making staff aware of the need for this change. 'Place' would be undertaking the necessary training to implement the policy. The price is then two-fold. First, there is the cost to the organization of retraining, developing new systems, etc. Secondly, the individual staff member may pay a 'psychological price' such as stress, uncertainty, loss of status, time spent learning new skills.

7.7   Pricing and ethical issues

As previously stated, pricing has increasingly undertaken an ethical element. This is due in part to the fact that organizations are under greater scrutiny from pressure groups and government bodies, but also due to the adoption of business strategies containing a strong ethical dimension. Put simply, ethical business makes good commercial business sense.

Subsequently, pricing strategies need to be seen as fair and ethical. Some segments of a given market will happily support higher prices when such prices bring social justice. For example, food products carrying the 'Fair Trade' logo may be relatively expensive, but the consumer is assured that Third World farmers are not being exploited.

Jobber (2001) outlines several key ethical areas relating to price setting. These include price fixing, predatory pricing, deceptive pricing and dumping.

- **Price fixing**   Legislation exists to protect consumers from groups of companies colluding to keep prices high. Illicit cartels could conspire in order to remove the elements of price competition which benefits the consumer (see the Manchester United example).

- **Predatory pricing**   This is the reverse of price fixing. Here competition is so intense that a competitor may cut its prices to a loss-making level. The aim is to drive specific competitors out of business by sustaining artificially low prices, thus creating a monopoly market position. While

> **Illustrative example 7.3**
> **Manchester United: price fixing and the OFT**
>
> The Office of Fair Trading (OFT) uncovered price fixing among major football teams, kit manufacturers and retailers in key sales periods such as the launch of new strips and participation in major football championships. The OFT is critical of sports businesses appearing to exploit the family market by taking advantage of parents under pressure from children to purchase the latest kit. The OFT's investigation found firms entered into price fixing agreements for top-selling adult and children's Manchester United and England replica football shirts. Under new rules the OFT has the power to levy heavy fines on firms guilty of price fixing behaviour.
>
> In 2000, the OFT found that replica kits were constantly priced at around £40. However, since launching the investigation the kit prices have fallen, with customers able to shop around to benefit from a wider range of prices.
>
> Fines handed out include: Manchester United £1.65m, the Football Association £158 000, JD Sports £73 000, Umbro £6.6m and Sports Connection £20 000. The firms do have the right of appeal against such fines.

the consumer benefits in the short term from dramatic price reductions, in the long term they would be faced with limited/no choice.

- **Deceptive pricing**   This situation occurs when the buyer is misled by pricing strategies. This could include misleading price comparisons, confusing/unspecified pricing structures and limiting product availability at the reduced price.

- **Dumping**   The practice of 'dumping' involves selling surplus goods into a market at below the normal market price. The practice may occur to make use of surplus manufacturing capacity, or to get rid of dated products/stock. The problem for domestic competitors occurs when the 'dumped' product is priced at below their cost of production. Potentially, this could destroy local industries.

7.8   e-Marketing perspective

The development of Internet marketing has had a profound effect on price. Arguably, pricing is the mix element most affected by Internet developments. Such developments have witnessed: (1) lower operating costs

> **Illustrative example 7.4**
> **Pricerunner.com: compare before you shop**
>
> The Pricerunner.com website provides potential consumers with informed choice relating to product specification, performance and price. It provides an independent price comparison and detailed product information from both on-line and store-based retailers. Pricerunner.com is not owned by, or dependent on, any product manufacturer or retailer. Consumer product experts and independent organizations provide product reviews, advice and recommendation. While partly funded through advertising, it emphasizes that editorial content is never compromised to accommodate advertisers' views. Pricerunner.com does not sell products, it is purely an information provider. Users are able to examine product specifications and review the price of a product from a range of different vendors. For example (at time of writing) Pricerunner showed vendors charging prices ranging from £8.99 to £18.37 for the Elton John CD 'The Greatest Hits 1970–2002'.

leading to lower price, (2) more price-based competition as the consumer has access to a far wider range of potential suppliers and (3) greater price transparency, as increasing access to information enables the consumer to make rapid price comparisons (see Pricerunner.com example).

Summary

Traditionally, pricing has been seen as the least important of the 'mix' elements. This view is surprising, as pricing produces revenue. Effective pricing strategies require a cross-organizational approach to be truly effective.

Pricing objectives include a balance between financial and marketing issues. As such, objectives need to cover return on investment, profit optimization, cash generation, market stability and gaining market share. Marketing managers consider pricing in terms of market skimming and market penetration. Additionally, the price will need to be adapted to meet current business conditions. Some industries now adopt a revenue management approach – looking to optimize revenue streams for different operational conditions.

Ethical issues are of vital importance in the development of pricing policy. An ethical dimension to pricing covers predatory pricing, price fixing, deceptive pricing and dumping.

Discussion questions

1 Compare the concept of pricing from economic, accounting and marketing perspectives.

2 Illustrative example 7.1 on 'easyCinema' shows an attempt at a dynamic pricing model. Discuss this model using a demand curve.

3 Analyse the pricing objectives of National Express (Illustrative example 7.2).

4 Using additional reading, review the concept of 'revenue management'. What factors drive revenue management?

5 Give an example of a 'non-price' price you have paid.

References

Adcock, D., Halborg, A. and Ross, C. (2001) *Marketing Principles & Practice*, 4th edn. Financial Times–Prentice Hall.

Burgess, C. and Bryant, K. (2001) Revenue management – the contribution of the financial function to profitability. *International Journal of Contemporary Hospitality Management*, Vol.13, No. 3, pp. 144–50.

Jobber, D. (2001) *Principles and Practices of Marketing*, 3rd edn. McGraw-Hill.

Kotler, P. (1999) *Kotler on Marketing*. The Free Press.

Shapiro, B.P. and Jackson, B.B. (1978) Industrial pricing to meet customer need. *Harvard Business Review*, Nov.–Dec., pp. 119–27.

Promotion

About this chapter

Perhaps the promotional element of the marketing mix would be better termed communication. Essentially, promotion means any method, or combination of methods, used to communicate with a target audience. The aim is to get the right message to the right target group in a timely and cost-effective fashion.

After reading this chapter, you will understand:

- The principal factors affecting successful communication.

- Strategic and tactical approaches to promotional activities.

- The nature, benefits and limitation of the communications mix.

- Development of integrated marketing communications.

- Ethical issues relating to promotional activity.

8.1 The communications mix

Those with only a passing knowledge of marketing tend to equate marketing with advertising (plus other related techniques). This premise, while wrong, is understandable. Promotional tools and techniques represent the 'visible' element of marketing. In other words, promotion represents what the potential consumer is told, by a provider, about a product offering.

Marketing communication involves answering the following questions: *who* is the target audience, *what* should be communicated and *how* should it be communicated? Communication is a multifaceted process and the overall image projected by a provider is critically important. To this end, a range of promotional techniques can be used – the communications mix. Jobber (2004) views the mix as having six key elements (see Figure 8.1):

1 **Advertising**   This involves using media channels such as TV, print and cinema. As such media are used to convey a message, idea or product, advertising is a 'non-personal' form of communication, i.e. advertising is aimed at the mass market as opposed to the individual.

2 **Personal selling**   Personal selling is the process of identifying customer needs and matching such needs with the benefits offered by a provider's products. The process consists of direct person-to-person interaction and communication.

3 **Direct marketing**   Uses specific and often interactive media, targeted at the individual as opposed to addressing a mass audience. It can involve the use of direct mail and telephone marketing.

4 **Internet and on-line marketing**   Electronic media are used, as opposed to traditional methods. The approach can be targeted (as per direct marketing), e.g. e-mail marketing, or involve advertising on the Internet (see Illustrative example 8.1).

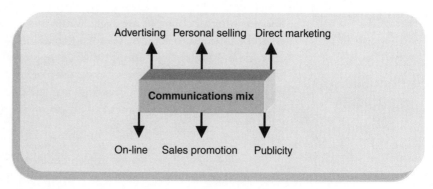

Figure 8.1
The communications mix

> ## Illustrative example 8.1
> ### Intelligent Finance: interactive marketing
>
> Intelligent Finance (IF), the Internet and phone banking service, has mailed out an information pack to 50 000 customers encouraging existing customers to switch from phone-based services to Internet banking. The information pack contained a CD-ROM that demonstrates the on-line service. This demo allows customers to 'test-drive' the service before making a commitment to switch.

5 **Sales promotion** Incentives, inducements and point-of-sale material designed to stimulate trade and/or consumer demand. For example, free samples, discount vouchers and competitions.

6 **Publicity** Creating a favourable view by influence and the development of good media relationships. The process looks to place information in the media (without purchasing advertising space) and is defined by the Institute of Public Relations as:

> The deliberate, planned and sustained effort to establish mutual understanding between an organization and its publics.

8.2   Integrated marketing communications

Consider a typical organization where advertising is controlled by the marketing department, selling is the responsibility of the sales department and the website is controlled and maintained by IT services. These three departments will have differing agendas, priorities and budgets. How do we ensure that the potential customer receives a consistent message from all three sources? The answer lies in integrated marketing communications (IMC). Integrated marketing communications attempts to fuse together the various communications messages/tools used by the organization into one meaningful coherent message. While this view makes intuitive sense, it can be difficult to achieve. Factors such as internal politics, demarcation of work and budget allocation can all conspire against this seemingly logical approach. Such problems can be overcome by a systematic approach to communication and by creating a specific senior management role which oversees the development of all communications activities.

Smith *et al.* (1997) define IMC in such a strategic fashion:

> The strategic analysis, choice implementation and control of all elements of marketing communication which efficiently, economically and

> ### Illustrative example 8.2
> ### The London Underground adopts IMC
>
> The London Underground has something of an image problem. The tube network is often associated with crowded commuter trains packed with weary rush hour travellers. The underground is now attempting to establish itself as a brand as opposed to simply a means of transport. Currently, thousands of seats remain empty at times outside the daily rush hour. To make use of this capacity, it is attempting an ambitious integrated marketing communications campaign. A series of press and poster adverts will encourage people to use the tube to visit London's famous attractions (e.g. The British Museum). This will be followed up with two TV ads.

effectively influence transactions between an organization and its existing and potential customers, consumers and clients.

Interestingly, this definition acknowledges that IMC must embrace all stakeholders (e.g. clients), not just customers.

The adoption of IMC has led to the development of **media neutral planning**. As opposed to finding creative uses for a given medium (e.g. TV advertising), media neutral planning focuses on solving specific communication problems. The starting point is the problem, as opposed to a favoured type of medium. Media planners are then free to explore a wide range of options.

Doyle (2002) outlines five factors important in determining the relative importance of elements in the communications mix. These can be summarized as follows:

- **Resources and objectives**   The relative size of the available communications budget can determine the formulation of the mix. For example, television advertising is very expensive in comparison to public relations. Additionally, what the campaign is trying to achieve is likely to determine which communications media are more likely to succeed.

- **Characteristics of the target market**   Marketing communicators need to consider market size and diversity of consumers. First, overall market size will determine whether mass media (giving wide coverage) is applicable or not. Secondly, diversity must be considered. If consumers are likely to display a diverse range of needs, and effectively form not one segment but a number of sub-segments, then more customized approaches to communication (e.g. direct marketing) may be applicable.

- **Product type**   More complex products tend to be perceived as having increased levels of risk. Therefore a more personal approach to communication, such as personal selling, could be beneficial. For example, a pension scheme is a complex long-term investment, and is more likely to be sold by a sales person as opposed to bought through an advert.

- **Push *vs.* pull strategy**   A 'pull' strategy involves communicating directly with the end-user. This aims to stimulate demand that 'pulls' the product through a distribution channel. Media advertising could achieve this. A 'push' strategy involves motivating distributors to 'push' specific products to consumers. This could be achieved via sales promotion such as trade discounts.

- **Market evolution**   As markets, and products, develop towards maturity, it is likely the communications mix will change. Press advertising could be used to create initial awareness. Once the product is established in the market place, direct marketing could foster customer loyalty.

8.3   The communications process

So far in this chapter we have considered the mechanisms available to communicate with a target audience. However, communication is more then simply sending a message. It is a two-way process, in as much as the message also needs to be received, understood and possibly acted on. For example, an advertising message may not be interpreted in the way the sender intended. Doyle (2002) defines communication as '*the transmission and receipt of a message*'. Whether the message is received and how it is interpreted by a target audience is affected by many extraneous factors. Such factors are collectively known as 'noise'. Noise is normally outwith the control of the sender and can distract or distort the intended message. Examples of noise include: (1) advertising clutter – where the message is lost as the target is overloaded with information; (2) cultural differences – when different cultures interpret images, words, symbols and colours in ways other than intended; (3) peer group pressure – people conform to the views of their peer group, thus interpreting a communication as their peers would. The action taken by the potential customer can be immediate (e.g. purchase an item, request more information, change behaviour, etc.) or it can be longer term (e.g. building awareness, will to consider, loyalty). Equally, a negative response is possible, such as reinforcing negative viewpoints, ignoring the message or switching to another supplier. Figure 8.2 summarizes the process.

One common model used to consider the effectiveness of communication is AIDA. The **AIDA** model is based on the principles of advertising and

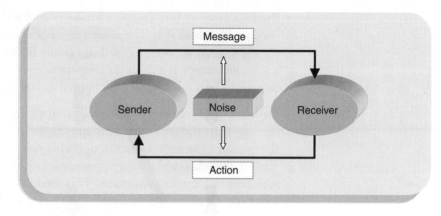

Figure 8.2
A sender/receiver
communications model

aims to take the consumer through a series of stages:

Awareness – Attract the audience's attention.
Interest – Have an impact, which stimulates and holds the audience's interest.
Desire – Generates a desire and preference for a product.
Action – Motivates the potential customer to actually become a customer.

While this model retains 'classic' status, and provides a useful communications framework, it is subject to some criticism. First, it does not address the important issue of repeat purchase and therefore is limited to converting non-buyers to buyers as opposed to buyers to loyal customers. Secondly, there is little evidence supporting the premise that interest leads to desire. The potential consumer may display interest but take the matter no further. Many alternatives exist. One of the most common models in advertising is **DAGMAR** (Defining Advertising Goals for Measuring Advertising Results), which splits the communications process into four stages: awareness, comprehension, response and conviction. While, widely quoted, this model is subject to the same criticisms stated above.

Alternative models highlight the importance of reinforcement. The **ATR** model (Lancaster and Massingham, 2001) highlights the importance of both trial and message reinforcement. The need to reinforce the message periodically is viewed as critical to successful communication. ATR is defined as: Awareness, Trial and Reinforcement.

8.4   Developing a communications strategy

So far, this chapter has examined the types/combinations of marketing communication vehicles available and the communications process from a customer perspective. Now, the overall process of developing a communications strategy is considered. The seven-stage process is summarized in

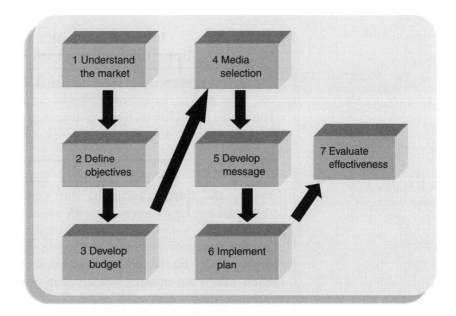

Figure 8.3
Developing a
communications
strategy

Figure 8.3. Note, any communications strategy needs to be prefaced with a marketing strategy appropriate to the organization (see Chapter 2).

While the stages are presented in a sequential fashion, it is important to remember that decisions relating to budget, message development and media selection are, by necessity, developed in parallel. Each stage is now considered.

Understand the market

The initial decision in any communications strategy is to identify and understand the target audience. This would involve segmenting the market (see Chapter 5) and providing an understanding of what motivates and interests the key target groups. For example, what criteria do buyers use when evaluating a product offering, or who do target groups identify with? Additionally, the potential of a given segment(s) may need to be considered: Where can we best gain competitive advantage? Case example 8.3 illustrates.

Define objectives

Clearly there is a need to define objectives. Objectives are particularly important as they are often used to brief external bodies such as advertising agencies. They would then develop a creative campaign based on these objectives. Objectives normally relate to:

- **Informing a target group** Informing the audience aims to create awareness relating to the provider's existence or ability to effectively

> ### Illustrative example 8.3
> ### Trojan condoms target UK women
>
> Trojan, the USA's leading condom brand, has a dilemma in the UK. How do you challenge a market leader as dominant as Durex? The Durex brand has such strong awareness it has become, within the UK, a generic term for the product category.
>
> One possible solution is to target an alternative market segment – women! Trojan felt that traditional male orientated 'laddish' imagery and rhetoric associated with condom marketing campaigns did not have a resonance with women wishing to take control of their own sexual health. For example, a recent Durex advert featured condoms spelling out play-on-words phrases such as 'Roger More', 'Ejaculater' and 'Longer Screws'. Trojan's research found that while modern women were more sexually confident and concerned about health issues, they perceived condom advertising as male-orientated.
>
> The female-orientated Trojan poster campaign featuring a young woman experiencing ecstasy and using the line 'Her pleasure', will be backed up with TV advertising and a website. Durex have now recognized the potential of this market, and recently launched a similar product.

meet a given need. Additionally, there is a need to remind existing consumers of the product and reinforce brand loyalty.

- **Persuading a target group**   Here, the aim is to alter opinion or promote action, such as a trial purchase. For example, a comparison could be made between brands to encourage brand switching.

- **Image development**   Image is often used to build a brand and help differentiate products from competitors. Image development, and maintenance, is a critical weapon in positioning strategy. Such strategies look to form positive associations relating to a brand/product.

Develop a budget

It is often said that 'money oils the wheels of business' and business communications are no different, ultimately being dependent on finance. There are several ways that a communication budget can be formulated. One common approach is simply to match the competition and spend approximately the same as any rivals. Equally simplistic methods include: (1) spending a given percentage of current sales revenue on future communications activity or (2) spending what is deemed to be affordable given the organization's current situation. The most logical method is to match task and objectives. While complex, this aims to budget on the basis of achieving specific communications objectives.

Media selection

Selection of appropriate media is normally done in parallel with message development. Four key issues affect the media decision, and the overall process is driven by the target audience. Which medium, or combination of media, is most effective for a given audience? The key factors are:

- **Reach**   What is the likely market size, and how much of a total market can we hope to target? For example, TV advertising is likely to cover more people than a local newspaper. However, reaching more people does not equate automatically to greater effectiveness.

- **Frequency**   How often is a possible consumer going to be exposed to a communications message within a given period? Is it better to have one high impact campaign, or should the approach be more gradual, using reinforcement over time?

- **Interactivity**   Do we wish to establish a dialogue with the potential consumer? Hollensen (2002) classifies communication media as ranging from one-way communication, such as simply passing on information (e.g. an advert that imparts information) to two-way communication which is interactive (e.g. personal selling that establishes a dialogue) (see Figure 8.4).

- **Cost**   The available budget will of course drive media decisions. Whatever is done has to be affordable.

Develop a message

Message development is the creative side of communications. It aims to grab attention and promote some form of unique selling proposition (USP). The message produced needs to have resonance with the target audience. In other words, it needs to be important to them, and form a basis for action/activity. Message development has to be perceived from

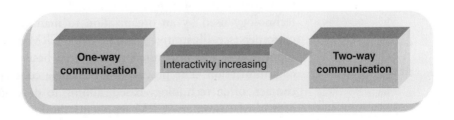

Figure 8.4
Degree of interactivity
in media

the consumer viewpoint. For example, it is important to use the customer's own preferred style of language as opposed to the language of the provider. Messages tend to focus on: functional features, trust, reassurance and belonging. These are often the emotive issues that connect with the customer. Remember, communication is more than words; image, colour, typeface and graphics all have a part to play.

Implement the plan

Once designed, any programme has to be implemented. This involves scheduling the media and translating the desired message into an appropriate format.

Evaluate effectiveness

Given the importance of communication, it is important to evaluate its effectiveness. Having clear objectives, in the first instance, is a key to effective evaluation. Evaluation can be both by pre-testing (before the campaign is launched) and post-testing (after launch). It can look at factors such as: attitude before and after the campaign, effect on actual sales and usage and recall of adverts and brand names/association. One advantage of direct marketing is that it is more 'accountable'. Direct marketing campaigns normally have short-term, well-defined aims. Thus direct response methods of communication are more directly evaluated. For example, factors such as cost per enquiry or cost per sale can be easily established.

8.5   Customer relationship management

Gronroos (1996) defines relationship marketing as:

> To establish, maintain and enhance long-term customer relationships, so that the objectives of both parties are met. This is done by mutual exchange and fulfilment of promises.

This is to say, real benefits stem from long-term relationships between provider and customer, with the loyal customer being recognized as a valuable business asset.

Customer relationship management (CRM) is processes, techniques and technology used by an organization to manage its relationship with a customer (see Illustrative example 8.5). CRM has become increasingly sophisticated and now offers a structured basis from customer contact/communication. The process offers a single coherent point of customer contact, often technology-based, aiming to develop a relationship with individual customers. CRM represents the interface with the customer,

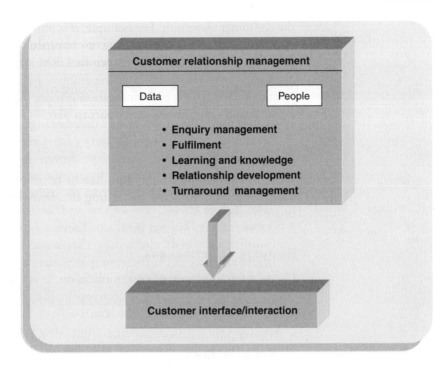

Figure 8.5
Customer relationship
management

and as such it is often the sole method of communication for both parties. Figure 8.5 summarizes the key elements of CRM.

There are two key elements in the development of a successful CRM. First, **data** need to drive the process. Accurate data need to be stored, analysed and accessed in order to support high levels of customer service. Customer service staff need to have immediate access to customer records in order to deal with enquiries/problems etc. Marketing managers can make use of stored data to develop customized marketing programmes and model customer response. This process is known as **data warehousing** (or data mining). For example, Amazon recommends books to potential buyers based on their previous purchases. Secondly, **people** employed in a customer contact role are vital in the development of customer loyalty. They need the correct training and support to deliver high levels of service. The other elements of CRM are:

- Enquiry management, which involves prompt and effective response to any customer enquiry. This includes both existing and new customers.

- Fulfilment, which is concerned with ensuring that all transactions are carried out in accordance with policy.

- Learning and knowledge relate to the data warehousing aspects of the process, and stress the need to develop and maintain a marketing database.

> **Illustrative example 8.5**
> **Unilever improves CRM structure**
>
> Unilever owns a wide range of consumer brands – Lever Fabérgé, Unilever Best Foods, Unilever Ice Cream and Frozen Food. Collectively, the group owns a diverse range of well-known brands. Examples include: Ben & Jerry's Ice Cream, Nino Cerruti fragrances, Persil, and Birds Eye frozen foods. The group has appointed a senior manager to coordinate and develop customer relationship management across its entire portfolio of products. The aim is to increase loyalty and determine opportunities to cross-market Unilever products. Previously, responsibility for communication was divided among the various business divisions. The move emphasizes the increasing importance that Unilever attaches to relationship marketing.

- Relationship development endeavours to foster higher levels of loyalty among customers.

- Turnaround management involves dealing with problems and handling complaints. Additionally, it may involve developing programmes to win back customers who defect to rival providers.

The importance attached to relationship-based communication has seen the development of **permission marketing** (Godin, 1999). Permission marketing aims to develop one-to-one communication with the consumer, where the consumer has given 'permission' for it to take place. If the consumer signals a willingness to enter into a dialogue with a provider then the chances of a positive consumer response are greatly increased.

8.6   Viral marketing

Viral marketing is a relatively new concept. In simple terms information is passed from one person to another just as a virus would be. The process relies on a message being transferred from person to person. Clearly, transmission rates are vastly increased when word-of-mouth type communication is enhanced by electronic (e-mail, Internet) means. Viral campaigns rely on transmission, with Chaffey (2003) defining three types of transmission: word-of-mouth, word-of-Web and word-of-Internet. Transmission is more likely when the communication is relevant to some common interest (e.g. pass this e-mail to a friend) or when there is an incentive to pass it on (e.g. introduce a friend and receive a discount). Additionally, transmission can be involuntary (e.g. attachments, adverts).

8.7 Ethical issues in marketing communication

As previously stated, marketing communication is the most visible element of the marketing mix. Given such high visibility, communications techniques and messages are often seen as a defining measure of the organization's ethical credibility. Ethics can be seen as our beliefs about what is right and wrong. From a corporate perspective, ethics provides direction and/or constrains decision-making. Additionally, there will be legally enforceable practices relating to what is acceptable. Note, ethics relating to marketing communication can vary greatly depending on the cultural background of the audience. What is acceptable to one group or society may be unacceptable to other cultures.

Hollensen (2002) highlights the following factors as possible ethical issues in the promotion element of the mix:

- Overstated claims for a product.

- Advertising to children.

- Sex or fear as an advertising appeal.

- Exaggerated product benefits.

- High-pressure or misleading sales techniques.

- Commission paid to 'push' certain products.

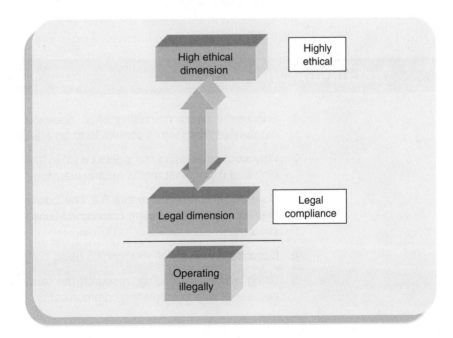

Figure 8.6
Ethical dimension to communication

It is vital that marketing managers are familiar with the ethical, social and legal constraints relating to the markets they operate in. Figure 8.6 shows a framework for planning an ethical communications strategy. Organizations tend to adopt an ethical standard somewhere on a continuum between highly ethical and simply adhering to the law.

Summary

Marketing communication involves targeting a specific audience with a communications mix. The communications mix is a diverse range of promotional techniques (e.g. advertising, personal selling, direct marketing and sales promotion). Ideally, such a mix needs to be formed into an integrated marketing communication (IMC) system. IMC aims to fuse together the communications methods most appropriate to a given target audience or situation.

Marketers need a fundamental understanding of how consumers respond to a planned communication strategy. Models such as AIDA, DAGMAR and ATR provide a useful understanding of the process. Planned campaigns typically have seven stages: (1) understanding the market; (2) defining objectives; (3) developing a budget; (4) media selection; (5) developing a message; (6) implementing the plan; and (7) evaluating effectiveness.

Given the importance of relationships in marketing, organizations can develop customer relationship management (CRM) processes as a means of fostering on-going relationships with their customer base. Additionally, it is important to approach communication from an ethical standpoint.

Discussion questions

1 Successful direct marketing often depends on having a marketing database. What factors contribute to an effective database?

2 Why would marketing managers be (a) in favour of media neutral planning and (b) against media neutral planning?

3 Consider Illustrative example 8.2 The London Underground. Discuss their attempt at developing communications in terms of 'push' or 'pull' strategy.

4 Describe an advert of your choice using both AIDA and ATR models.

5 Using additional reading, research the term 'data warehousing' and discuss its role in marketing communication.

References

Adcock, D., Halborg, A. and Ross, C. (2001) *Marketing Principles and Practice*, 4th edn. Prentice Hall.

Chaffey, D. (2003) *Total E-Mail Marketing*. Butterworth Heinemann.

Doyle, P. (2002) *Marketing Management and Strategy*, 3rd edn. Prentice Hall.

Godin, S. (1999) *Permission Marketing*. Simon & Schuster.

Gronroos, C. (1996) Relationship marketing; strategic and tactical implications. *Management Decision*, Vol. 43, No. 3, pp. 5–14.

Hollensen, S. (2002) *Marketing Management: A Relationship Approach*. Prentice Hall.

Jobber, D. (2004) *Principles and Practice of Marketing*, 4th edn. McGraw-Hill.

Lancaster, G. and Massingham, L. (2001) *Marketing Management*, 3rd edn. McGraw-Hill.

Smith, P., Berry, C. and Pulford, A. (1997) *Strategic Marketing Communications*. Kogan Page.

Place

About this chapter

Distribution arrangements are amongst the most important factors that affect the success in the market of an organization's products and services. Both public and private sector organizations are faced with a series of complex issues when dealing with the distribution element of the marketing mix.

After reading this chapter, you will understand:

- The traditional approach to distribution channels.

- The key issues of conflict and control.

- The increasing power of retailers in the consumer goods sector and the impact this has had on marketing channels over the past 30 years.

- The relevance of distribution decisions on public sector provision.

- The impact of e-commerce on distribution decisions.

9.1   Distribution channels

Distribution channels, sometimes referred to as marketing channels, are vital to an organization's success, whether it is involved in consumer, industrial, or service products, or in the public sector. Distribution has been one of the most neglected aspects of marketing, so much so that Drucker's claim that it was marketing's 'dark continent' (1973) still has some relevance. Distribution still fails to receive the same level of attention as other aspects of the marketing mix but for many sectors it is an area where the most crucial decisions have to be taken. What are channels of distribution?

Distribution channels are the structures by which groups of related organizations transfer goods or services from the initial producer to final domestic consumer or business user. The organizations that operate within these channels are called middlemen. The final selling price of any product or service includes the margins paid to these specialist middlemen. Therefore it is often thought that if you can cut out these middlemen the price of a product charged to the final customer can be reduced. This argument, however, overlooks the efficiencies middlemen bring to the distribution process. Middlemen fulfil three major roles, each improving the efficiency of the channel of distribution. These are:

- **Breaking bulk**   Middlemen buy from producers in large quantities, and break these down into smaller unit volumes for the end customer. This allows the producer to carry out large scale production benefiting from the accompanying economies of scale. On the other hand, customers can purchase in smaller quantities from middlemen releasing the consumer's capital as it does not require to be tied up in large inventories of unnecessary stock. This function of buying in bulk also allows a producer to manufacture a product at a time that is most convenient based on their production constraints. In contrast, the middlemen will be open at a time consumers wish to purchase. The location of production facilities can also be removed from the consumer. Many cars bought by consumers in the UK are produced overseas. This is possible because local middlemen provide the showrooms, test drive facilities and after sales services that consumers require in order to make a purchase.

- **Specialization**   Many middlemen specialize in distributing specific types of product. This specialization can allow them to create economies of scale to the distribution channel. For instance, a middleman may have developed specialist skills in the servicing and installation of a type of product. Rather than the producer having to replicate these skills, it is more economic for them to distribute their product through the existing intermediary. This allows the producer to concentrate on their own specialist areas of expertise, such as production or research and development. Middlemen can also provide a specialist sales force. In these circumstances the cost of a

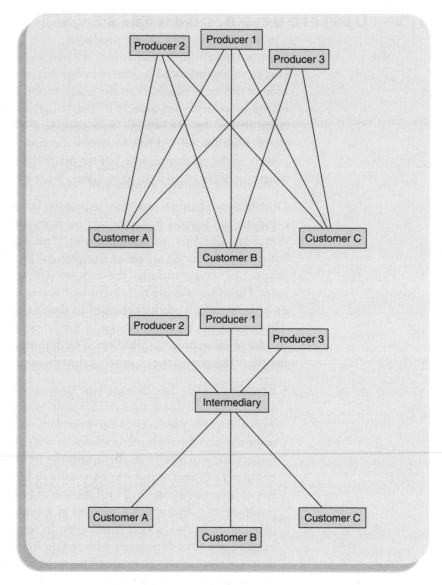

Figure 9.1
Transactional efficiency

sales representative can be spread over the several different producers'
products the intermediary carries. This would be a more efficient option
to a producer than employing their own dedicated sales force.

- **Transactional efficiency** It is not uncommon for middlemen to
  assemble a range of products from different producers. This allows them
  to offer the end customer an appropriate assortment for their needs.
  Thus a customer requiring a range of DIY tools can buy them all from
  one middleman rather than buying each tool separately from the
  specialist producer. This cuts down dramatically the number of transactions that are required in order to transfer goods from producers to
  consumers. Figure 9.1 shows how the intervention of one intermediary

reduces the number of transactions necessary in order for three consumers to buy products from three producers.

9.2   Marketing channels add value

A number of factors can affect consumers' perceptions of a product or service offering. These factors include:

- The customer services offered, such as the information and advice offered, the attitude of sales staff and the facilities for credit that are available.

- The convenience of the outlet in terms of opening times and locations. The ambience of the outlet is also a critical element in forming a consumer's perceptions towards a product offering.

- The depth and assortment of stock on offer.

All these factors are provided and controlled by the middleman and are critical in adding value to the basic product. Distribution channels should be seen as a vehicle by which an organization can add value to its product offering. These channels are therefore a significant component of the marketing mix as they can be an extremely effective way in which to differentiate a product from the wider competition.

9.3   Types of middlemen

There are a number of different types of middlemen that act in distribution channels. Some do not take title to the goods they handle nor sometimes even physically handle the product. There are important distinctions between the roles and characteristics of the most common intermediaries:

- **Agents** Agents differ from other middlemen in that they do not take ownership or physical possession of the products they represent (i.e. they do not take title to the goods). They will act on a producer's behalf and take a commission on any sales they negotiate with a third party.

- **Producers' agents** Producers' agents tend to work for a number of different producers and deal with non-competitive or complementary products in a specific geographic area. They are normally used by producers that have fairly limited product lines and the agent is only involved in delivering the sales function.

- **Sales agents** Generally sales agents only deal with one producer and deliver a full range of marketing activities for this specific client. These activities would include creating distribution, pricing and promotional policies and plans. These agents would also provide recommendations on future product strategy. Sales agents are commonly used by small companies with limited resources or by business start-ups. Sales agents can also be employed by producers that are moving into an unknown overseas market. In this situation the sales agent can provide essential local knowledge.

- **Brokers** Brokers endeavour to bring potential buyers and sellers together by negotiating specific deals. Brokers usually do not have a long-term relationship with either party involved in a negotiation. Brokers, like agents, do not take title to the goods, nor do they physically handle the product and they act on a commission basis.

- **Wholesalers** Wholesalers differ from agents in that they take title to the goods they handle and are involved in the physical distribution of those products. They sell principally to other middlemen or directly to industrial, commercial or institutional customers rather than individual consumers. Full service wholesalers carry out a broad range of marketing activities for their suppliers and customers. These would include services such as purchasing, sales, warehousing and transportation of goods. They may also offer additional services such as advice on accounting and inventory control procedures. In contrast, limited service wholesalers strip out non-essential services and as a result are able to offer cost savings to customers. An example of this in the UK are the cash and carry wholesalers who provide no onward transport of any goods purchased by the customer; in this case, these are normally small independent retailers.

- **Retailers** Retailers sell goods and services directly to the end consumer. Retailers take title to the goods they stock which, as will become evident later in this chapter, is a crucial factor in their relationship with their suppliers.

There are a number of other, less common middlemen. These include:

- **Purchasing agents** These agents usually have a long-term contract with an organization on whose behalf they will act. Their responsibilities may be wider than merely purchasing on behalf of the company but may also include receiving, inspecting, storing and shipping the goods to their client.

- **Resident buyers** Resident buyers are found in sectors such as the clothing industry. They are to be found in major clothing markets, for instance, London, Paris or Milan. They provide essential information to smaller retailers and will buy merchandise on behalf of these clients.

9.4   Distribution strategies

Given the various types of middlemen available, many writers have suggested that producers have to decide which of these intermediaries are the most appropriate route for them to use in distributing their products. This approach looks at distribution channels solely from the producer's standpoint. From this perspective, a producer has to decide on the optimal number of customers it wishes to reach, and then has to employ one of three different distribution strategies.

- **Intensive distribution**   This strategy is deemed to be appropriate when distributing products that are impulse purchases such as chocolates. It is also suitable for convenience products like bread. In both these cases consumers brand loyalty is likely to be low. They will be prepared to buy the nearest substitute product rather than going to another distribution outlet. In this situation the more outlets an organization can get to stock their product the more they will be able to sell. Therefore chocolate producers distribute through as many outlets as possible, including large store groups, small corner shops, garages, video shops, university refectories and vending machines in public places. To do this they will use many wholesalers and retailers and therefore will lose a lot of control in terms of the service given to the customer by the retailer.

- **Exclusive distribution**   A producer implements a strategy of exclusive distribution by restricting the number of middlemen that are allowed to stock a particular product. This type of distribution strategy is usually employed in situations where customers are willing to travel to obtain a product and where high levels of customer service have to be guaranteed. Limiting the number of distributors allows the producer to keep control of service standards offered by intermediaries in the channel. This type of strategy would be employed by exclusive brands found in markets such as the fashion industry or specialist sport cars.

- **Selective distribution**   This strategy lies somewhere between the two strategies previously covered. In this situation producers are faced by consumers who would be prepared to do some shopping around to gain their preferred product. However, if their search has to become extensive they will choose a substitute product instead. An example of a product that may be affected by this type of consumer behaviour would be good quality, rather than status symbol, watches. A producer of these watches would wish to have them in several outlets in a city the size of Edinburgh or Manchester. At the same time the producer would endeavour to ensure that these outlets reflected and reinforced the quality of the product.

Writers who take a producer perspective propose that, having made a decision on the distribution strategy they wish to employ, producers then have to make a decision on which middlemen to use. These middlemen should be chosen on the basis of cost, product characteristics and the degree of control necessary. Clearly the more middlemen involved in the distribution of a product the less control a producer is likely to be able to bring to bear. The producer could also decide to pursue a multi-channel

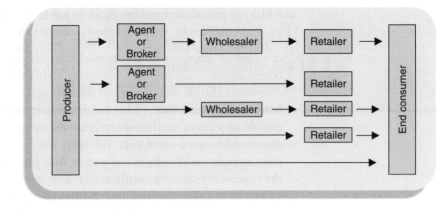

Figure 9.2
Typical channel flows for consumer products

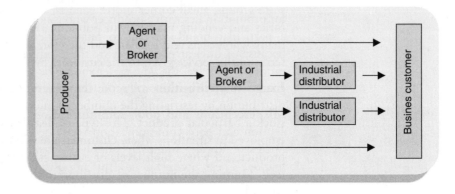

Figure 9.3
Typical channel flows for business-to-business products

strategy; this could be either complementary or competitive in nature. Competitive channel arrangements obviously have the potential to provoke conflict. Currently many financial institutions are offering their products not only through independent financial advisers, but also through direct telephone and Internet operations. These direct operations are an attempt to bypass the traditional middleman. It is a competitive channel arrangement and is understandably a potential source of conflict, i.e. independent financial advisers now find themselves competing directly with the producer of the insurance products.

There are a number of potential distribution channel structures that can be put together from the various intermediaries available. These options are shown in Figures 9.2 and 9.3 and include the option of a producer dealing directly with an end customer.

9.5 Channel conflict

Channel conflict is an important issue in channel management as it has the potential to damage a product's performance in the market. Channel conflict tends to arise for three main reasons:

- **Incompatible goals** Each member of a distribution channel in a commercial market will aim to maximize its profits. Therefore there is potential for frequent disagreement about margins and incentives. There can also be disputes about such things as who should pay for the holding of inventories. There can be conflicts caused by wider incompatible objectives such as when a producer wishes to increase market share while at the same time the aim of a key middleman may be to offer as wide an assortment of products as possible. This kind of situation inevitably leads to conflicts of interest

- **Unclear rights and responsibilities** Sometimes there is an area of overlap between channel members and it is unclear which party should be undertaking specific actions. A wholesaler may feel that responsibility for promotion lies with a producer who is not doing enough to promote a particular brand directly to retail outlets and the end consumer because of unclear policies set by the producer. At the same time the producer may feel the wholesaler should be putting more promotional energy into selling the product to the retailers they supply.

- **Misperceptions and poor communication** An example of misperception and poor communication is the decision of a number of producers of leading brands to supply Costco when it entered the UK market. These producers saw this opportunity as a way of expanding their distribution. The established supermarket chains however perceived this decision as being a threat to their market share and profit margins. The supermarkets' perception was that the producers were willing to offer favourable terms to the new entrant and as a result Costco were able to undercut the supermarkets' prices. As a result these supermarkets threatened to stop stocking the producer brands unless they were offered the same terms.

Channel conflict always has the potential to arise at some point in the relationship between channel members. The aim of a producer should be to minimize it in order to maximize the sales of their products. This can be achieved in a number of ways:

- **Involvement of middlemen in policy decisions** Producers can involve middlemen in the development of policy decisions. This can be achieved through the establishment of dealer advisory boards, or even by taking regular surveys of intermediaries' opinions.

- **Increase interaction between members of staff in the organizations** Mechanisms can be set up to increase levels of contact between members of staff of the various organizations in a channel. These mechanisms include setting up regular conferences, or weekend retreats for senior managers, or interchanging members of staff for short periods of time.

- **Focus on common goals** If there is a problem with the distribution of a particular product it is likely to affect the profitability of all channel members. Therefore bringing together the whole channel to concentrate on the development of a solution to a problem area should be a profitable exercise for all the parties involved.

So far we have examined distribution strategies and potential channel conflicts from a producer's perspective. Historically, the producer was the key player in any channel of distribution. In many areas, such as business-to-business, the producer is still the dominant partner in the distribution channel. However, in many markets, especially those involved in consumer goods, the situation is not as simple as has been outlined by taking a producer perspective.

9.6 The contemporary situation: channels of distribution *vs.* channels of supply

The reality today for many producers, particularly those involved in consumer products, is that they are not in a position to choose channels of distribution, but rather the situation is that middlemen choose channels of supply. The producer is not in the position of choosing a distribution channel unless they have a product or brand that a middleman particularly wants or feels it needs to carry. In many situations the

---

Illustrative example 9.1
Freesat

Channel 4 television recently signed a three-year extension to its deal with SKY for access to its satellite TV platform. ITV is also in negotiation to extend their contract with SKY. Both these developments have cast doubt on the BBC's ability to launch a rival free-to-air satellite system. As Channel 5 has four years left on its contract with SKY, of the key terrestrial networks, this would only leave the BBC channels on the Freesat platform unless ITV changed its mind. One of the key factors in Channel 4's decision was its need to continue to have access to the SKY platform for its pay TV channels, FilmFour and E4. In order to continue to operate these services Channel 4 required access to SKY's encryption service. As the situation stands there is no competition to SKY's control of UK TV satellite distribution.

producer's need for access to the middleman's distribution channel is greater than the middleman's need for a particular product. For instance, a major grocery supermarket like Tesco may feel it has to carry the leading brand in a category, such as Kellogg's Cornflakes, but does not need to carry a secondary brand. Thus the secondary brand's need for access to Tesco's distribution network is much greater than the supermarket's need to stock the secondary brand. This illustrates the shift in the balance of power in favour of the middleman, in particular, the retailer.

In many market sectors the past 25 years has seen the emergence of vertical marketing channels as the dominant form of distribution channel.

9.7 Vertical marketing channels

According to McCammon (1970):

> vertical marketing systems are centrally coordinated and professionally managed networks which are designed to create maximum impact in the market while achieving operating efficiencies.

In effect, one member of the channel emerges as a channel controller (sometimes referred to as a channel captain). That member coordinates the activities of the channel to take out inefficiencies. For instance, the channel controller is often in a position to be able to create centrally organized warehousing, data-processing and other facilities that provide scale efficiencies (see Figure 9.4).

Vertical marketing systems can be grouped into three main types: corporate, administered and contractual.

- **Corporate vertical marketing systems** In the corporate vertical marketing system all the stages of manufacture and distribution are owned by one organization, either through forward or backward integration. In theory corporate ownership of all aspects of production and distribution should indicate that the organization has complete control of the way in which a product is delivered to the market. In practice, executing delivery correctly can be just as difficult to achieve as with any other type of distribution channel. In fact there is potential that it may be more difficult as both the manufacturing operation and the distribution function know that the final sanction of taking business elsewhere is difficult to execute. MFI and the Co-operative Wholesale Society, which manufactures, wholesales and owns a number of retail co-operative societies, are examples of this type of vertical marketing system. However, there are fewer examples of corporate vertical marketing systems than there used to be. A number of organizations in the UK and Europe, particularly in

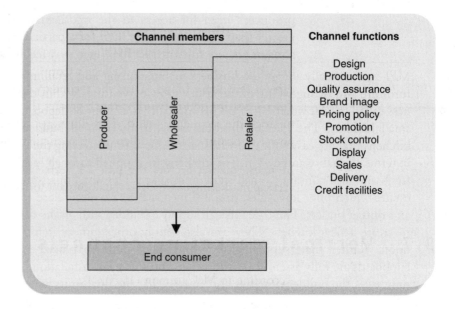

Channel members			Channel functions
Producer	Wholesaler	Retailer	Design Production Quality assurance Brand image Pricing policy Promotion Stock control Display Sales Delivery Credit facilities

End consumer

Figure 9.4
A vertical marketing
system

the clothing sector, have outsourced their manufacturing operations to the Far East. As a result they have effectively turned themselves into administered vertical marketing systems.

- **Administered vertical marketing system** Administered vertical marketing systems occur where one dominant intermediary coordinates the activities of the channel by virtue of its market power. Tesco in the UK would be a prime example as through its market power it can coordinate the activities of its suppliers in great detail. These activities can include all aspects of product design, quality, manufacture, branding, promotion, display, delivery, finance etc. (see Figure 9.4). There are many other examples of administered vertical marketing systems, such as Marks & Spencer, Sainsbury, Asda, B&Q and Dixons. Wholesalers can also become channel controllers, for example WH Smith is the UK's market leader in newspaper and magazine distribution. The company delivers to 22 000 customers daily and serves both independent and multiple retailers. Even producers such as Procter & Gamble, Unilever, Nestlé and Sony can still exercise high levels of channel control in certain sectors.

- **Contractual vertical marketing system** Within contractual vertical marketing systems independent organizations coordinate their activities on a contractual basis to create economies of scale and make an impact on the market. There are two main types:

  ○ *Wholesaler/retailer sponsored voluntary groups* Examples are organizations such as MACE and the Independent Grocer's Alliance, i.e. small grocery stores which have joined together to compete with the major chains.

Illustrative example 9.2
Howden joinery

MFI is a vertically integrated business manufacturing and retailing kitchen and bedroom furniture and fittings. One of the fastest growing ventures within the MFI group is a business called the Howden joinery. This company is a chain of depots that supply kitchens to small builders. The idea of the business is to meet small builders' needs by supplying kitchens that are easy to install whilst at the same time meeting the customers' expectations in terms of quality and design. The kitchens are supplied through local warehouses that hold stock and also contain a small showroom space. The warehouses are located on industrial estates which offer low rents, this also means they are often close to plumbers' merchants and timber outlets. These depots can supply a builder with all the component parts needed to create a new kitchen. They can also supply other joinery items such as windows and doors. Rather than supplying the component parts that need assembling, all kitchen cupboards are fully assembled by Howden and ready for installation by the builder. This not only saves the builder time but also ensures that the final units are of a high quality.

Howden promote themselves by contacting local builders with mail shots and by direct telephone contact. The relationship between local staff and local customers is seen as a crucial aspect of the business. Howden staff help the builders to draw computer designs of proposed kitchens and well as providing builders with brochures which they can show to their customers. Howden's customers are offered trade discounts and easy credit terms. The normal MFI store reaches maturity after around 18 months, however a Howden depot is still attracting new business four years after opening.

The aim is to have 350 outlets in the UK and MFI had also begun to consider the international expansion of the Howden business.

○ *Franchise systems* Franchise systems are the far more common variety of contractual vertical marketing systems. Franchises tend to consist of arrangements where a franchisee acquires the right to distribute a product or service; in return they have to adhere to service standards set by the franchiser. There will be specific services that have to be offered as well as normally a set of physical fittings that have to be installed in any outlet. There are a number of different franchise systems. These are:

1　Producer–retailer franchises, such as car dealerships and petrol stations.

2　Producer–wholesaler franchises such as Coca-Cola's country franchises.

3　Service sponsor–retailer franchises such as Avis's car rentals and Burger King's fast food restaurants.

The key advantage of a franchising system to the franchisers is that they are able to retain a high degree of control over the distribution channel without having to invest capital in setting up their own outlets.

9.8 Channel controllers

Increasingly in the UK, and throughout Europe and North America, in consumer goods markets the channel controllers are retailers. There are a number of reasons for this accelerating development that go back to decisions taken 40 years ago. In the early 1960s producers were very powerful and dominant organizations. However, from the mid 1960s onwards there has been a shift in the balance of power in favour of retailers. If the UK is taken as an example, this occurred for three main reasons:

- The UK abolished 'Resale Price Maintenance' (RPM) in 1964 for most product areas (books and pharmaceuticals were excluded). Up until 1964 producers set the price at which their product could be sold by the retailer. Once RPM was abolished retailers were free to set their own prices.

- Small and medium-sized multiple retailers were able to obtain discounts from manufacturers by buying in bulk. As a result larger retailers were able to set lower prices but maintain their margins by buying in bulk. In turn this led to the growth of large multiple chains. Growth took place at the expense of the small corner shops and independent retailers who could not match the prices set by the multiples.

- Once multiples became large organizations they began to develop their own branded goods (own label).

The market share figures of the four largest retailers in the UK grocery sector, shown in Table 9.1, illustrate the growth of multiple retailers' influence over a ten year period.

	1994	2004
Tesco	15.7	28.0
Sainsbury	17.0	15.3
Asda	8.9	16.9
Morrisons (incorporating Safeway sales)	11.4	13.6
Total market share	53.0	73.8

Source: based on Taylor Nelson Sofres, data from several published sources

Table 9.1
Percentage market share of the major supermarket chains in the UK groceries sector

> **Illustrative example 9.3**
> **AOL/Blockbuster**
>
> In June 2004 AOL the Internet service provider announced that it had reached agreement with Blockbuster to distribute its Internet access CDs at point of sale. Blockbuster has 720 branches throughout the UK. This deal will allow Blockbuster customers the opportunity to try AOL's 9.0 Internet service for free. In return AOL will advertise Blockbuster's online DVD service to its 2 million UK members through its entertainment channel. This agreement allows AOL to build a lead over its key rival Wanadoo in the retail distribution of Internet access CDs. It also provides Blockbuster with an Internet channel for its new online DVD rental service.

For the reasons outlined above, in consumer goods retailers have come to control the marketing channels as well as key elements of the retail marketing mix.

9.9 The retail marketing mix

The retail marketing mix consists of seven elements each tending to be controller by the retailer. The seven elements of the marketing mix are:

- **Product range**   Retailers are interested in offering a mix of products that will appeal to their target customer. Therefore they are less likely to stock the full range of a manufacture's product unless it fits in with their overall merchandising plans.

- **Product image**   To a large extent this is controlled by the retailer. Producers will attempt to create a distinctive brand image for a quality product through all elements of the mix including pricing and merchandising. However, a major retailer may decide to discount a leading brand potentially damaging the image the producer is attempting to retain. The producer is unlikely to restrict stock if the retailer is a large multiple that has a significant share of the market. The retailer therefore can control the product image. According to McGoldrick (1990), Hotpoint once found itself in this situation when the UK retailer Comet heavily discounted Hotpoint's branded products.

- **Consumer franchise**   Nowadays consumers tend to think in terms of retail brand names rather than producer's brand names. For instance, if buying an electric toaster a consumer is initially likely to think in terms of retail outlets that sell electrical goods rather than producers' brand names like Kenwood, or Swan.

> ## Illustrative example 9.4
> ### Asda
>
> In 1992 *Marketing*, the trade magazine, reported that Asda had embarked on the unprecedented move of threatening to de-list products unless their suppliers provided cash payments as well as lower prices and larger annual discounts. Asda had just bought the Gateway chain of supermarkets for £705m and had suffered a difficult financial year. It was not unusual for supermarkets to ask suppliers to pay for sponsored advertisements for new store openings, where their products would be featured. But in this case there didn't appear to be any incentives offered to the suppliers. This move by Asda caused resentment among their suppliers and producers of secondary brands were deemed likely to accept de-listing rather than make any cash payments. Producers of market leading brands would obviously have been in a far stronger position to negotiate with Asda then the suppliers of these secondary brands.

- **Shelf price**   As stated before, retailers now set retail prices, producers can only recommend.

- **Distribution**   Most multiple retailers now have central warehouses that producers deliver to. Thus the retailer decides where a product is distributed, in what quantity and at what time.

- **Shelving**   The retailer decides on the positioning of products within the store. There are obviously better sites in a store and a producer would have to offer the retailer strong incentives in order to gain the best space within a store.

- **Advertising**   Retailers are generally large organizations that can spend a great deal more on advertising than producers. Especially as producers give retailers allowances for joint advertising campaigns.

9.10   Public sector distribution

It is generally accepted that one of the most important factors in the success of any retail outlet is its physical location. However, the significance of location to the success of public sector facilities has had a much lower profile. A study of a centre providing community psychiatric services in the Bronx in New York (Perlman, 1975) showed that the vast majority of 'customers' came from within walking distance. That is, they came from within five blocks of the medical centre. This was in spite of the fact the centre was located on major public transport routes. Other studies have provided similar results. It appears that the time and effort, as well as the cost of the travel itself, are regarded as an integral part of the real cost of using the service. Even when it comes to health, once that cost passes a certain limit the consumer is unwilling to use the service offered. This is referred to as the Jarvis Law effect. Jarvis's Law states that 'utilization varies inversely with the square of the distance to the source of the care' (McStravic, 1977).

Research studies, such as the one discussed above, demonstrate the fact that location is obviously of major importance to the frequency of use of public sector facilities. However, there are a series of reasons why public sector facilities end up on sites that may not promote optimum usage. These are:

- **Inherited facilities**   Many institutions end up being located on a site because they inherit facilities. For instance, many hospitals in the UK are located on the site of nineteenth-century workhouses. Whiston Hospital on Merseyside is an example of a hospital that is on the site of a facility built in 1843 to house a Poor Law institution called the Prescott Union Workhouse and Infirmary. Once set up, relocating any facility such as a hospital would be very costly.

- **Donated land**   This is very often the case with recreational areas such as parks as well as a number of universities in the UK. Heriot–Watt University in Edinburgh relocated out of old city centre accommodation to a large greenfield site 6 miles from the city centre which was donated to them by Midlothian County Council. No site of that size would have been available in the centre of Edinburgh. However, some potential students may have preferred to be located in the city centre.

- **Centralized administration**   To make the administration of central or local government more efficient, departments are located in one principal administration building. This location has very little to do with encouraging use of the services by the end consumer. Flintshire County Council built County Hall one mile outside the rural town of Mold. Theatr Clwyd, the major theatre in North Wales, is located alongside. Neither is easily accessible to anyone without transport.

- **Site availability**   Facilities are sometimes located on secondary sites as prime sites are unavailable.

- **Inexpensive land**   This is probably the overriding factor in major location decisions. Generally it fails to take into account the cost of facilities being under-utilized because the location is unattractive to the consumer of the service.

In the public sector, as in the private sector, an organization requires a distribution strategy. This strategy first has to establish some clear objectives.

These can be set in a number of ways, such as:

- Response times required for emergency services to arrive after an emergency call.

- The number of books circulated in a particular time frame for a library service.

- The number of times a client is contacted in a period of time for a social services department.

Once clear distribution objectives have been established the organization then has to decide:

- How many outlets it needs in a particular area to achieve its objectives.

- Whether it should provide those services direct or through another agency whether public or private.

When making these decisions the organization should realize that services and facilities in some cases can be split, i.e. a physiotherapy service can be delivered direct to the client.

9.11   e-Marketing perspective

There are numerous ways in which e-commerce technology could affect existing marketing channels. These could be fairly benign developments undertaken by current intermediaries, such as the installation of IT systems that create cost reductions or greater efficiencies in particular business units or processes. In Germany, the world's fifth largest retail group Metro has been experimenting with developments in smart logistics. These developments include:

- Wireless electronic labels on supermarket shelves that can be changed automatically from a back office PC.

- Smart self-scan check-outs that can compare the weight of a shopping bag with the items a customer has scanned to ensure the store is not defrauded.

- Radio Frequency Identification Tags (RFID), or 'talking bar codes' attached to each unit of stock. These tags consist of a tiny micro chip with a small antenna and each holds a unique identification code. These tags are read as they go past readers and their location is reported to a central data base. Metro can track an individual product's progress through all stages of its distribution channel. The result has been that inventories are able to be kept up to date, shelves are kept fully stocked and stock losses are down. This system can alert shop staff as to when shelve stock is falling low or even when stock is reaching its sell-by date.

Illustrative example 9.5
Blackwell's Bookshops

Blackwell's has been operating academic bookshops for 125 years, but in November 2004 it announced that it was considering the future of some of its 61 stores in the light of intensive competition from Internet operators. Despite being the first online bookstore in the UK, in 2003 Blackwell's had sales of around £68m. Although Internet sales of books still only amount to 5% of the total market, Amazon, the market leader, had total sales (including non-book sales) of £250m.

Some researchers have speculated that e-commerce not only could increase the efficiency of existing channels but also could lead to the complete replacement of the conventional bricks and mortar retail operation or at the very least have a dramatic affect on a traditional retailer's market share and profitability (Christensen and Tedlow, 2000). Although there has been considerable growth in on-line retailing there has been little evidence of the demise of traditional intermediaries, apart from some very specialist markets such as those for computer software.

The growth of on-line retailing, however, has been rising almost exponentially. In January 1999 Fletcher Research was reported as predicting that the UK on-line retail market would be worth £3 billion by 2003. In December 2003, the Office for National Statistics reported that in the year 2002 actual on-line sales had reached the level of £23.3bn. Although key growth areas were books and CDs, a survey by IMRG estimated that on-line clothing sales alone made up £600m of that total. Although on-line sales in 2002 are impressive they still only accounted for 1.2% of all retail sales that year. This is a similar percentage figure that American on-line sales reached in 2003. The US Commerce Department indicated that on-line sales had reached $3.5 trillion, amounting to 1.6% of the total retail market (Note: These US figures do not include on-line travel services, financial brokers or ticket sales agencies.)

The interesting question is why there has been such growth in on-line retailing. Does it appeal to specific market segments and what need does this type of marketing channel fulfil? A study by Karayanni (2003) suggests that the Web-shoppers were more concerned with time efficiency, availability of shopping on a 24 hour basis and queue avoidance. These are time-pressured consumers who seek to save time on shopping activities and wish to undertake this type of activity at a point in the day that is convenient to their needs. It is easy to speculate that maybe this description fits some consumers all of the time; perhaps at times any consumer may need to purchase under time-constrained circumstances. However, another key aspect of the study was that Web-shoppers were less concerned with the enjoyable aspects of shopping that can be gained through physical outlets. A study of attitudes to shopping in the UK undertaken by Mintel in 1986 found that a significant percentage of consumers found shopping to be educational, creative, active, relaxing, social and fun. In fact a majority of consumers shopping for clothes reported these aspects as being important attributes of their shopping experience. It may be therefore that on-line shopping will emerge as a complementary rather than a competitive channel to the traditional bricks and mortar retailer.

Summary

Whether you are in the public, private, or non-profit-making sector, distribution is a critical factor in the success of your organization. Every organization should have a clearly thought out distribution strategy that will allow it to achieve its objectives. Distribution decisions are generally more expensive and longer-term than other areas of the marketing mix. For instance, if necessary, a pricing policy can be changed overnight. However, once a distribution facility is established, such as an out of town retail outlet, it is not easy to dispose of. Even channels of distribution can be hard to change, given the complex nature of the relationship between channel members. Distribution is no longer an overlooked area of the marketing mix, but an area that is of growing importance to organizations, especially to those that wish to differentiate themselves on the basis of quality service.

Discussion questions

1   If you were a producer of an exclusive sports car what areas would you want to have control over in the relationship with your dealerships?

2   Taking an organization of your choice, assess the advantages and disadvantages of its channels of distribution. Does this organization's current distribution relate to any of the strategies outlined above? If this organization was setting up from new, what channel of distribution would you suggest it chooses?

3   If you were given £500 to buy a new chair, how would you go about making the purchase? Would you go to a particular retailer?

4   You are the brand manager of Chillwood, a brand of frozen foods. The UK market is broken down as follows: brand leader 30%, retailer's own label 38%, Chillwood 12%, others 10%. A large supermarket chain

holding 15% of the UK market has asked you to make a substantial contribution to their advertising and promotional bill to help finance their store opening programme. In return you are promised no special treatment, however, you are aware that they are undertaking a review of the brands they wish to stock in future. What actions would you recommend to your manager over both the short and longer term?

5 Examine public sector institutions located in the areas where you live. Why is your local hospital located where it is? Where is your local leisure centre? Why?

References

Christensen, C.M. and Tedlow, R.S. (2000) Patterns of disruption in retailing. *Harvard Business Review*, Jan–Feb, pp. 42–5.

Drucker, P.F. (1973) *Management: Tasks, Responsibilities, Practices*. Harper and Row, p. 62.

Karayanni, D.A. (2003) Web-shoppers and non-shoppers: compatibility, relative advantage and demographics. *European Business Review*, Vol. 15, No. 3, pp. 141–52.

McCammon, B.C. (1970) Perspectives on distribution programming, in L.P. Bucklin (ed.), *Vertical Marketing Systems*. Scott Foresman, pp. 32–51.

McGoldrick, P.J. (1990) *Retail Marketing*. McGraw-Hill, p. 7.

McStravic, R.E. (1977) *Marketing Health Care*. Aspen Systems Corporation, p. 167.

Perlman, R. (1975) *Consumers and Social Services*. Wiley, p. 55.

10

Analysing competitors and competitive advantage

About this chapter

Business success is as much determined by the actions of competitors as the actions of the organization itself. For example, the success of Coca-Cola is partly determined by the actions of Pepsi Cola. This chapter explores the increasingly vital practice of competitive intelligence and examines how organizations can use such a function to support/develop successful marketing strategies. Gathering, analysing and disseminating intelligence relating to competitors' strategies, goals, procedures and products greatly underpins competitiveness.

Marketing strategy aims to generate sustainable competitive advantage. The process is influenced by industry position, experience curves, value effects and other factors, such as product life cycle. In any given market place, businesses must adopt defensive and attacking strategies. Such actions aim to maintain and/or increase market share. Organizations need to ensure their strategic position is relevant to current/future market conditions.

After reading this chapter, you will understand:

- The basic competitive intelligence cycle.

- The nature and development of competitive advantage.

- Experience and value effects.

- Offensive and defensive strategies.

- The use of the product/market matrix in strategic development.

- PIMS analysis.

10.1   What is competitive intelligence?

Competitive intelligence has something of an image problem. The term conjures up an image of elicit activities involving private detectives, telephoto lenses and hidden microphones. While such images are not completely unappealing, they are far removed from the truth. Put simply, competitive intelligence is a structured, ethical and legal process designed to gather, analyse and distribute data/information relating to current, and potential, competitors. The key to successful competitive intelligence is the ability to turn basic raw data into actionable intelligence. Actionable intelligence involves providing decision-makers with timely, appropriate information that facilitates action. Additionally, competitive intelligence stresses the need to protect business activities against competitors' intelligence-gathering operations.

The need for competitive intelligence (CI) has always been recognized. Indeed, Sun Tzu's *The Art of War*, written in China around 400 BC, makes many references to CI:

Know the enemy and know yourself, in a hundred battles you will never be defeated.

Such reference is equally applicable to today's business world. Given the established business trends of (a) globalization, (b) rapid technological development and (c) merger and acquisition, CI is likely to be a strategic priority for most organizations. Currently, management information tends to fall into two main categories. First, reporting and control information; this monitors what has happened internally within any given period. Secondly, information relating to key performance indicators providing measures of success/failure relative to pre-set benchmarks (e.g. accounting ratios, profit and loss accounts, etc.). Such data is of course necessary, but managers increasingly need to be forward-looking. CI serves this purpose.

Illustrative example 10.1
Nike: the sports footwear market

Reebok established that design and fashion, as opposed to functional performance, were increasingly driving the sports footwear market. Reebok viewed their products as being image-driven as opposed to Nike's performance-driven product development. At first, Nike ignored the Reebok product lines and subsequently lost significant market share. It took layoffs and a management restructuring before Nike acknowledged their competition. Nike paid the price for failing to pay close attention to one of their key competitors.

CI can provide a number of useful functions within any organization. These can be summarized as follows:

- **Anticipating competitors' activities**   The most obvious advantage of CI is in provision of system(s) to consider the likely action of specific competitors. The various strengths and weaknesses of the opposition can be considered and frameworks established to anticipate and pre-empt competitor initiatives. Early warning of competitors' actions enables the organization to judge the seriousness of a threat and develop appropriate responses. The process may also uncover potential competitors who are about to target your existing customer base or industry activities.

- **Analysing industry trends**   By examining the actions of groups of competitors within specific segments and/or market leaders it is possible to proactively establish growing trends. If management can spot the convergence of technologies and operating procedures, it is possible to 'steal a march' on competitors.

- **Learning and innovation**   The CI process offers tremendous opportunities to learn. CI forces managers to have an external focus. By constantly reviewing the opposition, we are better able to develop, adapt and innovate our own product offerings. For example, the process of reverse engineering – involving detailed examination of competitors' products – can provide a valuable insight into improving our own products. Scenario planning exercises, which anticipate competitors' actions, can enhance the organization's understanding of the competitive environment.

- **Improved communication**   Key principles of CI are: (a) the delivery of concise, timely information to decision-makers and (b) the ability to share information across functional boundaries and provide wider access to knowledge. These general concepts do much to enhance overall corporate communication and promote teamwork. Correctly applied, CI concepts enable staff to overcome many problems associated with information overload.

The reality is that most organizations have some form of competitive intelligence. For example, they conduct benchmarking exercises, commission market research or monitor competitors' prices. CI offers the opportunity to bring together the various strands of information that already exist into one cohesive, practical system.

10.2   The competitive intelligence cycle

Kahaner (1997) developed the concept of the CI cycle (see Figure 10.1). This basic concept is derived from government agency intelligence-gathering operations (e.g. the CIA).

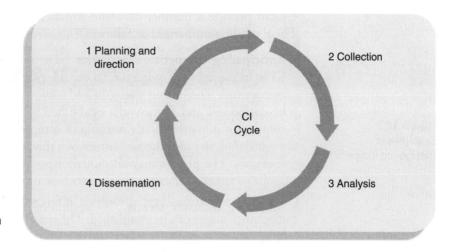

Figure 10.1
Competitive
intelligence cycle
(*Source:* adapted from
Kahaner, 1997)

Planning and directing

The cycle begins with establishing intelligence requirements. It is important to prioritize information needs and set appropriate time-scales/reporting periods. This phase requires a detailed understanding of what business decisions are being taken and how information will be used. When prioritizing information it is important to differentiate between 'targeted intelligence' – collected to achieve a specific objective – and 'awareness intelligence' – collecting general information, which will be 'filtered' in order to build a general picture of the competitive environment. Targeted intelligence is used to resolve specific problems, while awareness intelligence is designed to monitor the competitive environment on an on-going basis. The planning process is concerned with obtaining the correct balance between the two.

Collection

Based on established intelligence requirements, a collection strategy is now developed. Pollard (1999) advocates translating key intelligence requirements into more specific key intelligence questions and then identifying and monitoring intelligence indicators. These intelligence indicators are identifiable signals that are likely to precede particular competitor actions (see example in Figure 10.2).

Common sources of competitive information are considered later in this chapter.

Analysis

Analysis is concerned with converting raw data into useful information. The process involves classification, evaluation, collation and synthesis.

Key intelligence question(s)	Intelligence indicators
Is the competitor about to initiate a customer loyalty scheme?	Actively recruiting customer service staff
	Buying media advertising space

Figure 10.2
Examples of
intelligence indicators

Once information has been processed informed judgements relating to competitors' intent can be established. The classification stage may involve tagging data as: (a) primary – facts directly from the source (e.g. interviews, annual reports, promotional material, etc.) and (b) secondary – reported by third parties (e.g. newspaper comment, books and analysts' reports). Data can then be prioritized in terms of importance. When necessary, triangulation can be used to confirm findings. This involves cross-checking an item against a number of sources. The CIA (1999) offers the following guidelines relating to classification of data/information: (a) *Fact* – verified information, something known to exist or have happened; (b) *Information* – the content of reports, research and analytical reflection on an intelligence issue that helps analysts evaluate the likelihood that something is factual and thereby reduces uncertainty; (c) *Direct information* – information which can, as a rule, be considered factual, because of the nature of the sources, the sources' direct access to the information, and readily verifiable content; (d) *Indirect information* – information that may or may not be factual, the doubt reflecting some combination of the sources' questionable reliability, lack of direct access to information and complex content; and (e) *Sourcing* – depicting the manner, or method, in which the information was obtained, in order to assist in evaluating the likely factual content.

History teaches us the importance of evaluation and classification. Most military, political and commercial intelligence failures have not been due to inadequate information collection, but due to poor evaluation of available information.

Many analytical tools/techniques exist to facilitate management decision-making and such techniques provide vehicles for forecasting/speculating competitive intent. Common techniques included:

- **SWOT/Portfolio analysis** The classic SWOT or portfolio analysis (e.g. Boston Matrix, Ansoff Matrix, etc. see later) is applied to the competitor(s) in question.

- **Behavioural traits** While not an absolute indicator of future action, it is true to say that organizational leaders tend to repeat past successful behaviour and avoid previous mistakes. Therefore, to some degree, future behaviour is likely to be predictable. Understanding the behaviour and reactions of rival corporate leaders to given sets of circumstances can be highly revealing of future intent.

- **War gaming** In-house teams' take on the simulated role of competitors for a workshop exercise. The team is provided with actual data and asked to simulate the strategies/actions they believe the competitor is most likely to follow. Their responses are then analysed in a de-brief session. Numerous advantages stem from this process, such as: identifying competitors' weaknesses, enhancing teamwork and identifying information 'gaps' relating to knowledge of competitors.

- **Synthesis reports** Information from numerous sources is collated under common key themes. It is possible to electronically scan large amounts of text for key words (e.g. brand names, patent applications, etc.) and selectively extract/flag information. Techniques such as word and pattern analysis can identify underlying themes and trends.

- **Mission statement analysis** The main aim of analysis is to predict what a competitor will do. Therefore it is possible to analyse competitors' mission statements in order to establish their goals, values and generic strategies. Analysing how mission statements have changed or been interpreted over time is highly insightful. Rumours of likely activity can be checked against a rival stated mission. Does the rumour seem to equate with overall corporate aims?

Dissemination

CI needs to be tailored to meet user needs. Effective dissemination is based on clarity, simplicity and appropriateness to need. CI should (if merited) form the basis of competitive action plans. A useful test is to consider what are the implications of the intelligence not being passed on. If there are no real implications, it is questionable whether it is necessary. Research shows that many CI projects fail during this phase. Therefore, presentation of CI is critical. Pollard (1999) recommends developing structured templates for reports, as follows: (1) *Information* – bullet points, graphics, etc.; (2) *Analysis* – interpretation of information; (3) *Implication* – what could happen; and (4) *Actions*.

10.3   Strategy formulation: an overview

It is important to recognize that alternative methods of achieving objectives exist. The ability to identify and evaluate these alternatives

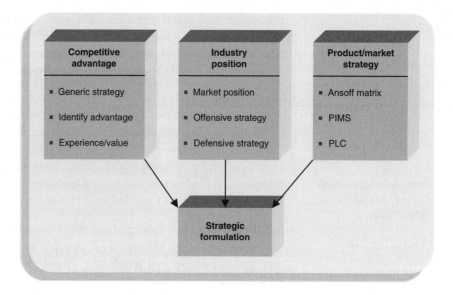

Figure 10.3
The formulation of strategy

forms the essence of strategy development. The goal is to obtain sustainable competitive advantage within predetermined markets.

Figure 10.3 summarizes the process.

10.4 Competitive advantage

The notions of competitive advantage and marketing strategy are intrinsically linked. Competitive advantage is the process of identifying a fundamental and sustainable basis from which to compete. Ultimately, marketing strategy aims to deliver this advantage in the market place.

Porter (see Porter, 1990) identifies three **generic strategies** – fundamental sources of competitive advantage. These are: cost leadership, differentiation and focus. Arguably, these provide a basis for all strategic activity and underpin the large number of marketing strategies available to the organization. Additionally, management needs to define the competitive scope of the business – targeting a broad or narrow range of industries/ customers (see Figure 10.4), essentially either operating industry-wide or targeting specific market segments. Each generic strategy is examined in turn.

Cost leadership

One potential source of competitive advantage is to seek an overall cost leadership position within an industry, or industry sector. Here the focus of strategic activity is to maintain a low cost structure. The desired structure is achievable via the aggressive pursuit of policies such as controlling

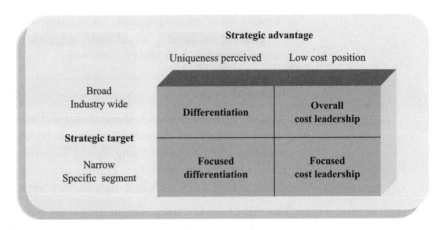

Figure 10.4
Competitive advantage
(*Source:* adapted from
Porter, 1990)

overhead cost, economies of scale, cost minimization in areas such as marketing and R&D, global sourcing of materials and experience effects. Additionally, the application of new technology to traditional activities offers significant opportunity for cost reduction.

Difficulties can exist in maintaining cost leadership. Success can attract larger, better-resourced competitors. If market share falls, economies of scale become harder to achieve and fixed costs, such as overheads, are difficult to adjust in the short-to-medium term. Additionally, cost leaderships and high volume strategy are likely to involve high initial investment costs and are often associated with 'commodity' type products where price discounting and price wars are common.

Remember, low cost does not need to equate automatically to low price. Products provided at average, or above average, industry price (while maintaining cost leadership) can generate higher than average margins.

The basic drivers of cost leadership include:

- **Economy of scale** This is perhaps the single biggest influence on unit cost. Correctly managed, volume can drive efficiency and enhances purchasing leverage. Additionally, given large scale operations, learning and experience effects (see later) can be a source of cost reduction.

- **Linkages and relationships** Being able to link activities together and form relationships can generate cost savings. For example a 'Just-in-Time' manufacturing system could reduce stockholding costs and enhance quality. Forging relationships with external organizations is also vital. If industry partners were to share development and distribution costs, or activities were 'outsourced' to specialist operators, a substantial reduction in overheads is possible.

- **Infrastructure** Factors such as location, availability of skills and governmental support greatly affect the firm's cost base. Given the development of information technology and the global economy it is possible to have a world-wide infrastructure and selectively place activities in low cost areas.

Differentiation

Here the product offered is distinct and differentiated from the competition. The source of differentiation must be on a basis of value to the customer. The product offering should be perceived as unique and ideally should offer the opportunity to command a price premium. Will customers pay more for factors such as design, quality, branding and service levels?

The skills base is somewhat different from a cost leadership strategy and will focus on creating reasons for purchase, innovation and flexibility. Remember, often it is the perception of performance as opposed to actual performance that generates differentiation.

There are several 'downsides' to this type of strategy. First, it can be costly, with associated costs outweighing the benefits. Secondly, innovation and other initiatives can be duplicated by competitors. Thirdly, customer needs change with time and the basis of differentiation can become less important as customers focus on other attributes. For example, in the car market, safety may now be seen as more important than fuel economy.

Common sources of differentiation include:

- **Product performance** Does product performance enhance its value to the customer? Factors such as quality, durability and capability all offer potential points of differentiation. Performance is evaluated relative to competitor's products and gives customers a reason to prefer one product over another.

- **Product perception** Often the perception of a product is more important than actual performance. Hopefully, the product has an enduring emotional appeal generating brand loyalty. This is commonly achieved via marketing communications (advertising, branding, endorsement, etc.) and direct experience of customer groups.

- **Product augmentation** We can differentiate by augmenting the product in a way that adds value. For example, high levels of service, after sales support, affordable finance and competitive pricing all serve to enhance the basic product offering. It is common for distributors, such as retailers, to provide the added-value augmentation. Product augmentation is dealt with in Chapter 9.

Focus

The organization concentrates on a narrower range of business activities. The aim is to specialize in a specific market segment and derive detailed customer knowledge. This focus, or niche, strategy can also generate the benefits of cost leadership or differentiation within a defined market segment (see Figure 10.4). For example, it may be possible to obtain cost leadership within a chosen segment or that segment may regard your product offering as differentiated.

Success within a specialist niche can attract competitors – perhaps much better resourced. Additionally, the narrow business base means more susceptibility to downturns in demand from key customer groups.

A focus strategy is based on factors such as:

- **Geographic area** Using geographic segmentation allows a product to be tailored to local needs. The local association may offer the potential to differentiate the offering (e.g. Champagne comes from a specific French region) and protect the market from larger predators. Another rationale for such segmentation is to serve markets too small or isolated to be viable on a large scale (e.g. rural communities).

- **End user focus** It is possible to focus on a specific type of user as opposed to the entire market. Specialization offers the opportunity to get 'close' to customers and have a better understanding of their needs (e.g. specialist hi-fi manufacturer). Additionally, within a narrow segment the focused organization may be able to offer the choice, service and economy of scale not available to more broadly based competitors. This strategy often works by selecting specific points on the price/quality spectrum within a given market (e.g. discount food retailer).

- **Product/product line specialist** The organization focuses on a single product type or product line. Value is derived from the specialization in terms of skills, volume and range (e.g. industrial power supplies).

Consistency and the alternative view

The 'Porter' view of generic strategy supports the need for consistency of approach. The organization needs to adopt a definite generic strategy. Attempting to mix the above strategies, within a defined market place, may result in failing to achieve the potential benefits and result in the organization being 'stuck in the middle of the road' – not low cost, differentiated nor focused. Figure 10.5 illustrates.

Porter's concept of competitive advantage advocates pursuing one generic strategy and thus avoiding a low profit 'stuck-in-the-middle' position. Alternative views exist. The adoption of common production, quality, marketing and management philosophies by industry competitors may mean that effective differentiation or absolute cost leadership is rarely achieved. Additionally, what managers aren't concerned with controlling costs? Therefore differentiation strategies need a cost focus. It is also possible

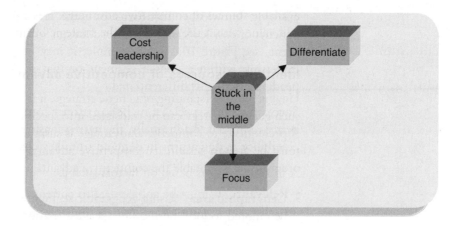

Figure 10.5
Inconsistent strategy

Illustrative example 10.2
SimplyOrg@nic Food Company Ltd: a niche 'e-tailer'

The food retailing business is highly competitive, with large super-market chains (e.g. Tesco) dominating the market place. However, potential exists for specialist retailers. The SimplyOrg@nic Food Company stocks a range of over 1500 organic products. These include fruit and vegetables, meat, fish, wine and beer, groceries, dairy and infant products. Telephone and Internet home shopping allows easy ordering, with products delivered to UK customers before noon on a day of their choice. The company has recently expanded its organic range to cover non-food products – gifts, fabrics and home care items.

While the large supermarket chains offer a range of organic goods, they operate on broad retail bases as opposed to SimplyOrg@nic's specific focus. As a home shopping 'e-tailer' – a dot.com company selling to the general public – focusing on organic goods, the poten-tial exists to create and sustain competitive advantage.

---

to follow '*hybrid strategies*' aiming to offer added value and lower cost. Indeed Fulmer and Goodwin (1993) point out that the two strategies (cost leadership and differentiation) are not mutually exclusive. For instance, total-quality-management programmes have resulted in superior quality and cost reductions.

The reality of modern business is that many successful organizations are 'stuck in the middle' within their competitive environments. This is not to decry the importance of establishing competitive advantage and con-sistency of approach. It merely serves to illustrate the competitive nature of modern business and the importance of uncovering and optimizing all available sources of competitive advantage. It is a question of how best to add value within the context of the strategic business environment.

Identifying sources of competitive advantage

Having an understanding of generic strategy, it is possible to consider how such general strategy can be translated into specific competitive advantage. A prerequisite to competitive advantage is sustainability. The organization must be able to sustain its competitive advantage over the long term. In order to be sustainable the competitive advantage must be:

- **Relevant**   It must be appropriate to current and future market needs. Additionally, it must be relevant to the organization – achievable within the available resource base.

- **Defensible**   There must be barriers to replication, otherwise success will simply be duplicated by competitors. Such barriers tend to be: (1) asset-based – tangible factors controlled by the organization such as: location, plant and machinery, brands and finance; (2) skills-based – the skills and resources required to make optimum use of the assets. Examples include: quality management, brand development, product design and IT skills.

Clearly, competitive advantage must be appropriate to the strategic nature of the industry. An interesting template that evaluates the strategic competitive environment has been developed by the Boston Consultancy Group. This matrix identifies four types of industry (see Figure 10.6). The industries are classified in terms of: size of competitive advantage and number of possible ways to achieve advantage.

- **Stalemate industries**   Here the potential for competitive advantage is limited. Advantages are small and only a few approaches exist to achieving these advantages. Technological advances are commonly adopted by all industry 'players' and we see rapid convergence in product design/performance. Such industries tend to be mature, highly

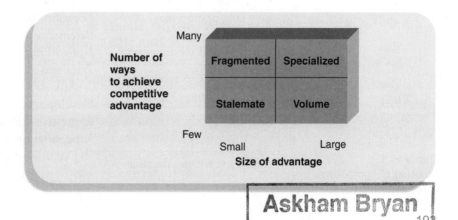

Figure 10.6
BCG strategic
advantage matrix

193

competitive and often akin to commodity type products where price is the key buying criterion (e.g. manufacturing desktop computers).

- **Volume industries** Here few but highly significant advantages exist. These industries are often capital-intensive and are dominated by a few large players who achieve economies of scale (e.g. volume car manufacture).

- **Fragmented** The market's needs are less well defined and numerous ways exist to gain advantage. The industry is often well suited to niche players and profitability may not be linked directly to size. Commonly, organizations grow by offering a range of niche products to different segments – a multi-segmentation strategy (e.g. computer software).

- **Specialized** The potential advantage of differentiation is considerable and numerous ways exist to achieve this advantage. Profitability and size are not automatically related. Such industries include those developing customized solutions to specific problems (e.g. management consultancy) and firms involved in the development/application of innovative technology (e.g. biomedical engineering).

Understanding generic strategies and the application of competitive advantage to the business environment is fundamental to success. Davidson (1997) offers an alternative view and states that competitive advantage is achieved:

whenever you do something better than competitors. If that something is important to consumers, or if a number of small advantages can be combined, you have an **exploitable** competitive advantage. (emphasis added)

Instinctively, this view appeals to the industry practitioner. The most potent sources of competitive advantage are summarized in Table 10.1.

Source of competitive advantage	Examples
Actual product performance	Robust, economic, easy to use
Perception of product	Brand image, product positioning
Low cost operations	Location, buying power
Legal advantage	Patents, contracts and copyright
Alliances and relationships	Networking, procurement
Superior skills	Database management, design skills
Flexibility	Developing customized solutions
Attitude	Aggressive selling, tough negotiation

Source: adapted from Davidson, 1987

Table 10.1
Sources of competitive advantage

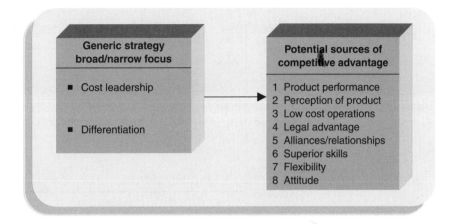

Figure 10.7
Generic strategy and
potential competitive
advantage

Such advantages are underpinned by the previously summarized generic sources of competitive advantage (Porter) and Figure 10.7 illustrates this concept.

10.5 Experience and value effects

Perhaps it is to state the obvious to say experience and ability to create value are closely linked and a major factor in successful marketing strategy. In considering these factors, two useful models are presented below.

The experience curve denotes a pattern of decreasing cost as a result of cumulative experience of carrying out an activity or function. Essentially, it shows how learning effects (repetition and accumulated knowledge) can be combined with volume effects (economy of scale) to derive optimal benefits (see Figure 10.8). With experience, the organization should produce better and lower cost products. The main influence of experience effects has been to promote a high volume/low cost philosophy aiming at a reduction in unit cost. However, in today's competitive business world, organizations cannot simply rely on a 'big is beautiful' strategy based on economy-of-scale and market share. It is important to recognize the importance of learning effects on factors such as product quality and service levels. Such factors hold the key to future success and greatly influence the ability to 'add value' to product offerings.

Eventually, cost and learning effect will display diminishing returns and an optimum level is reached. However, the process never stops. The advent of new technologies may mark a shift in experience and offer new challenges. For example, the large monolithic market leader could be in danger as newer, more forward-thinking competitors readily embrace new technology and the subsequent benefits it brings to today's business environment.

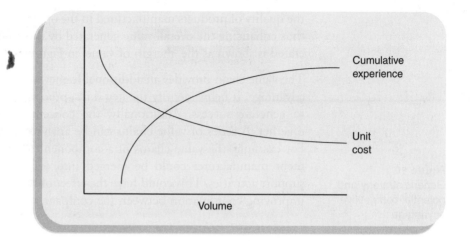

Figure 10.8
Experience curve

Figure 10.9
The value chain
(*Source:* Porter, 1990)

The concept of a **value chain**, developed by Porter, categorizes the organization as a series of processes generating value for customers and other stakeholders. By examining each value creating activity, it is possible to identify sources of potential cost leadership and differentiation.

The value chain (Figure 10.9) splits activities into: **primary activities** – in-bound logistics, operations, outward logistics, marketing/sales and service – and **secondary activities** – infrastructure, human resource management, technology development and procurement. These secondary activities take place in order to support the primary activities. For example, the firm's infrastructure (e.g. management, finance and buildings) serves to support the five primary functions. While each activity generates 'value', the linkages between the activities are critical. Consider the interface between in-bound logistics and operations. A just-in-time logistics system, supported by computerized stock ordering (technology development – secondary activity) could reduce stock costs and enhance the quality of products manufactured in the operations phase of the chain, thus enhancing the overall value generated by the process. The value generated is shown as the 'margin of value' in Figure 10.9.

The value chain provides an additional framework to analyse competitive advantage. It helps identify the key skills, processes and linkages required to generate success. Additionally, the concept can link organizations together. A series of value chains can be analysed as one overall process. For example, the value chains of a component manufacturer and equipment manufacturer could be merged into one system, with common support activities. This could have the effect of reducing overall costs and improving coordination between the companies.

10.6   Industry position

Clearly, strategy formulation must consider the position held within a given industry and the organization's resource base relative to competitors. Successful strategy amounts to implementing plans that meet customer need while effectively dealing with rival competitors. This section examines strategies relative to the competition.

Competitive marketing strategy draws heavily on military strategy. Indeed, many strategic principles can be traced to the analogy of the market place as a battlefield, with competitors as enemy forces. It could be argued that Sun Tsu's classic work from 400 BC on military tactics and philosophy, *The Art of War*, provides as much of an insight into the principles of modern day strategic marketing as it does to military campaigns.

Market position

The position of the organization (or product) within a given market will clearly influence the strategic options available. For example, when comparing the market leader with a smaller 'niche' competitor, it is likely that marked differences exist in: aims, capabilities and resources. When considering a market, competitors break down into four general categories: market leaders, market challengers, market followers and market nichers. Each will be examined in turn.

Market leaders

A market leader is dominant within the given industry or segment. This dominance is normally due to market share. However, some organizations may achieve 'leadership' via innovation or technical expertise. Additionally, the organization may only be a leader in a given segment (e.g. geographic area). Be careful how the term 'market' is defined when talking about market leaders.

The market leader will be a constant target for aggressive competitors and must remain vigilant and proactive. Common strategies include:

- **Expanding the market**   If the total market expands, the leader tends to gain the largest share of this expansion. This can be achieved by finding new users or new uses for the products and by encouraging more use by existing customers.

- **Offensive strategy**   By aggressively pursuing market share, the fight is taken to the competitors.

- **Defensive strategy**   Equally, it is important to protect your existing customer base and ensure that market share is retained.

Offensive and defensive strategies are applicable to all industry 'players' not just market leaders.

Market challengers

Market challengers will seek confrontation and aggressively pursue market share. Often, such organizations are large and well resourced. They are seeking market leadership and present a long-term sustained challenge to the current leader.

Strategies available to challengers include:

- **Selective targeting**   The challenger can target specific competitors. It may attack smaller (perhaps regional) competitors or firms that are equivalent in size and resources. Basically, the challenger is looking to attack weaker competitors – those failing to satisfy the customer in some way, or those under-financed or resourced. By picking-off weaker competitors, challengers enhance their market position.

- **Attack the leader**   The challenger can directly challenge the dominant player. This is often a long-term war of attrition and it is unlikely that market leadership will change over night. Commonly, direct attacks sustained over time erode market share gradually.

Market follower

Being in second place, third or even further down the rankings within an industry may still be an attractive position. Market followers tend to 'shadow' the market leader as opposed to challenge them, unless there is a high degree of certainty that a challenge will be successful – they follow the leader. In simple terms, followers duplicate (to greater or lesser degree) the actions and product offerings of the bigger industry players and avoid 'rocking the boat'.

Typical strategies are:

- **Duplication**   The product offering is duplicated in every possible way, even down to the packaging and promotion. Such strategies are potentially open to legal challenge in the areas of patents and copyright.

- **Adaptation**   Here we adapt the basic product offering. If we can improve on the concept, then potential exists to differentiate ourselves. For example, we may sell the same/similar products but have a reputation for higher levels of customer service.

Market niche

Niche players focus on specific market segments. They are more specialized in nature and seek to gain competitive advantage by adding value in some way appropriate to specific target groups.

Focus strategies, adopted by niche players, were outlined earlier and commonly involve: geographic, end-user or product line specialization.

Offensive and defensive strategies

Two fundamentals exist in the battle for market share – the ability to gain market share and being able to retain existing market share. To achieve these objectives, organizations need offensive (attacking) and defensive strategies. Kotler *et al.* (1999) identify a number of attacking and defensive strategies. Such strategies are used in combination by organizations in order to successfully compete in the modern business world.

Offensive strategies, designed primarily to gain market share, are shown in Figure 10.10. Each is summarized in turn.

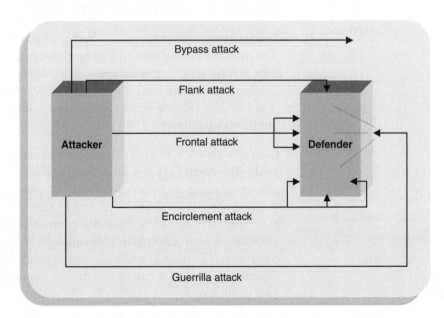

Figure 10.10
Attacking strategies
(*Source:* Kotler *et al.*,
1999)

- **Frontal attack**   This is an all-out attack on a competitor. Generally, such an attack requires a sustained effort. Attackers must be certain they have the resources to endure a long hard struggle and survive potentially heavy initial losses. They are likely to face a well-established competitor with broadly the same product offering. Therefore, the attacker needs a clearly defined advantage. For example, the attacker may have a cost advantage or its brands may be perceived more positively.

- **Flank attack**   This draws on the analogy of the battlefield, where the flanks were always the weakest point of any army. Equally, this can be the case in the business world and 'flanking' is achieved by attacking selective market segments where the competitor is relatively weak. By concentrating resources on narrow areas it is possible to achieve superiority. The key to success is to identify worthwhile, under-served segments. For example, a computer manufacturer may feel a rival only offers a limited, and somewhat dated, range of laptop computers. This could be a weak 'flank' vulnerable to attack.

- **Encirclement attack**   Here the aim is to offer a range of products that effectively encircle the competitor. Each of these products will tend to stress a different attribute and leave the competitor's product facing a series of more focused rivals. For example, in marketing soap powder, the market leader could be encircled by three rival products each stressing a different attribute: cleaning power, low cost and environmentally friendly. The combined effect of the three rivals is to undermine the positioning of the market leader. One obvious danger of this strategy is that it leads to a proliferation of products. These may compete with each other and are likely to drive up cost.

- **Bypass attack**   Perhaps more a policy of avoidance rather than attack. The attacker moves into areas where competitors are not active. This may involve targeting geographic areas, applying new technologies or developing new distribution systems. For example, a tour operator could bypass existing retail distribution outlets and sell direct to the public via mail order.

- **Guerrilla attack**   Tactical (short-term) marketing initiatives are used to gradually weaken the opposition. Sudden price cuts, burst of promotional activity or other such tactics are used to create product awareness and slowly erode market share. Such attacks may be a precursor to a longer, more sustained attack. Additionally, guerrilla attacks are not restricted to marketing – legal action such as lawsuits can be used to harass and restrict competitors. The key to success is the unpredictability of such attacks and their ability to destroy morale and deplete resources, such as management time or finance.

Illustrative example 10.3
Marks & Spencer's new style lingerie stores

Marks & Spencer aim to maintain its market position within the lingerie sector. By way of a position defence, it plans to offer a value-added product in the women's lingerie market. M&S will open a number of smaller specialist outlets which will only sell ladies' underwear. The stores will be branded as 'msl' (short for M&S Lingerie), and have a different retail format – softer lighting, specialist staff, etc. This move aims to strengthen M&S's current position in the market and make the company less vulnerable to specialist operators and 'designer-label' products. Thus, 'msl' displays the classic characteristic of a position defence.

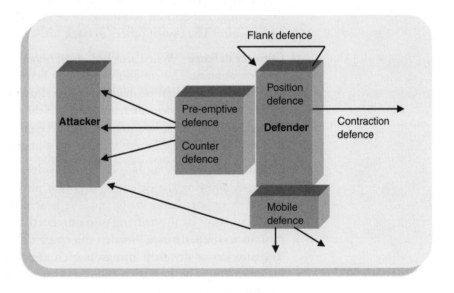

Figure 10.11
Defensive strategies
(*Source:* Kotlet *et al.*, 1999)

It is true to say that for every offensive move a defensive counter exists. Indeed, the 'backbone' of any marketing strategy must be to maintain market share. Regardless of market position, firms must continually defend their current business against competitors. A strong defence should deter, as well as repel, rivals and allow the organization to build on its strengths. Common defensive strategies are summarized by Kotler *et al.* (1999) in Figure 10.11.

- **Position defence** A position defence aims to strengthen the current position and shut out the competition. The aim is to use the distinct competencies and assets of the organization to build an unassailable position in the market place. If the defending firms can offer a differentiated, value-added product to customers its market position will be maintained, if not enhanced. Defending a market position is often dependent on brand management, service levels and distribution.

- **Flank defence**   Not only do organizations need to protect their main areas of operation, but they must also protect any weak spots (flanks). First, managers must identify weak areas and the potential impact of an 'attack' on the core business. Secondly, they need to be sure that the flank defence is sustainable. For example, a food retailer may see its flank as frozen products. Here it competes with specialist frozen food retailers. The flank could be protected by maintaining several 'loss leader' (sold at below cost) products.

- **Pre-emptive defence**   This involves striking at potential competitors before they attack. The aim is to pre-empt their actions and reduce the potential competitive threat. This may involve using, or threatening to use, the attacking strategies (e.g. guerrilla attack) shown in Figure 10.11. Large, powerful 'players' deter competitors by routinely threatening, but seldom actioning, price cuts or increased promotional expenditure. They warn others to back off.

- **Counter defence**   When attacked, most organizations will respond with a counter-attack. The counter-attack may be immediate or a more considered response might be made once the situation has settled down. By nature, counter defences are reactive, and if the position defence is strong enough no additional counter may be necessary. For example, a strong well-established brand loyalty may see off a price-cutting competitor.

- **Mobile defence**   A mobile defence involves a flexible and adaptive response, allowing the defender to switch into new areas of interest as threats or opportunities materialize. It is achieved by broadening current markets or by diversifying into unrelated activities. To illustrate, an insurance company may broaden the range of financial services offered to customers or diversify into areas such as estate agency and property management. The key is to build a strategic presence in a range of lucrative areas/segments.

- **Contraction defence**   It may prove impossible to defend all operational activities. Therefore, a selective strategic withdrawal could be the best option. By sacrificing some activities, resources are freed to defend core activities. For example, consider a computer company. It could withdraw from the high volume/low margin personal computer market and focus on more profitable areas, such as maintenance and software development.

10.7   Product and market strategies

Product/market strategies are detailed in nature. They address the specific market impact of a product or product line. This section examines three

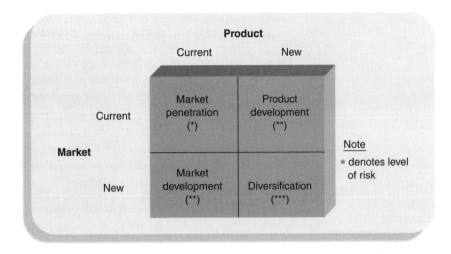

Figure 10.12
Product/market matrix

concepts useful in formulating such strategies: the product/market matrix, PIMS analysis and the product life cycle.

Product/market matrix

Ansoff (1975) developed a policy/market matrix (or 'Ansoff' matrix) which provides a useful linkage between products and markets. The matrix (Figure 10.12) considers four combinations of product and market. Each combination suggests a growth strategy.

The organization's potential is determined by the combination of current and new products within current and new markets. Additionally, the element of risk must be considered. As organizations move away from existing markets and products the potential risk factors increase.

- **Market penetration** The aim is to increase sales of existing products in current markets. An aggressive marketing drive, via factors such as competitive pricing, sales promotion or advertising, can expand the share of an existing market. Dealing with familiar customers and products is low risk and provides a starting point to planned growth. However, the potential for market penetration is often limited and strategic plans may require additional options to be pursued.

- **Market development** Referring to Figure 10.12, market development aims to find new markets for existing products. This could involve new geographic markets (e.g. exporting), adding distribution channels or finding new market segments. For example, a manufacturer of sports clothing may try to position its products as fashion items and target a different set of retailers.

- **Product development** Organizations must up-date their product portfolio to remain competitive. Ideally, a balanced product portfolio

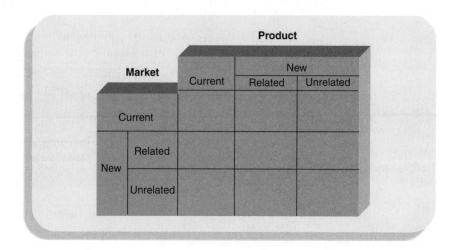

Figure 10.13
Expanded
product/market matrix

should exist, with established products generating funds for product development.

• **Diversification** This involves moving beyond existing areas of operation and actively seeking involvement in unfamiliar activities. Diversification can be related – having linkages to existing activities – or unrelated – venturing into totally new activities. While unrelated diversification may spread risk, it can be difficult to achieve.

The product/market matrix can be expanded to consider the degree to which new activities are related or unrelated (Figure 10.13) to the core business. As previously stated, it is more difficult to achieve success in unrelated activities. Hence, unrelated diversification of product and/or markets is often tackled via joint ventures, mergers and acquisitions.

10.8 PIMS analysis

Many influential marketing studies have examined the link between profit and marketing strategy. These PIMS (profit impact of market strategy) studies aimed to identify the key drivers of profitability and have recognized the importance of market share as such a driver. Generally speaking, profits will increase in line with relative market share. This relationship (Figure 10.14) has influenced marketing thinking, promoting actions aimed at increasing market share as a route to profitability.

While such a relationship is often true, it is not universal, and some industries display a 'V-shaped' relationship. Here, profitability can initially fall until a critical mass, in terms of market share, is reached. The effect of the 'V-curve' is polarization – industries with small niche players and large dominant companies. Medium-sized firms see profits fall until critical

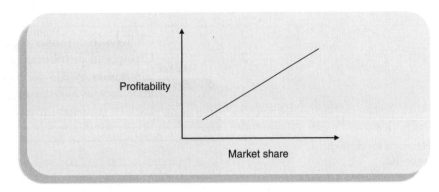

Figure 10.14
Profit related to market share

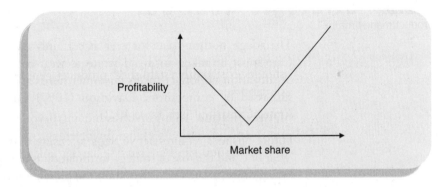

Figure 10.15
V-shaped profit/market share relationship

Illustrative example 10.4
Nike: targeting the women's market

Nike recognizes the global importance of the women's sports market. In order to achieve a dominant position in this market, Nike has announced the formation of a new unit. The unit combines design, manufacturing and sales and specifically aims to increase the company's share of the international women's sportswear market.

Nike's strategy can be considered in terms of the 'Ansoff matrix'. The company appears to be looking at a process of market penetration and product development (see Figure 10.12 – the product/market matrix).

mass is reached. This makes it very difficult for small/medium companies to grow. Figure 10.15 shows the relationship.

Clearly, the marketing strategist must consider the nature of these relationships and not blindly pursue market share. It should be possible to determine the optimal market share/profitability position.

1	Changes in customer requirements
2	Changes in distribution systems
3	Innovation by competitors
4	Poor control of company costs
5	Lack of consistent investment
6	Ill-advised changes in successful strategy

Table 10.2
Reasons for strategic wear-out

10.9 Strategic wear-out

The adage 'nothing lasts for ever' is certainly true of marketing strategy. Care must be taken to avoid strategic wear-out. This occurs when the organization no longer meets customer needs and the pursued strategy is surpassed by competitors. Davidson (1997) summarizes the causes of strategic wear-out (see Table 10.2).

Future business requires active steps to ensure that your strategy does not 'wear out' and the role of strategy formulation is to develop/maintain a marketing orientation. This is based on the premise of defining customer need and prospering through customer satisfaction and loyalty. Sound general and financial management should underpin this orientation and the entire corporate focus should relate to the key asset of any business – customers.

10.10 Difficult market conditions

Marketing strategy is often linked to a premise of favourable market conditions. For example, strategies tend to work well when we are experiencing incremental growth – the market demand grows annually. However, many industries (arguably the majority of industries) are now experiencing static or declining demand. Such markets are hostile in nature and feature factors such as: volatility, over-capacity, price discounting, reduced profit margins and 'down-sizing'.

Given these conditions Aaker (1995) advocates a number of strategic options for declining and/or hostile markets. These include:

• **Generate growth** Can we revitalize the industry by finding growth? This could be possible via: (1) encouraging existing users to increase usage, (2) developing new markets for our products and (3) finding new applications for existing products or technologies/skills. The Ansoff matrix (see Figure 10.12) provides a useful analytical framework for this purpose.

> ### Illustrative example 10.5
> ### Apple iMAC
>
> Despite increasing levels of sales, the PC market has proved highly hostile. The market has massive price discounting, domination by software suppliers, as opposed to hardware manufacturers and an increasing number of global competitors. Despite such market conditions prevailing Apple's iMAC PC went on to become the company's fastest selling product. iMAC achieved a growth rate of over 210% in the UK home market and heralded a dynamic turn-round in the company's fortunes. The product presented a fresh and innovative challenge to existing, slow, boringly styled, difficult to use Windows-based PCs. The product made a virtue of consumers' benefits such as speed, ease of use and simplicity. It helped widen the potential user base for Apple products and attract back the software developers so essential to future developments.

- **Survival**   Organizations can survive by effectively managing cost and clearly signalling their commitment to the industry and its customers. Clearly, there is a need to manage cost structures, with experience effects and economy of scale becoming vital. Organizations may rationalize their product portfolios and focus on larger more profitable customers. Conversely, perhaps correctly, organizations may actually expand their product range, aiming to cover the maximum number of customers by offering a wide range of price points. We may witness take-overs, mergers and acquisitions, as organizations aim to reduce cost and generate economies of scale. A portfolio approach can be taken, with 'cash cows' supporting operations/products which are currently struggling but are deemed to have long-term potential. A useful strategic option is to reduce industry exit barriers by selectively buying-out elements of a competitor's current business. For example, we could take over their commitment to supplying spare parts and maintain existing products. This 'shake-out' inevitable leaves the industry with fewer but larger competitors.

- **Exit strategy**   If business conditions are particularly unfavourable, prudence may dictate withdrawal from the industry. Such action will involve overcoming exit barriers such as the costs associated with downsizing (e.g. redundancy, legal costs of breaking contracts, etc.) and handling commitments to existing customers. Exit strategy can be rapid – withdrawing immediately – or a slow phased withdrawal with activities being gradually run-down. Remember exiting a market may have repercussions for other activities and products, as it affects 'goodwill' and customer confidence.

10.11   e-Marketing perspective

A key question is: do we require a separate e-marketing strategy? Arguably, the Internet, and associated technologies, should be integrated into existing strategic plans. However, such views tend to relegate the Internet to 'just another form of advertising'. Given that e-marketing is an enabling technology, a separate strategy may be required to fully develop the interactive advantages of such media. Such plans need to tackle strategic issues and be integrated into existing value-adding activities, otherwise planning tends to focus on superficial design aspects (e.g. website layout). To summarize, a separate e-marketing strategy will:

- Optimize the interactive benefits of the technology.

- Foster integration of technologies into one integrated system.

- Quantify required investment for e-marketing development.

Chaffey *et al.* (2000) outlines three levels of strategic development:

- First generation: Simple website providing 'brouchware'. The site provides one-to-many communication (e.g. user can download product information).

- Provides some degree of activity, with users being able to check product availability, order on-line and conduct basic queries/searches for information. The communication is still mainly one-to-many.

- Fully interactive site, which offers customized one-to-one communication and 'learns' customer preferences. The communication is now one-to-one, and may provide market research information.

Internet marketing needs to generate competitive advantage by providing a 'value proposition'. A value proposition provides a clear rationale for the customer to purchase an item, use a service or return to the website in the future. The proposition should define the provider's competitive advantage. Ideally, the Internet would add additional value to existing offerings. The value proposition should:

- Differentiate the website from other providers.

- Enhance existing product offering (e.g. provide at lower prices).

- Engage the potential user, generating both brand and website loyalty.

Kumar (1999) suggests that organizations need to decide if the Internet will complement existing activities or replace them. Replacement strategies are more likely when:

- Customer access to the Internet is high.

- The Internet can provide better value then existing activities (e.g. a lower price).

- The product/service can be provided directly over the Internet. For example, where the product is purely information-based.

- Products are standardized and don't require the user to try out, evaluate or examine (e.g. books).

Summary

Strategy formulation offers alternative methods of achieving objectives. The process has three components: (1) competitive advantage; (2) industry position; and (3) product/market strategies. The importance of having constant and sustainable strategies cannot be underestimated.

Three generic (fundamental) strategies exist – cost leadership, differentiation and a focused approach. Porter (1990) stresses the importance of adopting one generic source of competitive advantage and thus avoiding the strategic equivalent of 'being stuck in the middle'. These strategies can be expanded upon to generate specific sources of competitive advantage. For example, superior products, perceived advantage or scale of operation are all exploitable competitive advantages. Additionally, it is important to understand the effects of the experience curve and value chains within the individual industry. The primary and secondary activities of a value chain, coupled with experience effects, should support the organization's strategic thrust.

Companies need to examine their position within the market place. They can occupy the role of market leader, challenger, follower or niche player. Marketing strategy needs to be appropriate to the position occupied, relative ambition and resource base. All organizations actively pursue offensive and defensive strategies. The need exists to protect your core business and your flanks (weak areas), while taking the fight to competitors via appropriate offensive options (e.g. bypass or guerrilla attacks).

Ansoff's product/market matrix provides a useful summation of product and market strategies. Organizations can consider market penetration, market development, product development or diversification as key marketing initiatives. Much product/market strategy focuses on gaining market share. PIMS analysis has proved highly influential and has linked market share to profitability. While this relationship is often true – don't blindly chase market share as it is not universally applicable.

Additionally, an awareness of the product life cycle (PLC) is important. The strategist needs to understand the PLC shape and how the marketing mix varies in the introduction, growth, maturity and decline phases.

Organizations need to be watchful and avoid the pitfall of strategic wear-out and strategies need to address hostile and declining markets.

e-Marketing should provide opportunities to enhance the organization's competitive advantage. To this end, a separate e-marketing strategy may be required, with providers having to decide if the Internet will support or replace existing activity.

Discussion questions

1 Consider the CI cycle and discuss the problem associated with dissemination.

2 Give an example of an organization using the strategies outlined in Figure 10.4: Competitive advantage.

3 Analyse the airline industry's use of the offensive and defensive strategies outlined in this chapter.

4 Discuss the following statement: 'PIMS forms a basis to develop marketing strategy. However, it must not be blindly followed.'

5 Select a brand that you consider to be underperforming and evaluate its underperformance using the key factors in strategic wear-out.

References

Aaker, D. (1995) *Strategic Market Management*, 4th edn. Wiley.

Ansoff, I. (1975) Strategies for diversification. *Harvard Business Review*, Vol. 25, No. 5, pp. 1110–25.

Chaffey, D., Mayer, R., Johnston, K. and Ellis, F. (2000) *Internet Marketing*. Prentice Hall.

CIA (1999) www.CIA.gov

Davidson, H. (1997) *Even More Offensive Marketing*. Penguin.

Fulmer, W. and Goodwin, J. (1993) Differentiation: Being with the Customer. *Business Horizons*, Vol. 101, No. 5.

Hooley, G., Saunders, J. and Piercy, N. (1999) *Marketing Strategy and Competitive Position*, 2nd edn. Prentice Hall.

Kahaner, L. (1997) *Competitive Intelligence*. Touchstone.

Kotler, P., Armsrong, G., Saunders, J. and Wong, V. (1999) *Principles of Marketing*, 2nd edn. Prentice Hall.

Kumar, N. (1999) Internet distribution strategies. *The Financial Times*, special insert Mastering Information Management, March, pp. 6–7.

Pollard, A. (1999) *Competitive Intelligence*. Pitman Publishing.

Porter, M. (1990) *Competitive Strategy: Techniques for Analysing Industries and Competitors*. Free Press.

Taylor, J. (1993) Competitive intelligence: a status report. *Journal of Marketing Management*, Vol. 8, No. 2, pp. 117–25.

11

Targeting, positioning and brand strategy

About this chapter

The subject of targeting and positioning builds on the segmentation techniques that were covered in Chapter 5. This chapter now explores criteria by which the attractiveness of a market segment can be judged. The targeting process is then examined before a discussion on a range of product positioning techniques is undertaken. Central to this discussion is the issue of brand strategy.

11.1   Introduction

At a fundamental level marketing strategy is about markets and products. Organizations are primarily making decisions about which markets to operate in and which products/services to offer to those markets. Once those essential decisions have been taken the company then has to decide on what basis it is going to compete in that chosen market. Segmentation is therefore at the heart of strategic marketing decision-making. In essence it is a strategic rather than an operational issue and has to be treated as such.

Initially any organization has to identify how it can, in general, gain competitive advantage. The stage that we will now explore is concerned with creating a specific competitive position. The first crucial step is to decide in which specific market segments to operate. Chapter 5 examined the criteria that can be used to identify discrete segments within a market. Once segments have been identified they then have to be evaluated in order that an organization can decide which particular segments it should serve. Target marketing, or targeting, is the common term for this process.

Once target markets have been chosen an organization then has to decide how it wishes to compete. What differential advantage can it create that will allow the company's product or service to hold a distinctive place in the chosen market segment. This process is normally called positioning. Targeting and positioning are critical processes that require the attention of senior management.

11.2   Evaluating market segments

To effectively evaluate different market segments it is necessary to systematically review two issues: the market attractiveness of the competing segments and the organization's comparative ability to address the needs of that segment. There are a number of criteria that can be used to judge the attractiveness of a market segment. These fall under three broad headings: market factors, the nature of competition and the wider environmental factors. At this point it is important to stress that marketers need to recognize that many of the criteria that can be used to evaluate the attractiveness of a market segment are qualitative rather than quantitative in nature. This has implications for the manner in which the process is managed. We will return to this topic later in the chapter. First we need to review the criteria themselves.

Market factors

When assessing market attractiveness the particular features of a market will affect any evaluation.

- **Segment size**   A large segment will generally have greater sales potential. This in itself will make it more attractive but it may also offer the potential of gaining economies of scale because of the larger volumes involved. Large segments with their potentially larger sales can justify the higher investments that may be necessary for organizations wishing to operate within them. However, large segments may not always be the most attractive. Large segments can be more competitive as their very size will attract other companies into them. Smaller organizations may not have the resources to address a large market and therefore may find smaller segments more appropriate for their attention.

- **Segment's rate of growth (measured in terms of real revenue growth after inflation)**   Segments that are growing are normally seen as being more attractive than segments where growth has peaked or even begun to decline. Segments in growth are seen as having a longer-term potential and therefore justify any investment necessary. Once again, however, these segments are likely to be more competitive as other companies also recognize their potential.

- **Segment's profitability**   What is the total profitability of the segment? If an organization is already operating in this segment it is not its profitability alone that should be reviewed. In order that all segments are evaluated on a consistent basis it is the profitability of all companies operating in the segment that should be calculated. This will have to be an estimate based on analysing competitors' activities.

- **Customers' price sensitivity**   Segments where consumers have low price-sensitivity are likely to be more attractive as higher profit margins can be gained. Consumers will be more concerned about quality and service rather than price alone. Price-sensitive segments are more susceptible to price competition, which leads to lower margins.

- **Stage of industry life cycle**   Entering a segment that is in the early stages of an industry's life cycle offers the advantages of potentially high growth in the future. In the early stages there are also likely to be less competitors. However, the early stages of the industry life cycle are characterized by the need for high investment in new plant, promotional activities and securing distribution channels. This occurs at a time when there may only be modest sales revenue. There will be a drain on cash into the new area of business that the company has to be able to fund. Businesses that are more interested in cash generation or profits in the short term may consider mature markets more favourable. These markets are likely to require a more modest level of investment.

- **Predictability**   The potential value of a market will be easier to predict if it is less prone to disturbance and the possibility of discontinuities. In the long term a predictable market is likely to be more viable.

- **Pattern of demand**   The attractiveness of a segment will be affected by any seasonal or other cyclical demand patterns it faces. A large percentage of sales in the gift and card market take place at Christmas in Western countries. An organization has to be able to withstand the cashflow implications of this skewed demand. The same problem occurs in other industry sectors such as travel and tourism.

- **Potential for substitution**   In any market there is the potential for new solutions to be developed that will address consumers' needs. An organization should review markets to establish whether new innovations could be used in the segment. Where substitutions are likely, an organization may decide not to enter on the basis that it makes the segment less attractive. If, however, the organization has the ability to deliver that innovatory approach it may make the segment a prime target as the company has the skills to change the nature of competition to their advantage.

Nature of competition in the target market and the underlying industry structure

- **Quality of competition**   Segments that have weak competition are more attractive than segments where there are strong and aggressive competitors. It is not the number of competitors operating but the nature of their competition that is critical in judging an opportunity.

- **Potential to create a differentiation position**   A segment will be more attractive if it contains unsatisfied customer needs that allow the company to create a differentiated product or service and gain a higher margin by charging a premium price. If it is a commodity market then competition is likely to be driven by price and the segment will be less attractive.

- **Likelihood of new entrants**   Segments that currently have limited competition may appear attractive. However, the potential for other companies to enter this market has to be taken into account.

- **Bargaining power of suppliers**   An organization will be in a stronger negotiating position where there is a range of potential suppliers. If, however, supply is in the hands of a few dominant companies the balance of power in negotiations will lie with the suppliers, making a segment less attractive.

- **Bargaining power of customers**   Customers may be the end customer but they can also be a customer in the channel of distribution, i.e. a major supermarket. If customers are in a strong negotiating position they will try to push suppliers' prices down, reducing margins. A market segment will be less favourable when a few major customers dominate it or the channels of distribution.

- **Barriers to entry in the market segment** There may be entry barriers to a segment that will reduce its appeal. These can be in the form of patents, new specialized plant or machinery necessary, or the need for high promotional expenditure. It may be that the overall level of investment necessary to successfully enter an area may be unrealistic for some companies. These same barriers may also put off other potential entrants. Therefore if a company calculates that it can overcome these barriers it may be able to enter a segment where there is little direct competition.

- **Barriers to exiting the market segment** There may be barriers that make exiting a segment difficult. Expensive facilities may have to be built that can only be used in servicing a particular market segment. Therefore withdrawing from this segment would leave expensive plant redundant. Other barriers could include service agreements to provide spare parts to customers for a number of years into the future, or plant and machinery that would be expensive to decommission. Organizations would have to anticipate the potential barriers to exit when they are initially evaluating a segment's attractiveness.

Environmental factors

- **Social** Social changes can lead to newly emerging segments that are not currently served by any organization. There can be a significant advantage to companies that are the first to move into these areas. Organizations also need to review the impact that any likely changes in social trends will have on a particular segment.

- **Political** Changes in the political environment can create new segments in a market. The deregulation of the utilities market created several new market segments that organizations could address. The political environment may also make certain segments less attractive. Segments that are located in particular geographic areas may be affected by political instability. There may also be regulatory changes that will affect a sector such as pharmaceuticals.

- **Economic** Economic trends may make segments more or less attractive. The growing affluence of older people in Western economies is making them a much more attractive group than twenty years ago.

- **Technology** Technological changes have to be taken into consideration when evaluating a segment. A judgement will have to be made as to whether new entrants will be able to enter a segment competing on a different basis by using technology to create innovative ways of delivering a product or service.

- **Environmental** Consumers' and governments' concerns about environmental issues have become much more important in recent years.

Therefore an evaluation of the environmental issues that may affect an organization's ability to service a segment will have to be considered.

Companies will not be capable of supplying every attractive segment that is identified. Having analysed a segment's market attractiveness it is then necessary to compare the needs of that group of consumers with the organization's capabilities. An organization's strengths can be judged by analysing its assets and competencies.

11.3 Establishing organizational capability

Organizational capabilities will be made up of specific assets and competencies. The key areas to identify are where the organization is superior to the competition.

In summary, assets are organizational attributes, tangible or intangible, that can be utilized to gain advantages in the market (see Figure 11.1).

Scale advantages	→ Market share → Relative and absolute media weight → Leverage over suppliers	→ International presence → Sales/distribution service coverage → Specialist skills due to scale
Production processes (plant, machinery + information systems)	→ Level of contemporary practice → Level of flexibility	→ Economies of scale → Capacity utilization → Unique items
Customer franchises	→ Brand names → Brand franchises → Databases	→ Customer relationships → Unique products/ services → Patents
Working capital	→ Quantity → Ready access	→ Location → Access to credit
Sales/distribution service network	→ Coverage → Relationships with external distributors	→ Size → Quality
Relationships with other organizations	→ Suppliers → Financial institutions → Joint ventures	→ Joint exploitation of assets (technology or distribution)
Property	→ Type → Location	→ Ability to expand → Quality

Figure 11.1
Examples of assets that create a competitive advantage (*Source:* adapted from Davidson, 1997)

Obviously assets should not be viewed in isolation, it is also important to establish any competencies that give the organization advantages. The value chain is a useful framework to use to identify these areas of unique competence. Key competencies may lie in primary activities. These include activities such as in-bound logistics (e.g. inventory control), operations (e.g. manufacturing), out-bound logistics (e.g. global delivery), marketing (e.g. brand development) and service (e.g. installation). Other key competencies may lie in support activities such as procurement, technology development, human resource management and the organization's infrastructure.

When trying to identify these competencies, rather than using the generic value chain, it may be more effective to develop a value chain that reflects the specific operations that face a particular business sector. The primary activities for an organization offering management consultancy are outlined in Figure 11.2.

An organization's key competencies once identified will normally fall into the areas of marketing, selling or operations (see Figure 11.3).

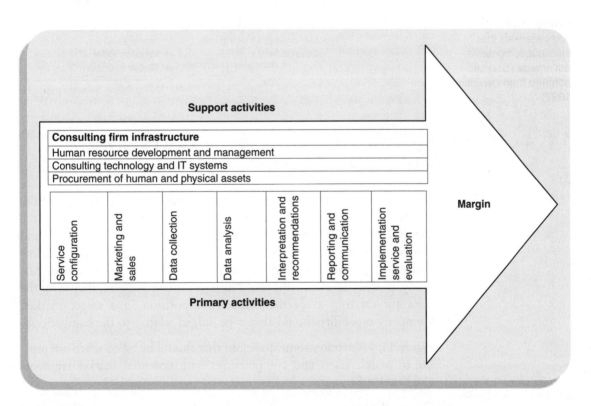

Figure 11.2
The value chain of a management consultancy practice (*Source:* adapted from Buckley, 1993)

Figure 11.3
Figure 11.3
Examples of
competencies that
create a competitive
advantage (*Source:*
adapted from Davidson,
1997)

11.4 Strategic alignment of assets and competencies (targeting)

The critical stage in the segmentation process is matching the capabilities of the organization to attractive market segment opportunities. At a largely operational level management analyse organizational assets and competencies to identify the skills and resources available to build low cost or differentiated positions. Where these assets or competencies currently, or with development, could surpass the competition, they form the basis for creating a specific competitive position in a target market. Company capability should always be judged relative to the competition.

Figure 11.4 illustrates some questions that should be asked when attempting to match assets and competencies with potential market segments (Jobber, 1995).

Overall the organization has to establish whether entering a particular segment is consistent with its long-term aims and objectives. If not, then no

Marketing assets
Does the market segment allow a company to take advantage of its current marketing strengths? Successful situations are more likely to occur where a company's current brand identity, or method of distribution, is consistent with those required to enter the new target market

Cost advantages
Entering a price-sensitive segment would be consistent with the capabilities of an organization that has a low cost base

Technological strengths
Where the organization has access to superior technology, is its use compatible with the market segment, and will it allow the company to gain any advantage?

Managerial capabilities and commitment
Does the company have the technical and managerial skills necessary to successfully enter a market segment?

Figure 11.4
Examples of assets and competencies matching with potential market segments

matter how tempting, entering the segment should be resisted. It will only divert company resources and management time away from the core goals of the enterprise.

Once the key areas of a company's capabilities have been identified they can be aligned with the attractive market segments already identified. An organization should enter segments that allow it to exploit current assets and competencies, or will allow potential capabilities to develop into strengths. This is an area where adapting portfolio models, more normally used to evaluate current products or business units, can be useful. The Shell directional policy matrix for instance can be adapted to analyse market segment opportunities against corporate strengths. An adapted version of this model is shown in Figure 11.5.

Weighted criteria are used, as in the traditional usage of the model. In this case a selection of market attractiveness factors, from those discussed earlier, that are considered relevant in evaluating a particular sector are weighted according to their importance as judged by the organization's management. The same exercise is then undertaken of selecting a range of assets and competencies deemed relevant to this particular sector. These are again weighted. Choosing factors in relation to the specific area being considered ensures that the model is custom-made to the particular situation and organization under review.

Every potential market segment is then evaluated on a rating scale, normally of 1 to 10 (1 = poor, 10 = excellent) on each of the criteria. The overall position of the segment on each axis is established by multiplying the ratings by the weighting given to each factor (see Chapter 6 for full details). The result of such an exercise for an imaginary situation and organization is shown in Figure 11.6.

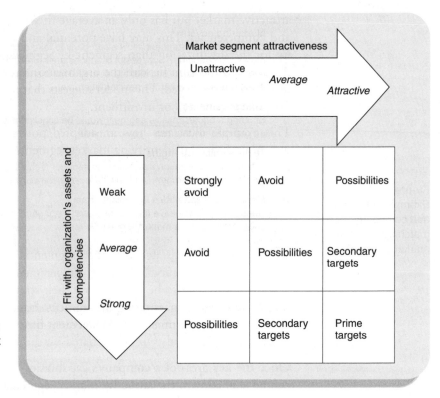

Figure 11.5
Adapted Shell
directional policy matrix
applied to target market
selection (*Source:*
Shell Chemical
Company, 1975)

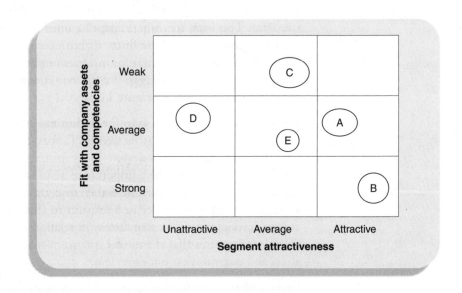

Figure 11.6
Evaluating market
segments for an
imaginary
organization/situation

The most attractive segment is B, as it lies in the box that is attractive on the horizontal axis representing segment attractiveness and has a strong fit with the company's assets and competencies as represented on the vertical axis. This segment should be a priority for the company. Segment A is an attractive market but has only an average fit with the organization's assets and competencies. This may have potential and would be a higher priority for the organization than segment E. Segment E has medium attractiveness and medium fit with the organization's competencies and should be selectively managed. The model suggests that targeting segments C and D is likely to be a poor investment.

This example illustrates how an adapted portfolio model can act as a screening device for identifying market segments that should be targeted.

11.5   The strategic nature of making target segment choices

As has already been stated, however, segmentation is a strategic process where qualitative and creative judgements have to be taken. Opportunities have to be evaluated on their strategic fit. Not only do the assets and competencies of the organization have to have synergy with a particular market segment, but wider issues have to be considered as well. Opportunities have also to be evaluated on the following somewhat subjective criteria:

- Ability to allow the creation of a sustainable market position.

- Compatibility with the corporate mission.

- Consistency with the organization's values and the culture. Segments that are a radical departure from current practice may challenge the prevailing values in the organization and the established status quo. The new segment may challenge the current power structure within the organization, which will create influential barriers to implementation.

- Ability to provide a focal point for action and future development in the organization.

- Ability to facilitate an innovative approach to market entry.

- Ability of the current organizational structure to service the target market. Does this opportunity lie between two areas of responsibility in the current organizational structure? This may lead to the opportunity never being seriously addressed.

- Compatibility with current internal information flows and reporting lines. Difficulties will arise where a segment does not sit easily with the current data collection or distribution systems. Segments in an innovative area may cause managers problems in terms of how to allocate targets and monitor progress. If this is linked to the problem already discussed under organizational structure, it may complicate issues such as areas of responsibility and reporting lines even further.

These factors of compatibility with the internal practices of an organization are likely to prove critical to the successful implementation of a new segmentation strategy. The newly entered segment has to have clear departmental ownership. Reporting lines and information flows have to be able to monitor its progress. In short, individuals within the organization have to wholeheartedly embrace the development of the new segment or failure will follow, no matter how attractive the segment or how well the organization's overt assets and competencies might fit.

A successful selection process will have identified a market segment (or segments) that are in alignment with the company's assets and competencies and is also compatible with the wider organizational issues.

11.6   Positioning

Having selected a target market or markets, the organization then has to decide on what basis it will compete in the chosen segment or segments. How best can it combine its assets and competencies to create a distinctive offering in the market? This has to be done in such a way that consumers can allocate a specific position to the company's product or service within the market, relative to other products. Consumers have to cope with a huge amount of product information. Customers will position a product in their mind in relation to other products on the market based on their perception of the key attributes it contains. Consumers will see the key attributes of Volvo as safety and durability. BMW's main attributes are based on performance, hence the 'The Ultimate Driving Machine' advertising slogan. When consumers consider the car market these two companies' products will be positioned relative to each other based on these perceptions. Companies can attempt to associate various qualities to their product as a way to help shape consumers' perceptions of their position in the market. A brand can be positioned using a range of associations, such as (Kotler *et al.*, 1996):

- **Product attributes**   Heinz positions its products on the attributes of no artificial colouring, flavouring or preservatives.

- **Product benefits**   Volvo positions itself using the product benefits of safety and durability.

- **Usage occasions**   The convenience store SPAR eight-till-late shops are positioned on the usage occasion. Customers use the shops when they need to shop out of normal hours or near to their home. Kit-Kat ('Have a break have a Kit-Kat') links the brand to tea and coffee breaks in the UK market.

- **Users**   Ecover cleaning products are positioned as environmentally friendly products for the green customer.

- **Activities**   Lucozade is positioned as an isotonic drink for sporting activities.

- **Personality**   Harley Davidson motorbikes are positioned as a macho product with a free spirit.

- **Origin**   Audi clearly illustrates its German origins in the UK market by the use of the 'Vorsprung durch technik' slogan. The hope is the product will be linked to the German reputation for quality engineering.

- **Competitors**   Pepsi-Cola positions itself as the choice of the next generation, reflecting the fact that in blind tasting tests younger people preferred Pepsi over competitors' offerings.

- **Product class**   Kellogg's Nutrigrain bars are positioned as 'morning bars', a substitute for the traditional breakfast.

- **Symbol**   Esso petrol has used the symbol of the tiger to position itself in the market.

These are the various ingredients that can be used by an organization endeavouring to influence consumer's perceptions of the product offering. Companies have to decide which of these they can use and more importantly how they wish to position their product in the market *vis-à-vis* the competing options.

Four factors are of critical importance for successful positioning (Jobber, 1995):

- **Credence**   The attributes used to position the product have to be perceived to be credible by the target customers. It would be very difficult for a nuclear power generator to position itself as environmentally friendly.

- **Competitiveness**   The product should offer the consumer benefits which competitors are not supplying. Clairol launched a new shampoo Herbal Essences in the USA in 1995 which emphasized the brand's wholesome ingredients. By 1997 this was the fastest-growing brand on the market and ranked number two behind Pantene.

- **Consistency**   A consistent message over time is invaluable in helping to establish a position against all the other products and services fighting for a share of the consumer's mind. An organization that changes its positioning on a regular basis causes confusion in the consumer's mind. This will mean they have an unclear perception of exactly what are the key characteristics of the product.

- **Clarity**   The positioning statement an organization chooses has to create a clearly differentiated position for the product in the minds of the target market. A distinct message such as 'Bread wi Nowt Taken Out' underlines the wholemeal 'old world' nature of Allison's bread.

Illustrative example 11.1
Coca-Cola

Recent research using brain scans revealed that consumers reacted differently to the Coca-Cola brand than they did to the Pepsi-Cola brand. When the individuals participating in the experiment were shown the company logos prior to tasting the product, the Coca-Cola brand stimulated responses in the areas of the brain associated with cultural knowledge, memory and self-image. Pepsi failed to initiate these brain responses. This effect was so strong that researchers could identify what drink the individual had been shown merely by looking at the brain scan. The Director of the Brown Human Neuroimaging Laboratory at Baylor College, Houston, Texas, Dr Read Montague, is quoted as saying 'There is a huge effect of the Coke label on brain activity related to the control of actions, the dredging up of memories and self-image. There is a response in the brain which leads to a behavioural effect.' When the consumers were subjected to a blind product tasting between the two brands there was no preference for one product over the other. However, when they were shown the label prior to tasting the product, 75% stated they preferred the taste of the Coca-Cola product. The researchers believe the label is so influential, stimulating responses in the brain the Pepsi brand failed to reach, that it actually altered the individual's perception of the taste of the product.

11.7   Perceptual mapping

Mapping consumer perceptions can allow an organization to see where it is currently placed compared to competitors' offerings. A simple perceptual map is based upon two axes representing key attributes in a particular market. These attributes are identified through market research and are determined by consumers' perceptions of the important factors in a market. This could, for example, be price and quality, or style and performance or a range of other issues. Products/companies or more particularly brands can then be placed according to their position on these attributes (see Figure 11.7).

In the case of Figure 11.7, in the hotel market the key attributes are deemed to be the price and the facilities. Hotel A on this map is seen as expensive but with a full range of facilities. Hotel B is perceived to be

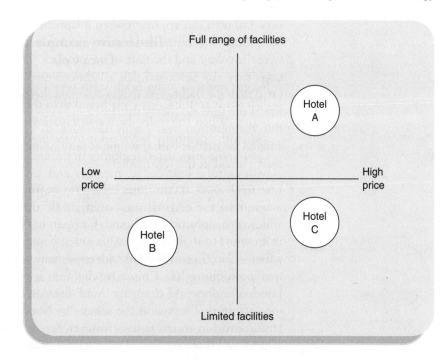

Figure 11.7
A perceptual map of
various hotels

inexpensive but with limited facilities. Both of these are reasonably consistent offerings. Hotel C, however, is seen as expensive but with an intermediate level of facilities. This position does not offer any unique aspects. There may of course be more than two key attributes in a market. Figure 11.7 does not map out quality. Hotel C may be seen as having high service quality for instance. To gain a fuller picture obviously more than one positioning map can be developed. There are also more sophisticated three-dimensional mapping techniques available for marketers to use.

Through the use of perceptual maps marketers can establish the current situation in a particular market. There will then be a number of alternatives from which to choose.

11.8   Positioning alternatives

In a seminal work, Ries and Trout (1981) claim that when considering positioning there are three principal options open to an organization:

- An organization can build on a current position to create a distinctive perception of the brand by consumers. Avis famously uses the 'We Try Harder' slogan to make a virtue out of being number two in the market.

- Having established the attributes that are most important to the consumer, the organization can look to see if there are any unoccupied positions that are desirable in consumers' minds and therefore viable opportunities.

IDV Ltd used this approach when it launched Croft Original Sherry. The key product attributes in the sherry market from a consumer's perspective were the colour and the taste of the product. Consumers favoured a sweet taste, they also perceived that a light-coloured sherry was more sophisticated than the traditional, darker-coloured sherries (see Figure 11.8). There was at the time no sherry that had a light colour and a sweet taste and yet this combination was highly desirable to consumers. Croft Original entered the market with this unique positioning and now is the best-selling sherry brand in the UK market.

- Due to changes in consumer behaviour or where perhaps there has been a failure of the original positioning, a third option can be considered which is to reposition the brand. Campari has recently been re-launched in an effort to shake off its 1970s image based on the 'Wafted from paradise? – No, Luton Airport' advertisement with Lorraine Chase. The new positioning has a more macho feel; it even includes a notorious London underworld character 'Mad' Frankie Fraser in the advert. Both the soft drink Tango and the snack Pot Noodle have successfully been repositioned in recent years. However, repositioning can be difficult to achieve and there are several examples of brands that have been less successful at moving their position. Babycham abandoned the famous deer symbol and the trademark green bottle for a more masculine image in 1993. By May 1997 it revived both the bottle and the Babycham deer and went back to its original, more female-orientated positioning.

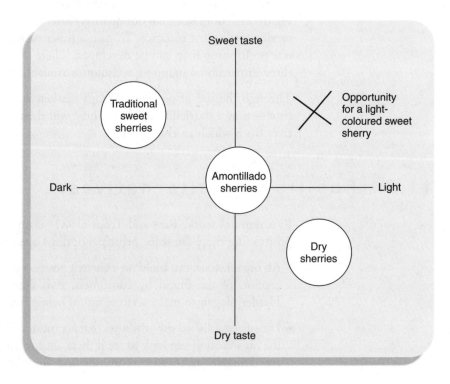

Figure 11.8
Perceptual map of the sherry market

There are alternative views on the correct approach to successful product/brand positioning. One view is that an organization should identify one unique selling proposition (USP) for a product and concentrate purely on that aspect. The whole focus of this approach is to be seen as the brand leader on that key attribute. For example, Gore-Tex fabric is seen as the leading fabric for breathable, waterproof, lightweight clothing material. The most effective USPs are based on quality, service, price, value or advanced technology (Ries and Trout, 1981).

An alternative approach to stressing a USP, based on a functional aspect of the product, is to concentrate on an emotional selling proposition (ESP). The product can be distanced from functionally similar rivals by appealing to unique emotional associations. An example of this is Alpha Romeo's positioning on the heritage and image of the traditional Italian sports car.

Both these approaches stress one key aspect of the product. However, there is a view that more than one factor can be used to position a product. As has been mentioned earlier, Volvo is positioned on safety and the compatible factor of durability. Whichever approach is taken, there are a number of positioning mistakes that can be made by an organization:

- **Underpositioning**   In this situation consumers have only a very limited perception of the brand and are unaware of any distinguishing features.

Illustrative example 11.2
Saga

Saga produces a wide range of products, including magazines, radio programmes, financial and travel services, for its estimated 6.5 million customer base of over-50s. The company is currently estimated to be worth around £1bn. However, the over-50s market is changing, and that has implications for the Saga brand. Recent surveys have revealed that a new over-50s market is emerging, one that has been termed the 'middle youth' market. Sainsbury Bank undertook a survey of individuals in their 50s, 60s and 70s and found many had the mindset of people in their 40s. Another GreyPower survey undertaken by Millennium, an agency that specializes in the mature market, found that 75% of consumers in their 50s and 60s would not consider taking a Saga holiday. In fact, 40% of those in their 60s, 70s and 80s thought the brand would be more suitable for people older than themselves. Saga now finds itself being challenged for the over-50s market by brands such as Secondlifestyle, which position themselves on the association of being for the active and young-in-mind customer.

- **Overpositioning** Consumers have a perception that the brand is only active in a very focused area, when in fact the brand covers a much broader product range.

- **Confused** Consumers have an unclear view of how the brand relates to competitive offerings.

Positioning is concerned with establishing an organization's product in the mind of a customer, in a position relative to other products in the market. Inevitably, therefore, making decisions about branding strategy will be a crucial aspect of this process.

11.9 Creating brand equity

The overall aim of branding decisions is to create an identity for the product or service that is distinctive and also in line with the targeting and positioning decisions already taken. Organizations should strive to produce a brand equity that delivers value to the consumer. This will result in either the customer showing greater brand loyalty or being willing to pay a premium price for the product. Brand equity according to Aaker (1991) is:

> a set of assets and liabilities linked to a brand's name and symbol that add to or subtract from the value provided by a product or service to a firm and/or that firm's customers.

Brands that contain high equity have strong name awareness, strong associations attached to the brand, a perception of quality and have high levels of brand loyalty (see Figure 11.9). To create a brand that exhibits these characteristics takes time and investment. For instance, of the top fifty UK grocery brands, four have their origins in the 1800s; 16 in the period

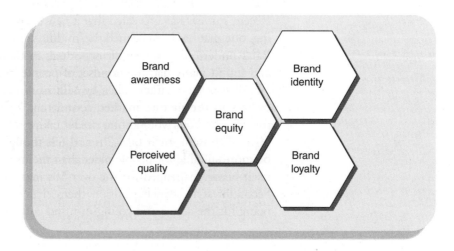

Figure 11.9
The constituents of brand equity (*Source:* Aaker, 1995)

1900–1950; 21 between 1951 and 1975; and only nine have been introduced to market in the years since 1975 (Hooley *et al.*, 1998). Once established, however, a successful brand will become a valuable asset to an organization in its own right.

11.10   Brand valuation

There has been a trend in recent years for companies to try to turn the general concept of brand equity into giving these organizational assets a specific financial valuation and to account for them on their company balance sheets separately from goodwill. Accountants have largely been at the forefront of this approach and have developed a range of factors seen as indicators of a brand's value. All are linked to the ability of the brand to sustain higher returns than competitors. These factors include:

- **Market type**   Brands operating in high margin, high volume and stable markets will carry higher valuation than brands in less profitable or stable sectors. The confectionery or beer markets have traditionally been seen as less liable to changes in technology or fashion. Deciding on the potential of a market type, however, is full of difficulties. Even the drinks industry now shows signs of more regular changes in consumers' behaviour. It should also be borne in mind that one of the aims of developing a strong brand is to allow a company to compete on other factors than price, allowing them to make strong margins even in what could be seen as commodity markets. The Andrex brand of toilet roll has consistently made strong margins in the UK market. More importantly it has gained higher margins than any of its competitors over the past 30 years from what is essentially a commodity product.

- **Market share**   Brands that are market leaders are deemed to command a premium because competitors will find it difficult to overcome consumers' tendency to buy the dominant brand. In effect, holding the market leadership position is seen as a barrier to entry for other brands.

- **Global presence**   Brands that either are, or carry the potential to be, exploited internationally obviously carry more value than brands within a purely domestic market. Development in e-commerce may lower barriers to establishing a global brand name and therefore do set a potential challenge to the high values placed on current global brands. There is also, obviously, the potential for the current global brands to end up as the dominant players in the e-commerce market thereby reinforcing their position and value.

- **Durability**   Some brands manage to maintain a contemporary appeal and retain their relevance to customers over a long period of time. These brands tend to have created strong customer loyalty and become an established player in the market. A study by Blackett found that brands such as Cadbury in the chocolate market, Gillette in razors, Kodak in film and Colgate in toothpaste, were all the brand leaders in their market areas over the period 1931–91 (Murphy, 1991). Such long-term brand leaderships are therefore likely to generate high valuations.

• **Extendibility** Brands that have the ability to be extended into related markets or stretched in new markets offer greater value than brands with more limited options. The Bic brand, for example, has been successfully extended from disposable pens into a number of other disposable markets such as cigarette lighters and razors. Andrex in 1987 had 39% of the toilet paper market, by 1994 this share had dropped to 28% due to increased competition from discounters (Kapferer, 1997). However, the potential to extend the brand allowed the company to enter related markets for products as such as kitchen paper, paper tissues etc.

• **Protection** Brands that have some protection from copying through patents or registered trademarks or designs, potentially offer greater value. However, this protection has in reality been limited. In particular, retailers have launched own label products with similar packaging to market leading brands.

The factors considered so far have generally been developments from an accountancy perspective. However, there are a range of other significant factors marketers perceive to be crucial in terms of judging the brand's potential value.

Illustrative example 11.3
Red Bull

The energy drinks market has been a fast-growing sector over the last few years and current sales are around £775m a year in the UK. In Western Europe Red Bull holds two-thirds of the market. This is a market that a company can enter with relatively low levels of investment and this has resulted in the launch of a rash of brands with similar characteristics to Red Bull. Some drinks have used similar names, such as, Red Rhino and Red Bat, some have used similar style packaging. In order to defend its brand Red Bull has resorted to legal action. So far it has won its case against a drink called Shark in the UK and other cases in the Netherlands and Australia. It is believed Red Bull has also settled out of court with up to twelve other drink brands in the UK. Red Bull believes unless it takes action not only will their brand suffer a lack of differentiation in the market but also the whole category will be damaged by the resulting customer confusion.

- **Superior products and services**   Brands that offer the consumer superior products and/or services than competitors create greater value. Brands that are perceived to deliver clear benefits to the consumer such as quality, style, or cheapness present the company with a clear asset in the market.

- **Country of origin**   The identity of the country of origin can either attach or deduct value from a brand. Association with Scotland is seen as attaching value to fresh food products in countries such as France. Association with Britain, however, has been deemed to have a negative image by consumers in certain market sectors such as telecommunications. This resulted in organizations such as British Telecom re-branding themselves as BT as a way of distancing themselves from their country of origin and appearing more international. Conversely, in the clothing market in the USA association with Britain is seen as positive, much to the benefit of brands such as Barbour (jackets etc.) and Church's shoes.

- **Market domination**   The brand's ability to gain extensive coverage in the market, a dominant position in the distribution channels and the ability to command good shelf positions are all assets of considerable value. Most of these attributes accompany brand leadership and merely add to the potential that market position gives a brand. There is some limited evidence however that affluent customers are now moving away from the major brands as a way of standing out from the crowd. In Japan there has even been the development of a retail clothing store, Seibu, successfully selling high quality clothing that carries no branded labels.

11.11   Strategic brand management

Successful brand development is reliant on far more than creating a strong image through the marketing communications mix. This is the area of which the consumer will be most aware but the less visible elements are crucial ingredients in creating a strong brand (see Figure 11.10). Factors such as providing product quality, continuous product development and high levels of service are potential components of a successful brand yet are not as visible as elements of the communications mix. Significantly, marketing communication skills are generally coordinated by agencies outside the organization, whilst the other components of successful brand development have traditionally been reliant on the company's internal assets and competencies. However, a number of alternative approaches to the structure and ownership of crucial elements of brand development and delivery have emerged over the past 30 years. Organizations now are faced with a number of decisions on the best way to gain access to the

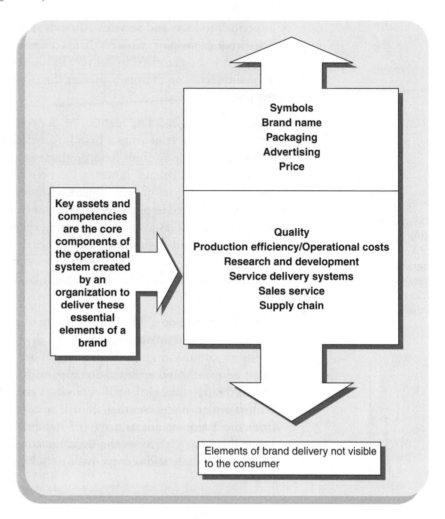

Symbols
Brand name
Packaging
Advertising
Price

Key assets and competencies are the core components of the operational system created by an organization to deliver these essential elements of a brand

Quality
Production efficiency/Operational costs
Research and development
Service delivery systems
Sales service
Supply chain

Elements of brand delivery not visible to the consumer

Figure 11.10
The visibility of core elements of a brand (*Source:* adapted from Davidson, 1997)

assets and competencies needed to successfully support a brand. This has led to a number of alternative ways of structuring the business functions that support successful brands. Organizations have the option of coordinating these activities without necessarily owning all the assets and competencies needed. The capability to support a brand can be obtained through various forms of relationships and alliances (see Figure 11.11).

Organizations have tended to use one of four main options in structuring their operations to gain access to the assets and competencies they require:

• **Manufacturer's brand system** Companies such as Kellogg only produce products under their own brand name. Kellogg owns the majority of the business operations except for the retail outlets selling the product. In some areas third party distribution systems may be utilized.

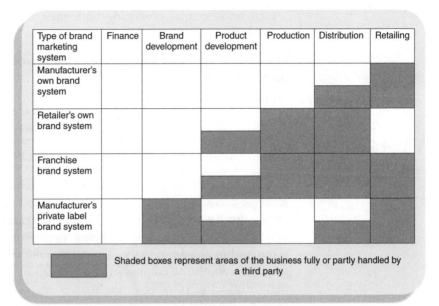

Figure 11.11
Options for the
structure/ownership
of key capabilities
necessary to support
successful brands
(*Source:* adapted
from Davidson, 1997)

Type of brand marketing system	Finance	Brand development	Product development	Production	Distribution	Retailing
Manufacturer's own brand system					▓	▓
Retailer's own brand system			▓	▓	▓	
Franchise brand system			▓	▓	▓	▓
Manufacturer's private label brand system		▓	▓		▓	▓

▓ Shaded boxes represent areas of the business fully or partly handled by a third party

- **Retailer's own brand system**   Retailers such as The Gap or Marks & Spencer only supply goods carrying their retail brand name. Manufacturers under contract to the retailer carry out production. Often distribution is contracted out. Product development is sometimes undertaken by a third party, such as a design agency, but more frequently it is a shared activity, with the retailer taking an active role.

- **Franchise brand system**   Organizations such as Benetton and Burger King are franchise operations. Benetton contracts out parts of its manufacturing activities. Key skills relating to core aspects of the brand's quality, such as pattern cutting and dying operations, are, however, kept in-house. Warehousing is also kept inside the company operations and is an area where considerable investment has been made to allow fast distribution around the globe. The retail outlets are mainly franchise operations. Although these retail outlets are one of the most visible aspects of the brand, this is not a core area of competence owned by the organization. Key competencies lie in the areas of product design, brand development, management of key areas of production and distribution, supplier and retail franchise management.

- **Manufacturer's private label brand system**   Some companies concentrate on manufacturing products to be sold under a retailer's own label, such as Marks & Spencer. These companies have no control over branding or the retail outlets; instead they create their competitive position through highly efficient manufacturing skills, customer service and new product development abilities. There are examples of organizations, such as Weetabix, producing both their own branded products and goods for retailers' own brands.

Optimizing the assets and competencies available to an organization is obviously a crucial step in creating appropriate operational systems to support a brand.

11.12   Brand name strategy

The operational structure an organization develops is not the only area of strategic decision-making associated with brand management. An organization also has to decide its policy for naming brands across all its products and services. Branding decisions for any new products can then be taken within this framework. The focal point of decisions on branding strategy is about the emphasis the organization wishes to place on creating a distinctive offering in the market against the weight it wishes to place on the origin of the product or service (see Figure 11.12).

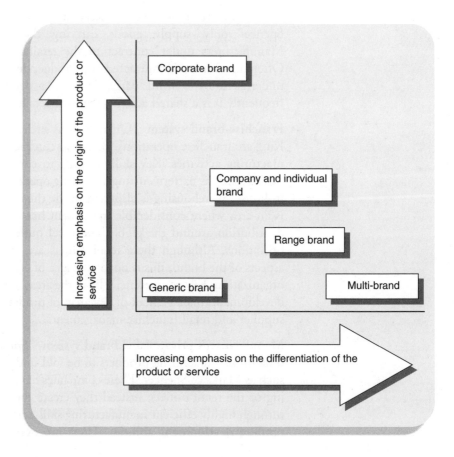

Figure 11.12 Alternative branding strategies (*Source:* adapted from Kapferer, 1997)

Between the extremes offered by these two approaches lie several options available to an organization when considering an overall brand strategy:

- **Corporate brand** Organizations following this approach use one corporate name across all its products. Heinz would be a classic example of this unified approach. Individual products merely carry a descriptive name under the corporate umbrella Heinz brand, hence Heinz Baked Beans, Heinz Cream of Mushroom Soup, Heinz Tomato Ketchup. Linking the individual products together creates a strong overall image. It also gives the opportunity to create economies of scale in marketing communication and possibly distribution. The clear danger is that if there is a problem with an individual product the reputation of all the products may suffer. Virgin has used the corporate brand name across their entire product portfolio. Their high profile problems with the Virgin rail franchise in the UK may over time have a negative impact across their other operations. The fact this does not yet appear to have happened is a testament to the strength of the core brand name.

- **Multi-brand** Multi-branding or discrete branding is the opposite of the corporate branding approach. With multi-branding each product is given a unique brand name. The aim is to build completely separate brand identities. This is appropriate if the organization is competing in a number of different segments and the consumer's perceptions of a product's position in one segment may adversely affect the consumer's perceptions of another product. A classic example of this approach would be Procter & Gamble, who produce a range of washing powders aimed at discrete sectors of the market, such as Daz, Ariel and Bold.

- **Company and individual brand (endorsed approach)** Traditionally Unilever practised a multi-brand approach with its washing powders but recently it has been moving closer to the strategy of linking a company name to an individual brand name. Their products now have Lever Bros as a high profile endorsement on the individual brands such as Persil, Radion and Surf. This can be used in different ways. Endorsing a product with the corporate name gives a new product credibility whilst at the same time allowing the new brand some degree of freedom. A fixed endorsed approach entails the corporate brand name being given a consistent profile against each individual product's brand name in the range. For example, all Kellogg's products give individual product brand names the prominent position on the pack, while the same secondary weighting is given to the company brand name. (Note: this is different to Heinz were the prominence of the corporate brand is sacrosanct.) Cadbury takes a more flexible approach to the corporate endorsement; it is more or less prominent depending on how independent they choose to make the brand.

- **Range branding** Some organizations use different brand names for different ranges of product, in effect creating a family of products. Ford has done this to an extent using Ford for its mass-market car range and Jaguar for the up-market executive car range. Volvo, Ford's latest acquisition, has its own distinct brand values that appeal to a particular market segment and therefore will become another brand family for the Ford group.

- **Private branding (distributor's own brand)** An organization may decide to supply private brands, in particular retail brands. In this case the private brand is owned and controlled by the distributor who will make decisions regarding the product's position in the market. The distributor is likely to use a strategy of either a corporate or a company and individual brand for its products.

- **Generic branding** This strategy involves the product having no brand name. The product's packaging merely states the contents of the package, for instance flour or washing-up liquid.

Each of the approaches to branding outlined above has advantages and disadvantages. These are summarized in Figure 11.13.

11.13 Combined brand strategies

Obviously large organizations may use a mixture of brand strategies to manage their large product portfolios.

3M employs a number of approaches to brand its broad range of products. The 3M brand name is used as an umbrella brand on all products aimed at the professional market, including cameras, overhead projectors and video tapes. On Post-it notes the individual brand name is accompanied by the 3M company brand name. This is also true of the company's general consumer products, where 3M is used as an endorsing brand name in small print.

The umbrella brand Scotch is used on most consumer products. This includes the company's video tapes aimed at the consumer market where the presence of a 3M connection is hard to identify. Initially 3M consumer scouring pads were sold under the generic product name and the Scotch-brite brand. In response to competitors' actions the scouring pad product was given the specific individual brand identity of Raccoon.

There are also some variations on these major branding themes within 3M. For instance, aerosol glue aimed at the professional market is branded with a large 3M logo but also carries the Scotch brand name in smaller print.

Each of these branding decisions at 3M has been taken to make the greatest competitive impact in a particular market. 3M is not alone in having

Branding strategy	Advantages	Disadvantages
Corporate brand	→ The strength of the corporate brand is conveyed to all products → Promotional costs are spread across all products	→ Any new product failure has the potential to damage the corporate brand → The positioning of the corporate brand constrains decisions on the quality and pricing for individual products
Multi-brand	→ Allows individual differentiation of brands → Allows products to be occupy different positions in the same market, i.e. a premium and a discount brand from the same parent company → Current brands are insulated from any new product failures	→ Each brand requires a separate promotional budget → Market sectors have to contain enough potential to support more than one brand → Highly focused brands are hard to reposition once a market enters decline
Company and individual brand	→ Product can be supported by the reputation of an existing corporate brand while at the same time the individual characteristics of the specific offering can be emphasized	→ A new product failure has the potential to cause some damage to the company brand → The positioning of the company brand constrains decisions on quality and pricing of the individual product
Range brand	→ The strength of the brand is conveyed to all the products in the range → Promotional costs are spread across all the products in the range	→ Any new product failure has the potential to damage the range brand → The positioning of the brand constrains decisions on quality and pricing for individual products
Private brand	→ Demands little promotional spend by producer → Producer can concentrate on gaining cost efficiency through volume production	→ Marketing decisions controlled by distributors → Removes the producer from direct contact with the market
Generic brand	→ Little promotional budget, reduced packaging costs	→ Competition becomes based mainly on price and service levels

Figure 11.13
Advantages and disadvantages of brand strategies (*Source:* adapted from Brown and McDonald, 1994)

such a sophisticated brand portfolio; many large organizations have quite complex brand structures.

The approach an organization adopts to branding is a crucial decision relating to the overall strategy the company has decided to pursue. The branding policy should be developed in the light of:

• The nature of the product or service.

• The pattern of consumer behaviour in the specific market.

• The company's competitive position.

When companies develop new products the branding decision will invariably be taken according to the general branding strategy of the organization. Multi-brand-orientated companies will tend to always create a new brand for the new product. For other companies the decision will depend on the nature of the target market. If it is very different from the organization's current markets they may decide to introduce a new brand. Toyota did this when they entered the up-market executive car market, introducing the Lexus brand. This is a rational approach where the target market is large enough and has the potential profitability to justify investing in creating a new brand. Companies may, however, choose to use a current brand name and opt for a brand extension or brand stretching policy.

11.14   Brand extension

There are occasions where an organization will try to extend the use of a brand name to new products in the same broad market. Brands that carry high brand equity are candidates for brand extension as they have the ability to increase the attractiveness of the new products. The Pretty Polly hosiery brand has been extended into the wider but related lingerie market (Tucker, 1998). The Pretty Polly brand is seen as fashionable, young, exciting and innovative, all qualities Sarah Lee, its holding company, feels can be extended to other markets.

11.15   Brand stretching

Brand stretching takes place when an organization stretches a brand into new unrelated markets. Virgin is an obvious example of this, moving from the recorded music industry to airlines, railways, financial services and cola drinks. Marks and Spencer and Tesco have both moved from mainstream retailing into financial services. Both are examples of brand stretching. This policy is more likely to be successful where the original brand values are compatible with the aspirations of the new target group.

Over a period of time, it is likely that an organization will be required to undertake actions to improve the performance of a brand. This can occur for a number of reasons, such as the advent of new technology, changing consumer behaviour or new competition. The options open to a company in these circumstances are either to increase sales volume or to raise the brand's profitability. Brand revitalization and brand repositioning are two approaches that can be employed to increase the sales volume of a brand.

11.16   Brand revitalization

Brand revitalization involves gaining sales volume by expanding the market for a brand. Four significant opportunities exist that can expand a market:

- **Enter new markets**   One approach is to expand into new geographical areas. Irn Bru, the Scottish soft drinks brand, has recently expanded into the Russian market as a way of increasing sales.

- **Exploit new market segments**   Once the initial market segment has been fully exploited a company can then expand by targeting new market segments. Johnson & Johnson's baby shampoo was stagnating until they moved the brand into a new market segment of adults who wash their hair frequently.

- **Increase the frequency of use**   This can be achieved by actions such as:

   ○ Appealing to consumers to use products on new occasions. Kellogg have been attempting to increase sales of their Cornflakes brand by promoting the proposition that the product should be eaten as a supper time snack as well as a breakfast cereal, thus increasing their sales.

   ○ Providing incentives to purchase, such as frequent flyer programmes which promote the sale of airline tickets.

- **Increase quantity used**   This can be achieved by:

   ○ Increasing the size of the 'normal sized container', such as the popcorn or soft drink containers offered in cinemas. If consumers accept this size as normal then consumption will increase. Alternatively, undertake advertising such as Weetabix promoting larger portions as normal – in their case suggesting eating three Weetabix at a time rather than two.

   ○ Removing barriers to consumption – thus companies can offer low calorie chocolate or soft drinks as a way of removing a major obstruction to consumer purchase.

11.17   Brand repositioning

Brand repositioning is undertaken in order to increase a brand's competitive position and therefore increase sales volume by seizing market share from rival products. When repositioning, companies can change aspects of the product, change the brand's target market or both. This gives four repositioning options (see Figure 11.14):

- **Image repositioning**   This takes place when both the product and the target market remain unchanged. The aim is to change the image of the

	Unchanged target market	Changed target market
Unchanged product attributes	Image repositioning	Market repositioning
Changed product attributes	Product repositioning	Total repositioning

Figure 11.14
Alternative options available for brand repositioning

product in its current target market. In the early 1990s Adidas were seen as reliable but dull. The company created an image of 'street credibility' in an attempt to reposition the brand to appeal to the consumer in the sports shoe market. Tango, the Britvic soft drink, has been transformed during the 1990s from a minor UK brand into a brand showing dynamic growth. This has been achieved by creating an anarchic image for the product through a major promotional re-launch that was aimed to appeal to consumers in the critical 16–24-year-old age group.

- **Market repositioning**   Here the product remains unchanged but it is repositioned to appeal to a new market segment. Lucozade, a brand of carbonated glucose drink, was originally targeted as a product for individuals suffering from illness, particularly children. In recent years it has been repositioned as an isotonic drink, aimed at young adults undertaking sporting activities.

- **Product repositioning**   In this situation the product is materially changed but is still aimed to appeal to the existing target market. In the early 1990s Castlemaine XXXX lager was altered, with its alcohol content being increased from 3.7% to 3.9% for pub sales and 4% for cans sold in supermarkets. The packaging was also changed as the size of can was increased from 440 ml to 500 ml. These moves were instituted to address the changes in consumer tastes in the product's target market.

- **Total repositioning**   This option involves both a change of target market and accompanying product modifications. Skoda has managed under Volkswagen's ownership to totally reposition itself. The product quality and design has changed significantly and the brand now has credibility with new, more affluent consumers. This has also allowed the brand to expand its sales outside its Eastern European heartland.

Illustrative example 11.4
Vimto

In the year ending March 2004 the UK cordial drinks market had grown by 5%. In the same period Vimto sales grew 6%. Despite outperforming the market, in July 2004 Vimto announced that it was going to repackage its cordial drink to emphasize its healthy attributes and to reposition the brand at the premium end of the market. The new design will feature images of fruit to underline the product's fruit juice content. Vimto has also launched a 250 ml container for the drink aimed at the children's lunchbox market. These were not isolated initiatives but part of a programme of brand management decisions, Vimto stating that it intended to launch other innovations over the next few months.

Raising a brand's profitability

If a brand is in a static or declining market and a company judges that the brand has finite potential then it may be prudent to force the maximum profitability out of the product. This can be achieved by:

- **Raising prices** Although this may lead to a drop in sales it is likely to dramatically improve margins. In a declining market competitors may be dropping out of the market, restricting consumer choice. Thus consumers who still purchase the product may have little choice but to accept the higher price.

- **Cutting costs** This action will obviously be a matter of management judgement, as it will obviously mean ceasing to invest in the brand and it may hasten its decline.

- **Cutting the brand's product range** Rationalizing the range of marginal product lines will save additional costs whilst having a limited impact on overall sales.

11.18 Brand extinction

Inevitably, over a period of time, brands die. They may last for decades or even in some cases centuries, but even well-established brands can falter. This can happen for a number of reasons:

- **Intense brand competition** Weak brands face increasing competition from both overseas brands entering domestic markets and the growth of retailers' own label brands. This leads to poor profitability for brands with small market share and in the end withdrawal from the market.

- **Acquisition and mergers** Companies that acquire brand names or undergo a merger often rationalize the portfolio of brand names owned by the new organization. Since acquisition, Nestlé has over time replaced the Rowntree brand name on its products.

- **Rationalization** Organizations periodically review their brand portfolio and may decide that in relation to their promotional budgets they cannot sustain the range of brand names that they have propagated. Over the past 40 years ceased to use such famous brand names as Triumph, Austin, Morris, Riley and Wolsey have disappeared. The Jaguar brand has been lucky to escape this cull.

- **Globalization** In order to create global brands, companies have also rationalized domestic brands in particular markets. Mars changed the name of Marathon chocolate bars in the UK to the Snickers brand name in order to create a consistent brand image internationally.

- **Weak brand management** Brands also falter through mediocre marketing, uncompetitive production costs or poor quality. It is an ignominious end for what should be the key asset of any organization.

Summary

Targeting aims to align an organization's assets and competencies to attractive market segments. Once these market segments have been identified an organization has to decide how it will position its product in the market, relative to the competition. One key aspect of this positioning process is branding.

An organization's assets and competencies can be used to create new products and services, to unlock the potential in market segments that are not currently served, either by the company in question, or by companies in general. Product development and innovation are critical issues to any organization and they are discussed in detail in Chapter 6.

Discussion questions

1 What factors should be used in establishing a segment's market attractiveness?

2 Apart from having synergy with organization's assets and competencies, what other criteria should a company use when evaluating a potential target segment?

3 Taking six brands of your choice identify with what associations are they positioned in the consumer's mind?

4 What factors are of critical importance for successful product positioning?

References

Aaker, D. (1991) *Managing Brand Equity*. The Free Press.

Aaker, D. (1995) *Strategic Market Management*, 4th edn. Wiley.

Buckley, A. (1993) *The Essence of Services Marketing*. Prentice Hall.

Brown, L. and McDonald, M. (1994) *Competitive Marketing Strategy for Europe*. Kogan Page.

Davidson, H. (1997) *Even More Offensive Marketing*. Penguin Books.

Hooley, G.H., Saunders, J.A. and Piercy, N.F. (1998) *Marketing Strategy and Competitive Positioning*, 2nd edn. Prentice Hall.

Jobber, D. (1995) *Principles and Practice of Marketing*. McGraw-Hill.

Kapferer, J. (1997) *Strategic Brand Management*, 2nd edn. Kogan Page.

Kotler, P., Armstrong, G., Saunders, J. and Wong, V. (eds) (1996) *Principles of Marketing: The European Edition*. Prentice Hall.

Murphy, J.M. (1992) *Branding: A Key Marketing Tool*, 2nd edn. Macmillan.

Ries, A. and Trout, J. (1981) *Positioning: The Battle for Your Mind*. McGraw-Hill.

Shell Chemical Company (1975) *The Directional Policy Matrix: A New Aid to Corporate Planning*. Shell.

Tucker, J. (1998) Pretty Polly set for lingerie push. *Marketing*, April 23.

12 Strategic implementation

About this chapter

Implementation is critical to the success or failure of any venture. Basic generic management principles (e.g. leadership, team building and delegation) contribute to the process. Marketing managers must evaluate the ease, or otherwise, of implementation and deploy project management techniques to achieve desired goals. Additionally, 'internal marketing' can ease the process of implementation.

After reading this chapter, you should:

• Understand the importance of implementation.

• Have an awareness of key management principles associated with implementation.

• Be able to apply the '7S' framework of implementation.

• Consider the role of people and politics in project management.

• Consider how internal marketing can drive successful implementation.

12.1　Implementation: stressing the importance

A key maxim in business is: never acquire a business you don't understand how to run. Equally, it would be true to say: never adopt a strategy you don't understand how to implement.

It can be said that, in terms of strategy, planning is the easy part. With a basic grounding in marketing, most managers could sit down with a blank sheet of paper and develop an outline marketing plan. This plan may contain all the correct 'buzz-words'. Ideas relating to market penetration, segmentation, globalization and competitive advantage would fill the page and a clear concise way forward formulated. However, it is not that simple. While many managers could produce such an outline – how many could implement it? Without implementation, the plan remains some ideas on a piece of paper.

In the context of marketing the goal will be to achieve and/or maintain a marketing orientation: success *by a process of understanding and meeting customer need*. It is doubtful if a marketing strategy can be implemented where this orientation does not exist. Achieving such a view is dependent on the quality of the organization's management and their understanding of marketing as a business philosophy.

It is reasonable to suggest that implementation is often a key determinant in the success or failure of any strategic activity. Therefore, it should be an integral part of any marketing strategy. This view is supported by examining the history of corporate strategy. Recent times have seen a move away from corporate planning to the concept of strategic management. The main difference is that strategic management addresses the issue of implementation.

12.2　Success *vs.* failure

Two dimensions determine the success of a strategy: the strategy itself and our ability to implement it. A useful starting point in considering success *or failure is outlined in Figure 12.1. Bonoma (1984) examines the appropriateness of the strategy and the effectiveness of execution skills thus establishing four general positions.

- **Success**　The ideal situation, an appropriate strategy and a strong ability to execute such a strategy. This should present little or no problem.

- **Chance**　Here the strategy is poor, perhaps lacking detailed analysis or not building on existing strengths. However, it may be saved by effective execution. This may be such that we can adopt and adapt from a weak

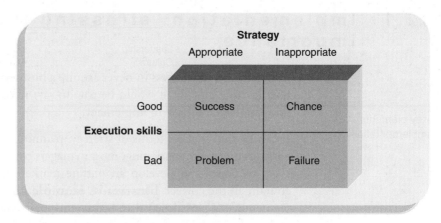

Figure 12.1
Strategy and execution
(*Source:* adapted from
Bonoma, 1984)

opening basis and, with luck, do what is required. Clearly, the degree of 'inappropriateness' is highly significant. Is the strategy saveable? Notwithstanding this question, this position always brings a high degree of risk.

- **Problem** We are doing the right things badly. The strength of strategic planning is dissipated by poor execution. Often the true value of the strategy is not fully recognized and it is dismissed as being inappropriate.

- **Failure** A no-win situation. With failure on all levels there is a danger of struggling on with implementation and simply 'throwing good money after bad'. Organizations should try to learn from such situations. Don't make the same mistake twice.

Clearly, there is an issue of subjectivity within defining good/bad and appropriate/inappropriate and it is all too easy to be wise after the event. It is simple to classify a strategy as inappropriate after it is deemed to have failed. The key quest is to ensure strategies fall into the 'success' category. Formulating an appropriate strategy has been dealt with in the preceding chapters of this text and we will now focus on the execution of strategy – in other words, implementation.

Effective implementation can be viewed in terms of:

- Understanding the fundamental principles of implementation.

- Assessing the ease, or otherwise, of implementing individual projects.

- Applying project management techniques.

12.3   Fundamental principles

Having stressed the importance of implementation, we turn to the issue of what factors are required for success. These are summarized in Figure 12.2.

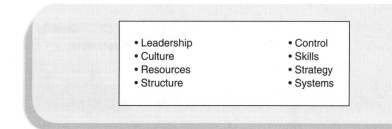

Figure 12.2
Key elements in
implementations

Illustrative example 12.1
Kall Kwik: implementing a national marketing strategy

Kall Kwik operates a UK wide chain of outlets, offering design, print and copy services to business. The organization faces the challenge of implementing clients' marketing strategies across a distributed, geographically dispersed, network. Kall Kwik Centre owners provide local service, while adhering to centrally set quality, pricing and production time standards. The network of local Kall Kwik Centres allows multi-site client organizations (e.g. retailers) to implement marketing campaigns without incurring the high distribution costs normally associated with centralized print purchasing.

Any successful strategy must be supported by each of the components shown below. These cover the human aspects of business and a more objective process approach to management. Note, these factors can either have a positive or negative effect on a given project. Each is considered in turn.

- **Leadership** The role of the leader is to get the best out of people and deal with the unexpected. Leaders should be viewed as facilitators. This is achieved by creating an environment where actions can take place. Leaders require effective people skills, such as negotiation and delegation. Often leaders acquire their leadership position by means of technical expertise. This can be dangerous; remember their primary function is to facilitate rather than undertake the work themselves. The leader needs transferable management skills in addition to technical and marketing competence. Adair (1984) summarizes leadership as:

1 Task needs – aiming to complete the project.

2 Group needs – developing team spirit and morale.

3 Individual needs – harmonizing the above with the needs of the individual.

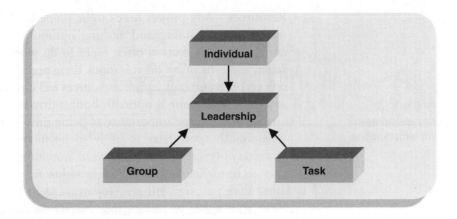

Figure 12.3
Leadership

Depending on circumstances, the leader will emphasize task, group or individual needs. Leaders need to adopt an appropriate **style** of management. If a crisis looms then a more direct autocratic style may be called for. However, under different circumstances a participative style may be best suited. Hence leaders can move from task, individual or group orientation depending on the circumstances.

- **Culture**   Much management theory relates to corporate culture. Culture can be defined as a combination of **shared values** and beliefs. These are commonly reinforced with corporate symbols and symbolic behaviour. For example, a company may wish to pursue a culture of openness and accessibility. The symbol of this may be to encourage all staff to dress informally on a Friday, to promote a more relaxed atmosphere. Great care must be taken when implementing strategy. If the strategy goes against the dominant culture it is likely to fail unless a major effort is made to develop and maintain support. This could be achieved via staff training, appraisal and restructuring. The strategist needs to be sensitive to the shared values that exist within the organization. Normally it is best to work with, as opposed to against, such values.

- **Structure**   The structure of any organization, or project, has two primary functions. First, it defines lines of authority denoting levels of responsibility. Current management thinking promotes a move towards flatter structures with more devolved authority. Secondly, structure is a basis for communication. Structures can filter out information making senior management remote from the customer. In the area of implementation consideration should be given to how communication occurs. In relation to developing marketing strategy, it can be advisable to have multi-functional teams. A group with a diverse range of backgrounds can promote ownership of projects, identify operational problems in advance and enhance overall quality.

- **Resources**   Any project needs to be properly resourced. Leaders have the role of obtaining and making optimum use of resources. The resourcing of projects is often more to do with internal politics than actual need. In many organizations there needs to be a more objective process of resource allocation. Resources will ultimately relate to finance and staff. Resourcing is normally budget-driven. However, there is now a recognition of the importance of being time-focused. For example, a three-month time delay is likely to be more serious than a minor budgetary overspend. The concept of 'time-to-market' is dealt with in a later section. Remember, implementation never takes place in a vacuum: things change and it is important to be flexible and build in an acceptable degree of contingency (additional resource to be called on) within any implementation strategy.

- **Control**   Control is simply a way of making sure what is supposed to happen actually happens. The term itself – 'control' – often appears to have negative connotations and is seen as limiting and coercive in nature. This should not be the case. Astute management can develop effective control systems. The basic approach is a simple feedback loop. You measure progress, compare against some pre-set standard and, if required, take action. Given the importance of control the concept is expanded upon in the next chapter.

- **Skills**   The appropriate skills mix is required in order to achieve any aim or goal. Within the context of implementing marketing strategy 'softer' human resource management (HRM) skills can be lacking. It should be remembered that project management is a skill in its own right. To summarize, successful implementation requires skills such as:

  ○ Technical/marketing skills, e.g. design, market research, industry analysis

  ○ HRM skills, e.g. delegation, performance appraisal, training

  ○ Project management skills, e.g. budgeting, resourcing, forecasting

- **Strategy**   To state the obvious, there must be a strategy to implement. However, the fact that a strategy exists may not be apparent to everyone. Additionally, the strategy may not be seen as appropriate by all staff. The project leader must ensure that people are aware of the strategy, the reason for it and their role in making it work. Potential strategy should be screened to ensure that it is appropriate to current circumstances. For example, what is the basis of competitive advantage? What organizational changes need to take place? The development of strategy is an on-going activity. During and after the implementation phase, management should review and adapt policy as required. While the overall objectives remain intact, there may be changes in how we set about achieving such targets. Figure 12.4 illustrates.

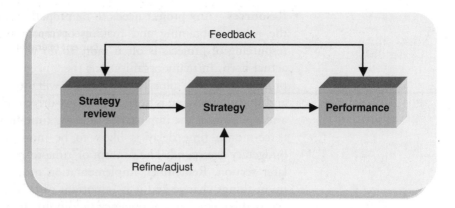

Figure 12.4
Reviewing strategy

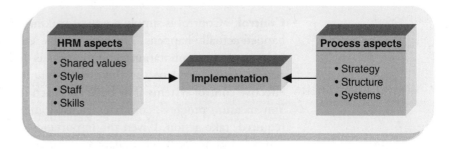

Figure 12.5
The Seven S's

- **Systems** Several systems are important in the implementation process and fall into two general groups: reporting and forecasting. It is necessary to have systems that aid management decision-making. (Note, these are aids to decision-making and not replacements for decision-making.) Such systems will cover areas such as finance and budgeting, project evaluation/refinement and market research. The key factor is often the interpretation of information rather than the system itself.

The Seven S's

The McKinsey & Co.'s 'Seven S' model provides a useful summation of these ideas. The model can be adapted as seen in Figure 12.5 and split into **human resource management** (HRM) aspects – dealing with the people-based aspects of implementation – and **process** aspects – the policy, procedures, reporting and systems aspects of implementation.

12.4   Assessing ease of implementation

It is now possible to test and evaluate the likely ease of implementation. First, strategic fit: how easily will the strategy fit into current activities?

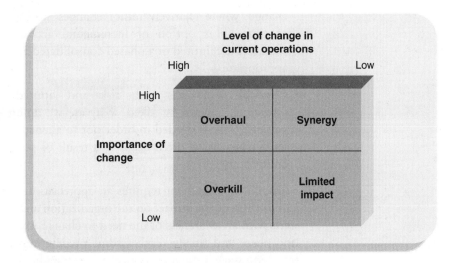

Figure 12.6
Strategic fit

Unsurprisingly, the easier the fit the less likely implementation problems are to occur. Note, it must be recognized that an 'easy fit' does not guarantee success; the strategy must be right for the business environment.

Primarily, the concern is with the level of change associated with the implementation. The greater the change, the greater the management challenge and the perceived benefit of the change needs to be. Hence there is a need to consider the potential pay-off and the amount of change required to achieve this. Figure 12.6 illustrates the relationship between change and importance.

- **Overhaul** Here implementation will have a significant impact and face significant challenges. Given that a high degree of change is likely, one must expect increasing levels of resistance and risk as the strategy has only a limited fit with current activity. There need to be compelling strategic reasons and significant support for this strategy's implementation. Such activities are likely to involve factors such as restructuring, downsizing, mergers and overhauling business culture.

- **Synergy** The word can be defined as 'working together'. The combined effect of high importance and relatively limited change offers a potentially 'easy ride'. Problems should be limited and risk of failure is reduced. However, great problems occur when a strategy is deemed to fall into this category, only to find it is not the case and far more change is required. Organizations should be doubly sure they have the required synergy before embarking on this route.

- **Limited impact** Here low levels of change affect relatively unimportant areas of activity. Often a series of such activities can yield incremental change. This could represent a stage-by-stage approach to change, where relatively minor changes are introduced over a period of time. This option of incremental activity can be used where resources are limited or a phased consolidated approach is deemed more appropriate.

- **Overkill** This has high risk and limited impact importance. Questions have to be asked. Why are we doing this and what is the pay-off? Care is needed in order not to alienate staff and disrupt activity. Such projects often occur as a result of political manoeuvring and compromise.

Successful management requires an appreciation of the nature of change and its subsequent impact on the organization and individual. The process starts with an awareness of the need to change, then progresses to a transition phase and finally reaches some predetermined state. Normally, the transition stage is the most critical as it is fraught with risk and uncertainty.

Management must assess the level of change associated with a project and deploy strategies relating to the management of change. For example:

- **Justification** Have supportive evidence in the form of facts and quantitative/statistical data. Hard data often proves a powerful ally.

- **Commitment** Try to involve others via group problem-solving, participation and communication. Such factors tend to generate commitment to change.

- **Learning** Change is often difficult to achieve and mistakes will be made. Learning from mistakes is important. Remember, experience is the name we like to give our mistakes.

- **Incrementalize** It may be better to have an overall strategy that can be broken down into a series of smaller on-going changes, as per the 'limited impact' strategy.

- **Operations** Ensure that change is reflected in operational activities through the appropriate systems, structures, policies and monitoring. In this way, change becomes a permanent feature and the organization avoids slipping back into old practices.

12.5 People, power and politics

When addressing the issue of implementation there are no panaceas. However, not all staff will be equally supportive of a given marketing strategy. Hence it is wise to consider the likely levels of support and resistance that may exist relative to a given project. Piercy (1997) sets out general categories into which staff can fall (see Figure 12.7).

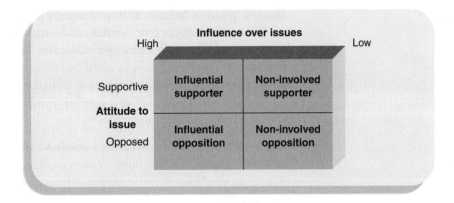

Figure 12.7
Key players matrix

Those with influence, often the appropriate decision-making unit (DMU), need careful consideration. Common tactics include:

- Converting or isolating opposition.

- Upgrading the status of influential supporters.

- Recruiting the active involvement of non-involved supporters.

- Negotiation and trade-off with vested interest.

In short, the success of any programme requires sufficient influence and support. This becomes more complex when the project generates high levels of change.

The issue of supporters and their influence tends to relate to the dreaded, but vital concept of internal office politics. Within the organization, political behaviour can be either desirable or undesirable; this often depends on individual perspective. Good strategies can flounder on the rocks of political self-interest and behaviour.

Kakabadse (1983) identifies seven common approaches to playing the political game.

1 Establish who the interested parties are – the stakeholders.

2 Consider their comfort zones. What do they value, fear or tolerate?

3 Work within these comfort zones.

4 Use networks – those interested or influential.

5 Identify 'gatekeepers' and adhere to the norms of the network.

6 Make deals for mutual benefit.

7 Withhold and withdraw. Consider withholding information and know when to withdraw from areas of conflict and dispute.

Arguably, political behaviour is an essential part of strategy implementation. This view requires management to identify key players and consider their potential reaction to strategic initiatives. Remember, the art of politics is about influencing people when one cannot rely on direct authority. By considering the political dimension related to the project it is possible to gauge resistance and support, develop justification and counter argument in advance of critical decisions.

Additionally, it may be possible to develop influence via various power bases. For example, controlling resources, having access to people and controlling the flow of information. These can all assist in playing the political game.

12.6   Internal marketing

No discussion relating to the ease, or otherwise, of implementation would be complete without considering the potential use of internal marketing. Internal marketing focuses on the relationship between the organization and its employees. Berry and Parasuraman (1991) define the process in terms of viewing employees (or groups of employees) as internal customers.

Definitions of this type encompass the work traditionally within the remit of personnel/human resource management function (e.g. recruitment, training, motivation, etc.). Few would argue with the importance of staff in relation to implementation. Therefore, can marketing techniques be used to motivate employees and ease the path of project implementation?

By applying the marketing concept internally, it may be possible to enhance the likely success of a project. Factors such as internal segmentation and application of the 'mix' may well have a role to play. Consider the following:

- **Segmentation**   The process of dividing groups into subgroups with similar characteristics. This is perfectly feasible within any organization. For example, senior managers may have different training needs from other staff. By grouping like types together more effective training and communication is possible.

- **Product**   This may well be the strategy and accompanying process of change. Equally, the individual's job or function could be viewed as an 'internal product'. The internal product, service or task is a component in delivering the overall strategy.

- **Promotion**   Clear communication has a vital role to play in establishing success. The project manager could design a 'promotional campaign',

Organization		
Segment I	Segment II	Segment III
Influential support	Influential opposition	Non-involved supporter
Internal mix I	Internal mix II	Internal mix III

Figure 12.8
Internal marketing

stressing the benefits of a new strategy. In all cases, communication is an issue that must be considered when planning implementation.

- **Place**   How to get the 'product' to the internal customer. Channels of distribution for information, services and training can be developed and optimized. These could include team briefings, seminars and day-to-day business interactions.

- **Price**   This is a complex issue. While it is relatively easy to cost factors like training, communications vehicles and other associated tangible costs, it is worth remembering a price is also paid by the group and/or individual. This 'psychological' price is difficult to measure, but important. It takes the form of uncertainty, loss of status, stress and loss (hopefully short term) of operational efficiency.

In its simplest form internal marketing offers a framework (the 4Ps) which can lay the foundations of successful policy implementation. It offers the marketing concept as a way to achieve specific strategic goals. Figure 12.8 illustrates how the concept could be applied to an organization. Here we segment by level of support. However, other criteria (e.g. department or management level) could be applied.

12.7   Applying project management techniques

The ability to manage a project is a skill in its own right. Such skills are 'transferable' and can be applied to any situation. Therefore, they adhere to general principles that can be learned by the marketing strategist.

Essentially, project management involves achieving unity of purpose and setting achievable goals within given resource and time scale parameters. Efforts tend to focus on integrating activity, building teamwork and

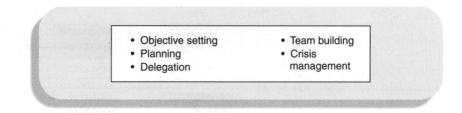

Figure 12.9
Project management

monitoring progress. Marketing projects are rarely simple and often have to be achieved while overcoming unforeseen problems and barriers. Effective project management deals with such problems as and when they arise.

Figure 12.9 summarizes common tasks in project management. Each task is reviewed in turn.

Objective setting

An overall strategic objective will be broken down into a series of 'sub-objectives'. It is important that these are clear, concise, understood and accepted by team members. A useful acronym is to develop **SMART** objectives. These add focus and relate to the task(s) required.

S   Specific. They should be clear and task-orientated.
M   Measurable. Objectives must be measured in order to establish progress.
A   Action. They should be task-related and promote activity.
R   Resourced. A realistic resource base has to be allocated to enable progress.
T   Time. There is a need to make the objective time-focused. How long will it take?

Planning

Having established what is to be achieved, planning breaks an activity into a series of structured manageable tasks, coordinates these tasks and monitors progress.

Tasks can happen in series or parallel. So-called 'parallel processing' – running several tasks simultaneously, has several advantages. Namely, it can reduce the overall time scale for the project and reduce the risk of a delay in one task delaying the entire project. Figure 12.10 illustrates.

Increasingly there is an awareness of being time-focused. Business is now adopting a time-to-market (T-t-M) philosophy. This T-t-M approach advocates the importance of reducing the overall time taken to implement

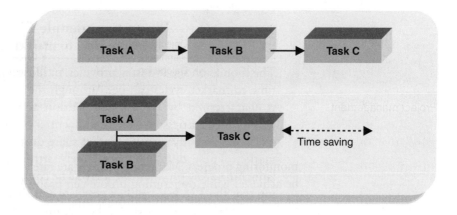

Figure 12.10
Serial *vs.* parallel
processing

a project. Consider the potential benefits of reducing implementation time. First, a commercial return is produced sooner. Secondly, by being early into the market the opportunity exists to gain a price premium and/or market share. The T-t-M focus is achieved by parallel processing and, conversely, spending more time developing a robust planning specification.

Delegation

Effective managers realize they cannot do everything themselves; they know that management is the art of delegation. The art is often to balance the degree of delegation with the appropriate span of control. The manager needs to understand the strength, weakness and group dynamics of the team members.

Many managers have a problem with letting go. Remember that delegation extends the capacity to manage and frees the leader from the mundane. Additionally, if staff are encouraged to take decisions, overall decision-making can be improved. The people 'on the spot' are more likely to have a fuller grasp of the situation and be able to make effective decisions.

Key principles of delegation include:

- Focus on the objective. Be crystal clear about what has to be achieved but flexible in how it is to be achieved.

- Delegate authority not just responsibility. Empower people to make decisions and manage resources.

- Test people on smaller and less important tasks and gradually give the more able employee greater scope.

Illustrative example 12.2
Ericsson: time to market

The mobile phone industry provides an illustration of how critical time-to-market cycles can be. Although the market is booming, it is characterized by intense competition and rapid technological development. Ericsson – the manufacturer of mobile phone handsets – has recently seen its market share drop within this growing market. These difficulties are largely attributed to the delay in launching a key product (the T28). The company is quoted as stating that the T28 was nearly a year late and that they had to cancel the T36 because it had only a short market life. Such delays caused Ericsson to miss out on demand for low cost handsets aimed at the expanding pre-pay mobile phone market.

- Explain how tasks are monitored and define circumstances in which they should refer back to senior management.

- Refrain from undue interference but be watchful.

Team building

Clearly there is a need to use the skills and capacity of the team to the optimal level. It is important to have a core goal as this gives the team a focal point. Each team member must understand his or her contribution to this collective goal. As Wickens (1997) states, teamwork does not depend on people working together but upon working to obtain the same objective.

A winning team has the right combination of skills. These should blend and complement each other. The environment should be positive and supportive but not complacent or overly relaxed.

Basic team building principles, which can be applied to a marketing project, are:

- Encourage a positive supportive environment. It's okay to make a mistake but ensure you learn from it.

- Show and encourage respect for each other. Encourage constructive criticism as opposed to personal attack.

- Link individual reward to group performance.

- Disagreement and discussion should not be suppressed and ideas should be listened to. However, this should not detract from effective decision-making.

Crisis management

There will be times when things go dramatically wrong and a crisis point is reached. The basic premise of crisis management is to take urgent action in response to unexpected events. By definition, the process is reactive in nature and invariably is a turning point. However, it does not negate prior planning. Management can develop a series of scenarios and have appropriate responses available as a contingency. This scenario planning allows a crisis management approach to be developed in advance.

Additionally, we may be given prior warning of a pending problem. Often there is a gradual worsening of events until the point of crisis is attained. If these signals are picked up early enough decisive action can be taken before the problem becomes a crisis.

A key idea is to maintain confidence and for management to be clearly in control. Basic techniques include:

- Assess the situation coolly and establish the facts before taking any rash action.

- Draw up a plan of action and establish a management structure.

- Set up a communications system to receive and disseminate information.

- Separate the trivial from the important and prioritize tasks.

- Be decisive and take responsibility.

Summary

Do not downplay the importance of implementation. Organizations need to consider not only the development of strategy, but address issues that turn strategy into reality.

The key to successful implementation is the application of basic management principles – leadership, systems and resourcing are all important. Such factors must be taken within the context of the organizational culture and business environment that exists.

Prior to implementation, it is wise to consider how easy the task(s) are likely to be. This relates to the importance of the task and the level of associated change. The attitude and influence of interested parties will also have a significant impact on the ease, or otherwise, of implementation.

Internal marketing techniques and the deployment of standard project management principles, such as objective setting, planning and delegation, facilitate a workable framework for the implementation of strategy.

Discussion questions

1 Discuss the following, illustrating with examples: Can good implementation save an inappropriate strategy?

2 Define an activity your are currently undertaking in terms of SMART objectives.

3 Examine the value of internal marketing in implementing strategy.

4 Using an example consider how the '7S framework' could be applied to marketing a new product.

5 Leaders need to adopt an appropriate style of management. Discuss this statement in the context of planning a marketing strategy.

References

Adair, J. (1984) *Action Centred Leadership.* McGraw Hill.

Berry, L. and Parasuraman, A. (1991) *Marketing Services: Competing Through Quality.* Free Press.

Bonoma, T. (1984) Making your marketing strategies work. *Harvard Business Review,* Vol. 62, No. 2, pp. 68–76.

Kakabadse, A. (1983) *The Politics of Management.* Gower.

Piercy, N. (1997) *Market-Led Strategic Change,* 2nd edn. Butterworth Heinemann.

Wickens, P. (1997) *The Road to Nissan.* Macmillan.

Control

About this chapter

Control mechanisms aim to translate strategic plans into specific actions. The purpose is to ensure that behaviour, systems and operations conform to corporate objectives/policy. Marketing managers need to be aware of a range of control variables: financial measures, budgets, performance appraisal and benchmarking.

After reading this chapter, you will understand:

- Basic control principles.
- What makes control systems effective.
- Management and financial control.
- Applying performance appraisal.
- The use of benchmarking in a control system.

13.1   Introduction

The term 'control' has received a bad press. The phrase smacks of coercive action, limiting freedom and keeping costs to an absolute minimum. The reality is somewhat different and managers should consider the control process as simply a mechanism to protect your strategic plans during implementation. Murphy's law states that 'If anything can go wrong, it will go wrong'. Hence a control system detecting and pre-empting the inevitable problems that accompany implementation is a valuable asset.

Control can be defined as attempting to guarantee that behaviour and systems conform to, and support, predetermined corporate objectives and policies. Such 'hard edged' views illustrate the importance of linking behaviour to overall strategic direction. This is a fundamental reason for having control systems.

13.2   Control: the basic principles

The basis of control is the ability to measure. In essence it compares what should happen with what actually happened or is likely to happen. Given the importance of measurement, a tendency exists to measure what is easy to quantify rather than what is important. Project managers must guard against this and focus on the key areas. Good control systems often detect and rectify problems before they become significant and managers should remember that prevention is better than cure. Try to be proactive rather than reactive.

The process is broken down into a series of simple steps. First, a target is set. Ideally, this is integrated into overall strategic planning. Secondly, a method of measurement has to be determined and implemented. Finally, measured results are compared with the predetermined target(s) and corrective action, if required, is undertaken.

There are two sides to the control equation – inputs and outputs. If only output is considered then the system is one of inspection as opposed to control. Correctly addressing both sides of the equation allows management to optimize the process and take a strategic view. Typical inputs include:

- Finance: Investment, working capital and cash.

- Operations: Capacity, usage, efficiency and application of machines, systems and other assets.

- People: Numbers, quality and skills of staff.

Output is measured in terms of overall system performance. Performance is derived from a combination of efficiency and effectiveness:

- Efficiency: How well utilized are the inputs? Do we make maximum use of finance, minimize cost and operate at optimal levels of capacity?

- Effectiveness: Are we doing the right things? This relates to actual performance and will include sales revenue, profit, market share and measures of customer satisfaction.

Remember, it is better to pursue effectiveness. For example, a company may be a very efficient producer (low cost, high volume, etc.) but relatively ineffective at finding buyers for its goods.

Control systems can operate as simple feedback loops. Figure 13.1 illustrates the concept. However, more sophisticated systems of *feedforward* control are possible. Such systems try to pre-empt problems by anticipating the effect of input(s) on overall performance. However, such systems are more complex and consequently more difficult to set-up.

Figure 13.2 illustrates the application of a basic control loop to the marketing management process. Here marketing objectives, such as increasing market share, are translated into performance targets. These targets define a specific measurable basis against which managers will be judged. The objective of increasing market share would be quantified. For example, we may aim at a 7% increase over 12 months. Responsibility for achieving the target is assigned and actual performance is evaluated against planned performance. The adjustment of the process is achieved by management action and/or altering the objectives or standards within the system. In this way, the system becomes flexible and can react to changes in performance and the business environment.

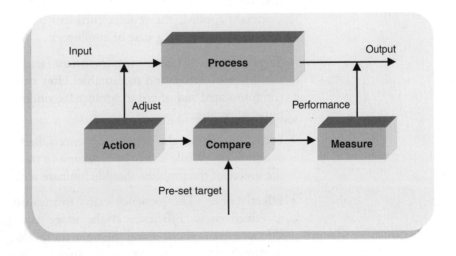

Figure 13.1
Feedback control

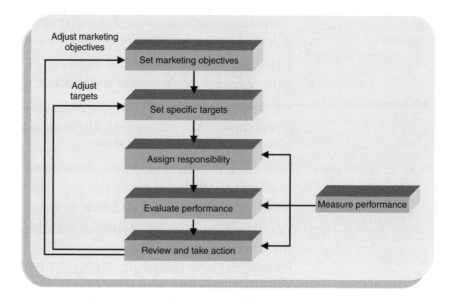

Figure 13.2
Marketing control
systems

13.3 What makes an effective control system?

Control systems require careful design. Generic principles exist which are common to all effective control mechanisms. As with management processes, it is important to retain a degree of flexibility and common sense. The project manager can deploy the following principles to ensure effective control:

- **Involvement**   This is achieved by encouraging participation in the process. Management can achieve desired results via consultation. For example, staff could contribute towards setting targets. Their own staff development needs could be considered along with the required tasks. Correctly applied, the process enhances morale, promotes ownership and develops the skills base of employees.

- **Target setting**   There are two important factors. First, the target criteria should be objective and measurable. How this is assessed needs to be communicated and agreed in advance. Secondly, it needs to be achievable but challenging.

- **Focus**   Recognize the difference between the symptoms and the source of a problem. While it may be expedient to treat the symptoms, tackling the source of the problem should eliminate it once and for all.

- **Effectiveness**   The tendency exists to measure efficiency as opposed to effectiveness. Efficiency is the usage and productivity of assets. Effectiveness is about doing the right things. Ideally, we want measures of efficiency applied to areas of effectiveness. In reality, we tend to apply

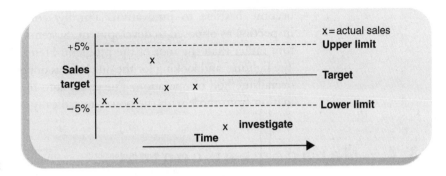

Figure 13.3
Tolerance control chart

efficiency measures to areas easiest to measure. Be careful to measure what is important, not what is easy to quantify. Additionally, measurement should be accurate, valid and consistent.

- **Management by exception**   Management attention is directed to areas of need. Identifying what constitutes an exception to the norm is a useful exercise in its own right. The process involves setting tolerances and benchmarks for normal operation. Management action only becomes a priority when pre-set limits are breached. Figure 13.3 shows a simple tolerance control chart. This is based on planned sales revenue plus or minus a tolerance of 5%. If the levels are broken, or in a proactive system appear as if they may be breached, management will begin to take an interest in the process.

- **Action**   Good control systems promote action. Such systems don't just detect problems; they solve problems. Basically, actions adjust the inputs to the process. For example, extra resources could be made available to deal with a back-log or a process or procedure could be redesigned to make it more effective.

Problems of control

A good control system is not easy to develop. The project manager requires an awareness of the general problems associated with control systems. Remember, no system is perfect and no control system offers one hundred percent accuracy. Often, the concern is keeping operations and plans within acceptable limits.

Three problems are commonly associated with control systems. First, such systems can be **costly**. Here the benefits of control and subsequent improvements are outweighed by the cost of the control mechanism. This often relates to large bureaucratic systems – layer upon layer of administration is built upon each other. This is self-serving rather than customer-focused, often absorbing resources that would be more effectively deployed in core activities. Secondly, control systems **stifle effort and creativity**. Such systems promote uniformity and conformance to pre-set targets. They become barriers to innovation. Thirdly, control promotes a view of **inspection as opposed to development**. Systems often deal with the symptom rather than the root of the problem. Here, we tend to be constantly 'fire fighting' and looking for the quick fix as opposed to developing a better overall method of operation. The effect is to filter and/or suppress information from those with the power to radically overhaul a poor system.

13.4   Management control

Having reviewed the basic concept of control, we can now focus on the key aspect of management control. Management control takes place at a number of different levels within the organization (see Figure 13.4). Control criteria apply to strategic, operational and tactical levels. The control variables at one level become targets for the next level down. Effectively, this means that a 'cascade' system of control is in operation. Senior/strategic levels use fewer, more critical, control variables. These are predominantly financial in nature and focus on divisional or strategic business unit (SBU) targets. The operational level relates to project or departmental activities and encompasses financial and non-financial information. The tactical level relates to group or individual performance and the focus is on productivity.

Good performance means that employees (at all levels) have a clear view of what the priorities are, what they should be doing currently, how their area of responsibility contributes to overall performance and what levels of achievement are acceptable.

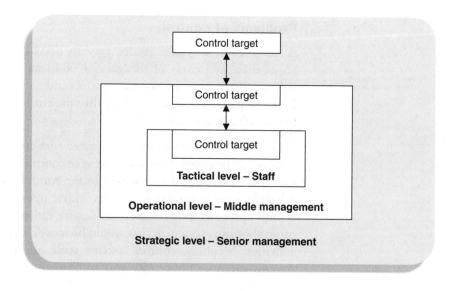

Figure 13.4
Cascade control

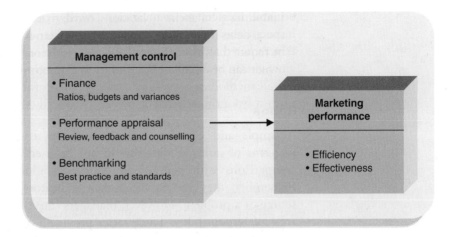

Figure 13.5
Management control
related to marketing

Management control will focus on: **finance, performance appraisal** and **benchmarking**. The relative importance of each may vary with level of management.

Financial measures will give both short- and long-term control data and are fundamental to decision-making. Performance appraisal examines the personnel and human resource aspects of management. Finally, benchmarking is a means of comparison and identification of best practice. As Figure 13.5 illustrates, management control is applied to marketing in order to establish marketing performance. Remember, performance is a function of efficiency and effectiveness.

13.5 Financial control

Financial control techniques are vital to successful strategy. Such techniques apply to both the planning and operational phases of projects. We will focus on three main financial control activities: ratios, budgeting and variance analysis.

A basic understanding of financial terminology is required. Remember, ultimately all business activities are measured in financial terms and managers require a grasp of accounting terms. Key terms include:

- **Assets** Items that have value to the business. Assets are subdivided into two categories: (1) *fixed assets* – retained by the business, in the long term, for continual use. Typical examples include buildings, machinery, vehicles and long-term investments. (2) *Current assets* – items that are readily convertible into cash or cash itself. Such assets are to be used in the short term. Examples include: stock, cash and debtors (those owing us money).

- **Liabilities**   Financial obligations owed to others. *Current liabilities* are those debts that must be paid in the near future. Therefore cash will be required to meet current liabilities. Additionally, *capital* invested by the owner can be classified as a liability as it is technically owed to the owners.

Ratios

A simple and effective control technique is to express performance in terms of ratios. Ratios should not be used in isolation. Trends and comparisons with planned or standards ratios should be considered. Remember, they are no more than indicators and rarely identify the source of a problem. However, managers can identify key ratios for their areas of responsibility. These ratios provide a quick and effective way to establish performance and highlight areas warranting more detailed analysis. Figure 13.6 outlines the uses of ratios.

Ratios represent a snapshot of the firm's financial/productivity position and fall into four general categories (see Figure 13.6): profitability, liquidity, debt and activity. Remember, when calculating ratios it is important to be consistent with the terms used. For example, how is profit defined – before or after tax?

- **Profitability ratios**   Here, effectiveness is measured by evaluating the organization's ability to produce profit. Profit margin is expressed in terms of a ratio of profit to sales. The profit margin is a key trading concern. Clearly, the profit margin can be enhanced by raising selling price and/or reducing costs. Return on Capital Employed (ROCE) is expressed as net profit as a percentage of capital. It examines to what extent an investment is paying off. It can be applied to an entire business or to specific projects requiring capital investment. ROCE is used to indicate the extent to which an investment is justified or to compare investment opportunities.

Ratio analysis	
Use	**Application**
• Trend analysis	• Profitability
• Comparison	• Liquidity
• Highlight key areas	• Debt
	• Activity

Figure 13.6
Use and application
of ratios

Examples:

$$\text{Gross profit margin} = \frac{\text{Profit}}{\text{Sales revenue}}$$

$$\text{Profit} = \text{Revenue} - \text{Cost}$$

$$\text{Net profit margin} = \frac{\text{Profit after tax}}{\text{Sales revenue}}$$

$$\text{Return on capital employed} = \frac{\text{Net profit}}{\text{Capital employed}}$$

- **Liquidity ratios**   Ratios that evaluate the ability to remain solvent and meet current liabilities. The firm needs to be able to convert assets into cash in order to meet payment demands. If the current ratio is more than 1, sufficient assets exist to meet current liabilities. The quick (or acid-test) ratio gives a stricter appraisal of solvency as it assumes stock is not automatically convertible into cash. Ideally, this ratio should be 1 to 1. However, many businesses operate with lower acceptable ratios. If the ratio is too high it may suggest that the organization does not make optimal use of its financial assets (e.g. holding too much cash).

  Examples:

$$\text{Current ratio} = \frac{\text{Current assets}}{\text{Current liabilities}}$$

$$\text{Quick ratio} = \frac{\text{Current assets} - \text{Inventory}}{\text{Current liabilities}}$$

- **Debt ratios**   These ratios help determine the company's ability to handle debt and meet scheduled repayments. They examine the extent to which borrowed funds finance business operations. If creditors begin to outweigh debtors this may signify overtrading – unable to collect money owed.

  Examples:

$$\text{Debt to assets ratio} = \frac{\text{Total liabilities}}{\text{Total assets}}$$

$$\text{Debt to credit ratio} = \frac{\text{Debtors}}{\text{Creditors}}$$

- **Activity ratios**   These ratios determine how effective the organization is at generating activity, such as sales from assets. These activities often relate to business cycles or processes, such as the time taken to turnover stock or collect debts. For example, the greater the stock turnover the better for the organization. An additional example, common in retailing, is sales per unit of floor space. This gives a measure of retail effectiveness.

Essentially, such ratios measure the relationship between inputs to outputs.

Examples:

$$\text{Inventory turnover} = \frac{\text{Sales}}{\text{Inventory}} \qquad \text{Sales per square foot} = \frac{\text{Sales}}{\text{Floor space}}$$

$$\text{Productivity} = \frac{\text{Units produced}}{\text{Number of employees}}$$

Budgeting

The processes of strategic development and budgeting are intrinsically linked. To be blunt; no budget equals no strategy! The budgeting process translates marketing strategy into financial terms which, whether we like it or not, are the way all plans are expressed, evaluated and controlled. Budgeting is the single most common control mechanism. It serves not only to quantify plans but also to coordinate activities, highlight areas of critical importance and assign responsibility. Many industry practitioners would agree with Piercy (1997). He talks about the 'hassle factor' – difficulty, time, negotiation, paperwork, etc. – associated with budgeting.

This serves to highlight two points. First, budgeting is about resource allocation. Secondly, budgeting is a political process (negotiate, bargaining, etc.) necessary to obtain required resources. Before managers can prepare a budget certain fundamental requirements exist:

- **Budget guidelines**   The organization's policy and procedure relating to budget formulation must be understood. These set out assumptions, method and presentational requirements.

- **Cost behaviour**   Management must understand what drives costs within their area of responsibility. Additionally, it is important to be clear on how costs are allocated. For example, what is the basis of overhead cost allocation?

- **Timescale**   A specific time period needs to be set. This could be for a fixed budgetary period, such as a financial year or alternatively a '**rolling budget**' could be prepared. Here, the budget is split into manageable time periods, and outline forecasts are updated at regular intervals. New periods are added as the budget progresses.

- **Objectives**   Specifically, what are we aiming to achieve and how is it being assessed? Corporate or departmental goals should be translated into resource and subsequent budgetary requirements.

Approaches to budgeting

Many approaches exist in formulating a budget. Most organizations have developed a historic way of approaching the task. Recent times have seen a move towards greater objectivity and the need to justify assumptions and requirements. Common methods of budgeting are:

- **Historic**   Traditionally the main determinant of a future budget is previous expenditure. Organizations simply base the budget on previous financial data. Adjustments are made for factors like inflation and level of activity. The model is basically incremental in nature; last year, plus or minus some factor, with managers concentrating on justifying or challenging changes.

- **Zero-based**   Budgets are systematically re-evaluated and senior management establishes priority within the context of overall financial constraints. The process involves examining activities and deriving the cost and resulting benefit from these activities. Alternative methods of achieving objectives are simultaneously considered and there is often a trade-off between activities. The method relates to analysing objectives and tasks and is highly 'political' in nature.

- **Activity related**   Here budgets are based on often crude measures of activity. Simple calculation rules such as percentage of sales, or average industry spend are used as precursors in determining available funds.

Variance analysis

Finally, in this section on financial control, variance analysis is reviewed. Basically, this examines the variation between actual and planned results and is a concept applicable to a range of activities. It is commonly used along with budgetary control. We compare the actual results with budgeted forecasts and then examine the variance in order to determine the reason for the difference. Variance analysis allows us to identify the main areas of concern and break problems down into component parts. For example, in marketing, variance analysis is often applied to sales price and sales volume. Standard formulae are useful in calculating the effect of these variables on overall revenue.

$$\text{Variance in sales revenue} = \text{Actual revenue} - \text{Planned revenue}$$

$$\text{Variance due to price} = \text{Actual volume}$$
$$\times (\text{Planned price} - \text{Actual price})$$

$$\text{Variance due to volume} = \text{Planned price}$$
$$\times (\text{Actual volume} - \text{Planned volume})$$

Consider the following example. We plan to sell 4200 units at £25 per unit. However, due to market conditions, we actually sell 3850 units at £16 per unit. Hence the variance in sales revenue is:

$$\text{Variance in sales revenue } (3850 \times 16) - (4200 \times 25) = -43\,400$$

Variance analysis can be used to determine whether the loss of sales revenue is predominantly due to the lower than expected volume or failure to maintain planned price.

$$
\begin{aligned}
\text{Variance due to price} &= 3850 \times (16 - 25) &&= -34\,650 &&80\% \\
\text{Variance due to volume} &= 25 \times (3850 - 4200) &&= \underline{\;-8\,750\;} &&\underline{\;20\%} \\
& && -43\,400 &&100\%
\end{aligned}
$$

Therefore, we can see that 80% of the failure to achieve planned revenue is due to the lower unit price. Management could then investigate why we failed to achieve the planned unit price.

Note, variance analysis is not limited to price and volume calculations. A wide range of factors can be analysed in this fashion (e.g. profit, cost and market size).

13.6   Performance appraisal

Performance appraisal concerns achieving better results from groups and individuals. A performance appraisal framework is based on: planned objectives, levels of achievement and competence. The focus is on the control and development of staff, and is critical to project implementation. Effective performance appraisal requires managers to have good people skills and appraisal should be constructive in nature. It is about doing a better job. Three key skills are involved: reviewing performance, giving feedback and counselling.

- **Reviewing**   The performance of individuals, or groups, should be reviewed continuously as part of normal management activity. Additionally, there may be a formal review which summarizes activity. Try to use objective criteria as a basis of review. Such criteria should be communicated and agreed in advance. Work and personal development plans should be considered in tandem with set criteria.

- **Feedback**   Feedback, relating to performance, is based on actual results, or observed behaviour. When giving feedback, one should be specific and describe rather than judge results. One should not just focus on the negative but try to give credit where it is due. By reference to specific actions and behaviours, managers can more readily focus on key aspects of improvement.

- **Counselling**   Performance appraisal should be positive in nature. In order to build on strengths and overcome weaknesses, management may well have to counsel staff. This is particularly relevant to areas of under-performance. Counselling needs to consider performance, not personality and invite a degree of self-appraisal. Aim to identify and agree problems then choose required actions.

13.7   Benchmarking

In order to be 'the best you can be', it pays to compare yourself with leading performers. Benchmarking provides a method of enabling such comparisons to take place.

Benchmarking is defined as:

> A systematic and on-going process of measuring and comparing an organization's business processes and achievements against acknowledged process leaders and/or key competitors, to facilitate improved performance.

However, benchmarking is more than just copying. The process is about continuous improvement and becoming a learning organization. The credo is one of adaptation rather than adoption. Ideas, practices and methods have to be screened and adapted to specific business situations. Benchmarking falls into three general areas:

- **Competitive analysis**   Reviewing competitors' activities, strategy and operations so we can improve our performance.

- **Best practice**   Determining the best way of undertaking an activity. This could involve examining activities in unrelated areas of business or industries. For example, a computer manufacturer could benchmark a mail-order retail company in order to improve its stock control system. Equally, best internal practice could be identified and spread to other units or departments within the organization.

- **Performance standards**   Benchmarks can be performance standards. Performance indicators become targets to be met or surpassed. As way of illustration, if the average industry conversion of enquiries into sales was 1 in 20 and we achieve 1 in 25, what does this say about our sales process?

The process of benchmarking

Benchmarking comprises a four-stage approach. This is illustrated using the 'Deming cycle' (Watson, 1993): plan, do, check and act (see Figure 13.7). The planning stage involves identifying what to study and who or what should act as the benchmark. Common areas to benchmark are: customer service levels, logistic and distribution methods, product quality and 'time-to-market' cycles. Organizations will benchmark against competitors, acknowledged leaders or successful internal activities. Next, conduct research. This may involve cooperation and direct contact with the benchmark. Alternatively, secondary data may be used to establish standards and actions. The data is then analysed. This involves establishing the extent of performance gaps and identifying assignable causes for such

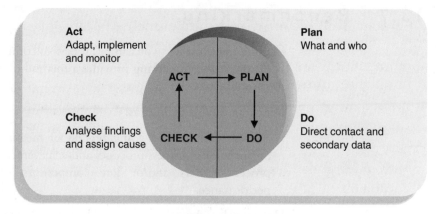

Figure 13.7
The Deming cycle
applied to benchmarking
(*Source:* Watson, 1993)

gaps. Finally, the lessons learned are adapted, as appropriate, and applied in order to generate improvement in performance.

13.8 Controlling marketing performance

In contrast to mechanical systems, marketing activities are inherently more volatile. This is due to a constantly changing business environment driven by the needs and wants of the market. Measuring marketing performance is a process of determining appropriate criteria by which to judge activity. Kotler (1997) identifies four main areas associated with the control of marketing activity (see Figure 13.8).

- **Annual planning**   This has the purpose of evaluating the extent to which marketing efforts, over the year, have been successful. Evaluation will focus on analysing: sales, market share, expenses and customer perception. Commonly, sales performance is a major element of this analysis. All other factors provide explanation of any variance in sales performance.

- **Profitability**   All marketing managers are concerned with controlling their profit levels. Examining the profitability of products, or activities, it is possible to make decisions relating to the expansion, reduction or elimination of product offerings. Additionally, it is common to break distribution channels and segments down in terms of profitability. Remember, it is important to have a systematic basis for allocating cost and defining profit.

- **Efficiency control**   Efficiency is concerned with gaining optimum value from the marketing assets. Managers are looking to obtain value for money in relation to marketing activity. The promotional aspects of marketing (sales, advertising, direct marketing, etc.) are commonly subject to such controls. Figure 13.9 displays examples.

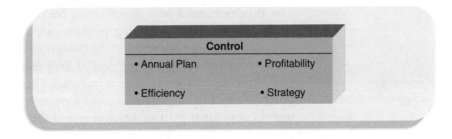

Figure 13.8
Control of
marketing activities

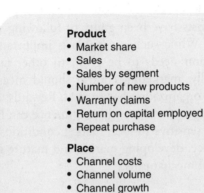

Figure 13.9
Control of marketing
activity

Product
- Market share
- Sales
- Sales by segment
- Number of new products
- Warranty claims
- Return on capital employed
- Repeat purchase

Price
- Profit margin
- Discount levels
- Price by segment
- Price comparisons

Place
- Channel costs
- Channel volume
- Channel growth
- Delivery time
- Stock levels

Promotion
- Cost per contact
- Media coverage
- Sales per call
- Awareness levels
- Enquiries generated

Illustrative example 13.1
British Airways: measuring marketing success

Organizations spend a great deal of time and money marketing their products; therefore they require objective measures relating to the effectiveness of such expenditure. British Airways is reported to evaluate marketing success via measurement of awareness, feedback on customer satisfaction and market share data. Additionally, a more focused approach is applied to specific promotions. These measure factors such as repeat business and level of sales.

- **Strategic control** There is a need to ensure that marketing activities are being directed towards strategic goals and that marketing is an integral part of the overall process of delivering value. A strategic review will aim to assess that marketing strategy, and subsequent implementation, is appropriate to the marketplace. A review of this nature will take the form of a marketing audit – a comprehensive examination of all marketing activity to assess effectiveness and improve marketing performance.

The aforementioned areas of marketing control are general in nature and specific measures of marketing performance are required. Performance measures and standards will vary by organization and market conditions. A representative sample of the type of data required to successfully control marketing activities is shown in Figure 13.9. The aim is to break the general areas (annual, plan, profitability, efficiency and strategy) into measurable component parts to which responsibility can be assigned.

Remember, in the context of marketing a balanced view is required. No one variable should dominate the control process. For example, marketing strategists have been guilty of following a credo of 'market share at any cost'. While such a variable is important, it is not a panacea and consideration needs to be given to other factors such as profitability. Additionally, marketing control should measure only dimensions over which the organization has control. Rewards, sanctions and management actions only make sense where influence can be exerted. Control systems should be sensitive to local market conditions and levels of competition. For instance, developing market and mature markets may require different control mechanisms.

Summary

The basic essence of control is the ability to measure and take action. Control systems are concerned with efficiency and effectiveness and often operate as simple feedback loops. In marketing terms, control ensures what is supposed to happen actually happens and is a mechanism to protect strategic plans when they become operational.

Effective control systems have focus, involve people and promote action. Management control extends to cover finance, performance appraisal and establishing and maintaining performance benchmarks. Marketing managers are concerned with the following control mechanisms: annual plans, profitability, efficiency of marketing and strategic control.

Discussion questions

1   Consider Murphy's Law – 'Anything that can go wrong will go wrong.' Discuss in the context of control.

2   Illustrating with examples, outline what makes an effective control system.

3   Develop a Deming cycle for an activity of your choice.

4   Illustrative example 13.1 considers British Airways. Discuss how BA could make use of (a) Strategic control and (b) Efficiency control within a marketing context.

5   Using additional reading, research the concept of feedforward control.

References

Kotler, P. (1997) *Marketing Management*, 9th edn. Prentice Hall.

Piercy, N. (1997) *Market-Led Strategic Change*, 2nd edn. Butterworth Heinemann.

Watson, G. (1993) *Strategic Benchmarking*. Wiley.

Index

Index

Procurement, 196
Product, 9, 107
  actual, 108
  augmentation, 190
  augmented, 108
  components of a product offering,
    107
  core, 108
  development, 203
  innovation, 128
  inseparability, 110
  intangibility, 109
  lack of ownership, 109
  life cycle, 110–113
  line specialist, 191
  market matrix, 203, 204
  market strategy, 188
  orientation, 4
  perception, 190, 195
  performance, 190
  perishability, 110
  portfolios, 114
  service element, 108
  variability, 110
Production orientation, 4
Profile variables, 75
Profit, 137
  impact, 205
Profitability ratio, 268
Project management, 248, 254
Promotion, 9
Psychographic variables, 75, 89
Public relations, 149
Public sector distribution, 176
Publicity, 149
Pull strategy, 151
Push strategy, 151

Qualitative research, 53
Quantitative research, 56
Questionnaire design, 57
Quick ratio, 269

Rapid skimming, 140
Ratio, activity, 269
  debt, 269
Ratios, 268
Red Bull, 230
Reference groups, 71
Relationship marketing, 6
Research methods, 52
Resource, 21
  allocation, 23
Resources, 248
Retail marketing mix, 175
Return on investment, 137
Revenue management, 142
Reviewing strategy, 250
Richmond Food, 120

Ries and Trout, 225, 227
Riley, 242
ROCE, 268
Rose and O'Reilly, 80, 82
Rowntree, 242
Ryanair, 13
Ryanair, 39, 113

Safeway, 120
Saga, 227
Sainbury Bank, 227
Sainbury, 24, 174
Sales, orientation, 4
  promotion, 149
  target, 265
SBU, 19
Secondary research, 52
Secondlifestyle, 227
Segmentation, 66, 254
  industrial, 92
  life-cycle, 77
  benefit, 87
  demographic, 76
  geographic, 83
  organizational, 92
  organizational, macro, 102
  organizational, micro, 102
  process, 68
  socio-economic, 80
  usage, 88
Segments, Euro-
    consumer, 86
  evaluating market
Selective, attention, 73
  distortion, 73
  retention, 73
Sender/receiver, 152
Serial processing, 256
Service mix, 9
Services, 10
Seven P's, 10
Seven S's, 250
Shared values, 250
Shell, 40
  directional policy matrix (DPM), 40,
    118, 119, 220
Sheth model of organizational buyer
    behaviour, 97–100
SimplyOrg@nic, 192
Skills, 25
  implementation, 248
Skoda, 240
SKY, 170
SKY TV, 80
Slow skimming, 140
SMART objectives, 256
Social class, 70
Social learning theories, 74
Societal marketing, 14

Sony, 172
  Librie, 130
SPAR, 222
Specialised markets, 193
Staff, 250
Stalemate, 193
Steers et al., 73
Strategic, advantage, 189
  control, 275
  fit, 250
  groups, 39
  marketing, 22
  marketing plan, 27, 28
  process, 21
  wear-out, 206
Strategy, and execution, 246
  and implementation, 246
  formulation, 187
Structure, 248, 250
Stuck-in-the-middle, 191
Style, 250
Sun Tzu, 183
Sunday Times, 16
Survey methods, 56
Survival, 206
Swan, 175
SWOT, 186
Synergy, 251
Systems, 250

Tactical marketing, 22
Tango, 226, 240
Target, audience, 153
  group, 153
  setting, 264
Targeting, 211, 218
Tasks needs, 247
Taylor Nelson research agency, 91
Taylor Nelson Sofres, 174
Technology development, 196
Telephone interviews, 56
Tesco, 171, 172 174, 238
The Cloud, 42
The Monitor framework, 91
The Times, 124
Time saving, 257
Time to market, 256
Tinson, 71
Torex, 21
Toyota, 38
Transactional efficiency, 164
Trend analysis, 268
Triumph, 242
Trojan Condoms, 154
T-t-M, 256
Tucker, 238
TVR, 38
Two-way communication,
    155